Enigma Books

Also published by Enigma Books

Hitler's Table Talk: 1941–1944
In Stalin's Secret Service
Hitler and Mussolini: The Secret Meetings
The Jews in Fascist Italy: A History
The Man Behind the Rosenbergs
Roosevelt and Hopkins: An Intimate History
Diary 1937–1943 (Galeazzo Ciano)
Secret Affairs: FDR, Cordell Hull, and Sumner Welles
Hitler and His Generals: Military Conferences 1942–1945
Stalin and the Jews: The Red Book
The Secret Front: Nazi Political Espionage
Fighting the Nazis: French Intelligence and Counterintelligence
A Death in Washington: Walter G. Krivitsky and the Stalin Terror
The Battle of the Casbah: Terrorism and Counterterrorism in Algeria 1955–1957
Hitler's Second Book: The Unpublished Sequel to *Mein Kampf*
At Napoleon's Side in Russia: The Classic Eyewitness Account
The Atlantic Wall: Hitler's Defenses for D-Day
Double Lives: Stalin, Willi Münzenberg and the Seduction of the Intellectuals
France and the Nazi Threat: The Collapse of French Diplomacy 1932–1939
Mussolini: The Secrets of His Death
Mortal Crimes: Soviet Penetration of the Manhattan Project
Top Nazi: Karl Wolff—The Man Between Hitler and Himmler
Empire on the Adriatic: Mussolini's Conquest of Yugoslavia
The Origins of the War of 1914 (3-volume set)
Hitler's Foreign Policy: 1933–1939—The Road to World War II
The Origins of Fascist Ideology 1918–1925
Max Corvo: OSS Italy 1942–1945
Hitler's Contract: The Secret History of the Italian Edition of *Mein Kampf*
Secret Intelligence and the Holocaust
Israel at High Noon
Balkan Inferno: Betrayal, War, and Intervention, 1990–2005
Calculated Risk: World War II Memoirs of General Mark Clark
The Murder of Maxim Gorky
The Kravchenko Case: One Man's War On Stalin
Operation Neptune
Paris Weekend
Shattered Sky
Hitler's Gift to France
The Mafia and the Allies
The Nazi Party, 1919-1945: A Complete History
Encyclopedia of Cold War Espionage, Spies, and Secret Operations
The Cicero Spy Affair
A Crate of Vodka
NOC
The First Iraq War: Britain's Mesopotamian Campaign, 1914-1918

Becoming Winston Churchill
Hitler's Intelligence Chief: Walter Schellenberg
Salazar: A Political Biography
The Italian Brothers
Nazi Palestine
Code Name: Kalistrat
Pax Romana
Lenin and His Comrades
Working with Napoleon
The Decision to Drop the Atomic Bomb
Target Hitler
Truman, MacArthur and the Korean War
The Eichmann Trial Diary
American Police: A History, Vol. 1
American Police: A History, Vol. 2
Cold Angel
Alphabet of Masks
Stalin's Man in Canada
Hunting Down the Jews
Mussolini Warlord
Election Year 1968
Spy Lost
Deadly Sleep

Thomas A. Reppetto

Shadows Over the White House

The Mafia and the Presidents

Enigma Books

Published by Enigma Books, New York

Copyright © 2015 by Thomas A. Reppetto

First Edition

Printed in Canada

ISBN: 978-1-936274-70-3
e-ISBN: 978-1-936274-71-0

Publisher's Cataloging-In-Publication Data

Reppetto, Thomas A.
  Shadows over the White House : the Mafia and the Presidents / Thomas A.
Reppetto. -- First edition.

    pages : illustrations ; cm

  Issued also as an ebook.
  Includes bibliographical references and index.
  ISBN: 978-1-936274-70-3

  1. Mafia--United States--History--20th century. 2. Presidents--United States--
History--20th century. 3. Political corruption--United States--History--20th century.
4. United States--Politics and government--20th century. I. Title.

HV6446 .R46 2014
364.1060973

Contents

Dedication

In memory of Virgil W. Peterson (1904-1989), FBI Special Agent and Special Agent in Charge, 1930-42; Executive Director of the Chicago Crime Commission, 1942-69. His vast knowledge of organized crime contributed greatly to the U.S. government's successful drive against the American Mafia.

Preface

The Mafia and the White House

Inquire of any American about what is the Mafia and they are likely to say it is a group of mobsters who killed President Kennedy. Ask a film critic to list the top dramatic movies of all time and he will surely include the *Godfather* series. Mafia stories have replaced westerns as the romantic portrayal of a way of life that fascinates Americans. Mafiosos and cowboys are pictured as strong men of action who live by a rigid code of honor. They put their mob families or saddle partners first in any situation. If one of their group is shot they don't run to the sheriff, but settle the score themselves. For many years law enforcement was split on the nature of the Mafia or even whether such an organization existed. As far back as 1903, a high official of the U.S. Secret Service called the Mafia "the most secret and terrible organization in the world." Harry Anslinger, who headed the Federal Bureau of Narcotics from 1930 to 1960, blamed the Mafia for the influx of drugs into the United States. In contrast, J. Edgar Hoover, long-time director of the FBI, denied that there was any national or international conspiracy and characterized the so-called Mafia as simply urban gangs that it was the job of local police to control.

In 1957, when New York State troopers raided a conclave of Italian-American gangsters being held on a local estate near Apalachin, New York, the most embarrassed man in America was Hoover, whose agents had known nothing of the meeting and who could not explain why so many men from all over the country were gathered in rural New York on that day. After that, even Hoover had to fall into line, although his heart was not in it. In the 1960s he explained that he had known all along about the Mafia but that its real name was La Cosa Nostra. He told a House of Representatives subcommittee:

> La Cosa Nostra is the largest association of the criminal underworld in this country, very closely organized and strictly disciplined. They have committed almost every crime under the sun... It operates on a nation-wide basis, with international implications, and until recent years it carried on its activities with almost complete secrecy.

Hoover did not mention that Anslinger's Narcotics Bureau had been circulating detailed reports on the Mafia for years, and some FBI field offices had submitted reports on local Mafia families. In the 1980s, after a long series of criminal trials in which whole Mafia families were convicted of racketeering and given 100-year sentences, top mafiosos and their lawyers finally admitted that such an organization did exist.

In the work which follows, I will refer to the predominantly Italian-American gangs, who once were loosely connected in a national syndicate, as the American Mafia. In some cities I simply use titles like the Chicago outfit, the Detroit Purple gang or the New York Genovese family. When I speak of Mafia gangs located in Italy, I will refer to them as the Italian Mafia. which is a separate entity from their American counterparts.[1]

*

So powerful was organized crime in America that it was sometimes able to work its will at the national level. Even before the rise of the

---

1. So common has the term Mafia become that Italian law enforcement officers no longer limit the use of the word to Sicilians but include the Neapolitan Camorra and the Calabrian Ndrangheta as "the Mafia."

American Mafia, the so-called "Ohio gang," which accompanied President Harding to Washington in 1921, put a virtual "For Sale" sign on the White House. As a result, bootleggers, drug dealers and tax evaders were able to bribe federal officials on a wholesale basis. At the end of Prohibition the American Mafia gangs became so powerful politically that their influence began to extend to 1600 Pennsylvania Avenue.

Though Franklin Roosevelt was a great president, in the 1930s and '40s he sheltered machine bosses, like Frank Hague of New Jersey and Ed Kelly of Chicago, from federal criminal charges because he needed their political support. This in turn was a boon for the American Mafia, which was protected by or even partners with Hague, Kelly, New York's Tammany Hall, the Brooklyn organization, and politicians in Boston, Buffalo, Cleveland, Detroit, Kansas City, and New Orleans.

In 1944 a coterie of machine bosses, some of them closely allied with the American Mafia, secured the nomination of Missouri senator Harry Truman as vice president. Since political insiders knew President Roosevelt was dying, this was tantamount to making Truman president. During his career in Kansas City the senator had been a key figure in the corrupt Pendergast machine which was allied with the local Mafia. Throughout President Truman's two terms, political bosses and the Mafia never had reason to regret their choice. The U.S. Parole Board gave an expedited release to half a dozen top Chicago mafiosos. When Congress tried to investigate the affair, Truman's Department of Justice refused to supply any information and the parole board resigned en masse rather than testify under oath. There was also extensive corruption in the Bureau of Internal Revenue, which went from being a fearsome agency to a pussycat under the leadership of Truman's ally Bob Hannegan of St. Louis. As in Harding's time, a "For Sale" sign hung on the White House.

In 1949 Truman attempted to block a Senate probe of organized crime in America. Only after the top two Kansas City Mafia bosses were shot and killed in the First Ward Democratic Club, and a picture of their bodies lying under a photo of the president appeared in every major newspaper in the United States, did Truman have to give way. The Senate then appointed an investigating committee headed by Estes Kefauver of Tennessee. The committee's findings would open the eyes

of the public to the nature of the American Mafia and its close relationship to political machines. Still, the shadow of Mafia influence
would hang over the White House for the next thirty-five years.

From 1961-63, President John F. Kennedy and his brother,
Attorney General Robert Kennedy, did more to combat the American
Mafia than any previous administration. Yet the Kennedys delivered
themselves into the hands of Chicago gangsters. In the 1960 presidential election, the candidate's father used Frank Sinatra to solicit the
support of Sam Giancana, boss of the Chicago syndicate. Later, some
of Robert Kennedy's assistants employed Giancana's hoodlums in an
unsuccessful campaign to eliminate Cuban dictator Fidel Castro. The
president himself became involved in a romantic triangle with a Las
Vegas courtesan who was a girlfriend of Giancana's.

President Lyndon Johnson was involved with men like Bobby
Baker, who was sent to prison for corruption. Though not connected
to mafiosos, Johnson, like Truman, sought unsuccessfully to prevent
an investigation of organized crime by a presidential commission.

Both the Nixon and Reagan administrations reached out to the
International Brotherhood of Teamsters (IBT), which, at the time, was
dominated by Mafia figures. After union president Jimmy Hoffa was
sent to prison by Bobby Kennedy, the Nixon administration released
him on parole with the provision that he not be able to hold union
office so that the temporary president, Frank Fitzsimmons, could
remain in power. Fitzsimmons, who had become subservient to the
Mafia, developed close ties with the Nixon White House through
Charles Colson, whose own criminality was revealed at the time of
Watergate. When Hoffa attempted to force his way back into power,
he disappeared and was presumably murdered by Mafia hitmen.

During Ronald Reagan's administration the president of the Teamsters International, Jackie Presser, who was both an FBI informant and
controlled by the Cleveland Mafia, was able to block federal investigations of his activities and exercise influence at the White House. When
this was revealed the president, the FBI, and the Department of Justice
came under severe criticism.

Thus, of nine presidents who served between 1933 and 1989, at
least five could have been accused of allowing Mafia influence to pene-

trate their administrations or, in the case of Kennedy, negligence for opening himself to Mafia blackmail.

Accounts of how the Mafia and corrupt politicians were able to assert so much power generally do not appear in books on American government. For example, the classic description of the workings of New York municipal administration, *Governing New York City* (1960) by two distinguished Ivy League professors, almost totally ignores the city's five families. Yet, in the 1940s and '50s, the Mafia played a major role in the election of New York mayors William O'Dwyer and Vincent Impellitteri. At the national level, despite the fact that mobsters had so much influence in various administrations their power is generally glossed over in works on the presidency.

Virtually from the day I was born, I have observed elements of the American Mafia close-up through either social contacts, or professional ones as a Chicago detective, sergeant, lieutenant, captain, and commander. Later, while earning a doctorate from Harvard, I had a chance to study the Boston Mafia close-up. As head of the Crime Commission of New York City for twenty-seven years, I was an observer of the federal and state efforts to bring down the city's five Mafia families. In a few instances I played a small role in the state government's anti-organized crime activities. I have also written two works on the American Mafia.[2]

The pages that follow will detail the relationships between organized crime, especially the Mafia, politicians, and the White House from Roosevelt to Reagan and address questions such as:

Why did President Roosevelt play ball with the corrupt political machines and ignore advice from members of his cabinet that he should prosecute bosses like New Jersey's Frank Hague and Chicago's Ed Kelly?

How did Harry Truman rise from machine lackey to president of the United States?

---

2. Like some economists, political scientists, and sociologists, I often write about the past. Thus, the media frequently refers to me as an historian, though I am not. My doctoral fields were law, public administration, criminology, and American government. My career has been spent in various facets of law enforcement and criminal justice.

Why did former crusading prosecutor and two-time presidential nominee Tom Dewey fail as governor to break open a murder case involving Franklin Roosevelt's closest ally in the labor movement, Sidney Hillman? Then, two years later, why did he release Mafia kingpin Lucky Luciano from serving a fifty-year sentence that Dewey himself had obtained as special prosecutor?

At the 1944 Democratic convention, was the labor leader Sidney Hillman pressured by the New York Mafia to support Truman's nomination?

How did a cabal of mobbed-up political machine bosses manage to control the 1944 convention?

Why did Truman's U.S. Parole Board release the top leaders of the Chicago syndicate on the very day they were eligible? Why did it quit en masse rather than submit to a congressional investigation.

What was the real reason FBI director J. Edgar Hoover resisted committing his agency to attacking the Mafia?

Why did Senator Kefauver go easy on the Chicago political machine and a police captain who was an integral part of the local Mafia?

Why did the Kennedy clan turn to the Mafia for help in getting elected and in overthrowing the Castro regime in Cuba?

Was the Mafia behind the assassination of President Kennedy?

Why did Lyndon Johnson as president attempt to block an investigation of the Mafia?

Did President Nixon receive $1 million from the Mafia to help with his legal expenses during Watergate?

What was the real story behind Jimmy Hoffa's disappearance and presumed murder?

Why did the Reagan administration make the same mistake as Nixon and get in bed with mobbed-up Teamsters chief Jackie Presser?

The final chapter will look at the way international organized crime may exert influence at 1600 Pennsylvania Avenue.

Shadows Over the White House

Chapter 1

The Fall of the Ohio Gang;
The Rise of the Mafia Gangs

The weather in Chicago was unbearably hot in the second week of June, 1920. Delegates who arrived in the city to attend the Republican presidential nominating convention had nowhere to seek relief. In that era hotels, restaurants, and meeting halls were not air-conditioned. At the packed Coliseum where the delegates met, a few blocks south of the Loop, the temperature in the convention hall was 90°. The Coliseum had been the scene of many dramatic events. In 1896, William Jennings Bryan would emerge from obscurity to receive the presidential nomination of the Democratic Party as a result of his "Cross of Gold" speech that electrified the delegates. In 1912, Teddy Roosevelt's attempt to wrest the Republican nomination from President Taft was beaten back. As a result, Roosevelt supporters withdrew and formed the Progressive Party, which nominated their hero to run for the presidency. The split between the Republicans and the Progressives led to the election of a Democratic president: Woodrow Wilson.

In 1920, Roosevelt would have been the Republican nominee but he had died the previous year and there was no front runner. General Leonard Wood had inherited some of Roosevelt's supporters. The Progressives (now back in the fold) favored Senator Hiram Johnson of

California. Others in the party lined up with Illinois governor Frank Lowden of Illinois. With the Wilson administration shattered, no matter who the party nominated, a GOP victory in November was almost certain and the new president would be in a position to shape the future of the nation.

Between 1868 and 1908 every Republican elected president was from Ohio, except Roosevelt.[1] The Ohioan in the field in 1920 was Senator Warren G. Harding, a man popular with his fellow senators but otherwise undistinguished. However, Harding's campaign was managed by a shrewd Ohio wheeler-dealer lawyer named Harry Daugherty. Even more importantly, given the different factions contesting and the bitterness between some of them—for example, Wood would never withdraw in favor of Lowden and vice versa—the nominee would likely be chosen by the bosses, mostly Senate colleagues of Harding's. Several months before the convention opened, Daugherty told reporters,

> I don't expect Senator Harding to be nominated on the first, second or third ballot, but I think about 11 minutes after 2 o'clock on Friday morning of the convention when 15 or 20 men, bleary-eyed and perspiring profusely from the heat, are sitting around the table some of them will say: who will we nominate. At that decisive time the friends of Senator Harding can suggest him....

By the fourth day the deadlocked convention, with sweating delegates running out of both money and clean shirts, had still been unable to agree on a nominee. On Thursday evening a meeting was held at the Blackstone Hotel in rooms, 404, 5, and 6, the suite occupied by Colonel George Harvey, publisher of the influential magazine *North American Review*. The honorary colonel was a national power broker with ties to both parties. Around 2:11 a.m. Friday morning, the men, in what came to be known as "the smoke-filled room," agreed to back Harding. The next day he was nominated, and in November was elected in a landslide.

*

---

1. Ohioan Benjamin Harrison was serving as governor of Indiana when he was elected president in 1888.

Corruption at the national level was not an unknown phenomenon in America. James Buchanan, who preceded Abraham Lincoln as president, had in his cabinet a secretary of war named John B. Floyd, who was indicted for mishandling government bonds and other financial crimes.[2] As a Confederate general in the Civil War, at the siege of Fort Donelson, Floyd fled, leaving a subordinate to surrender unconditionally to a newly minted Yankee brigadier, whom the press (playing on some of his initials—US) began calling "Unconditional Surrender" Grant.[3] During the 1869 to 1877 presidency of Grant, the savior of the union, there was massive corruption in the government. In 1884, House Speaker James G. Blaine, a Republican from Maine, became involved in so much graft he was defeated for president. State governments were notoriously corrupt. In the 1880s, young Theodore Roosevelt, a reform member of the New York State legislature, was unable to halt the charge of the "black horse cavalry," as the corrupt members of the lower House were known. Until 1912, state legislatures chose senators and it often happened that the successful candidate was the one favored by lobbyists for big banks and corporations, who spread money around on behalf of their choice.

When Harding became president, with Daugherty as his attorney general, a number of their fellow Ohioans came to Washington to fill jobs and seek favors for themselves or their clients. Old Washington hands referred to them as "the Ohio gang." The gang made its headquarters in a house at 1625 K Street where liquor was freely dispensed, courtesy of a local bootlegger, and high-stakes card games took place. The first was a violation of the Prohibition law and the second of a District of Columbia law. Some strong supporters of Prohibition who imbibed too freely at K Street or in the Capitol itself, had to be sobered up so that they could go on the floor of the Congress and cast their votes as Wayne Wheeler, an Ohioan who ran the anti-saloon league, dictated.

The gang was strategically positioned in the Department of Justice run by Daugherty. One of the key appointees there was William J. Burns, a native of Columbus, Ohio, where his father had been police

---

2. He would eventually beat the charges on legal technicalities.
3. His given names were Ulysses Hiram Simpson.

commissioner. Burns was known as America's greatest detective from his days as a famous U.S. Secret Service operative and later as head of his own private detective agency. In 1921 he was named director of the (federal) Bureau of Investigation where his number two man was twenty-six-year-old J. Edgar Hoover, who, as a DOJ official, had been in charge of combatting the Communists during the 1919-20 "Red Scare." During the period from 1914-17, Burns had worked for both the Allies and the Germans. Because of that and other scandals that he was involved in his reputation suffered. After the war he tried to restore his good name.

In September 1920 a bomb was set off outside America's leading investment bank, the House of Morgan, in New York's Wall Street area, killing thirty-nine people. Burns, though only a private citizen, inserted himself into the case, announcing that he had been retained by an unnamed client to investigate the crime and posted a $50,000 reward for the capture of the bombers. Some suspected Burns himself was the client. During the investigation he told reporters that the bombing was the work of the Soviet government of Russia which had taken power in 1917. After he became director of the Bureau of Investigation Burns announced that the man responsible for the bombing was a Polish anarchist named Wolf Lindenfeld who, when he was tracked down and arrested in Warsaw, claimed he had carried out the act on orders of the Communist International. Eventually Lindenfeld repudiated his confession and it was discovered that he had once worked for the Burns Agency.

Another Justice Department investigator was Gaston Means who, while working for the Burns Agency, had served its German clients. In the Imperial government's secret files he was listed as Agent F-13. A smooth talking North Carolinian, Means was a veteran con man who swindled many people. Once, claiming that the chain broke on the upper birth of his bed in a sleeping car, he sued the Pullman Company. It settled for $14,000, but there was suspicion that Means himself had sawn the chain. Despite the fact that he was fat and bald, Means was quite a ladies' man and in 1914 he took up with a wealthy widow. Allegedly he bilked her out of a half a million dollars and when her lawyers began asking questions about the affair, he invited his lady friend to take a walk down a country road and hunt for rabbits. Somehow the widow managed to "accidentally" shoot herself in the head with Means' gun. Though he was tried for murder he was acquitted by a friendly local jury.

As a special investigator for the DOJ Means told his many crooked friends that he could fix federal cases brought against them. While serving the Justice Department, he picked up the additional task of spying for Elmer Dover, an Ohioan who had been appointed assistant secretary of the treasury in charge of the internal revenue and custom services. Means' job for Dover apparently was to gather information on Treasury employees in case they decided to report their boss for corruption. He not only assured some bootleggers that he could quash indictments against them; he was also able to secure for them much sought after permits to obtain liquor supplies that were kept by the federal government for industrial purposes. The payoffs Means received explained how on a salary of $7 a day he managed to live in a townhouse in an exclusive neighborhood, employ three servants, and travel about in a chauffeur-driven Cadillac.

Attorney General Daugherty himself lived in a house on H Street. Because he feared to be alone at night, he shared accommodations with a fellow Ohioan, Jess Smith, whom he had brought along to Washington to act as his virtual right-hand man.[4] Smith soon became the man to see if a favor was required from the attorney general. One of those who paid him off was George B. Remus, a Cincinnati pharmacist who became known as "King of the Bootleggers." Remus not only paid Smith for liquor permits but kept him on a de facto retainer of nearly $100,000 a year. When federal authorities indicted Remus, Smith promised him the case would be fixed. Then, when the bootlegger was convicted, Smith assured him that the Court of Appeals would overturn it. During this time he picked up an additional $30,000 from Remus. Nevertheless, the bootlegger went to prison.

The Prohibition Commissioner was not selected by his nominal boss, the secretary of the treasury or Attorney General Daugherty. The appointment was in the gift of Wayne Wheeler, who was credited with

---

4. Daugherty's crippled wife, whom he very much loved, continued to reside in Ohio because it was felt her condition did not permit her to move to Washington.

doing the most in the fight to impose Prohibition and was regarded as the real author of the enforcing legislation known as the Volstead Act. Wheeler passed over many experienced law enforcement officers, and named the mayor of a small Ohio town to be commissioner of Prohibition. The Bureau was authorized just 1500 agents to cover the entire United States, and since they were exempt from civil service laws, they were invariably political appointees. Though their annual salary was in the $2000-a-year range, it was understood that they could easily make five times that amount, and in places like New York, $50,000 a year was the usual take. After just two or three years working in the Bureau an agent could amass a fortune well over a million dollars in today's money. Of course, the big money in Washington came from oil tycoons such as Harry Sinclair and Albert Doheny, who paid off for the rights to acquire naval oil reserves kept in reservations like the one in Wyoming known as Teapot Dome.

Organized criminals such as Arnold Rothstein, czar of New York City rackets, targeted a former Ohio pharmacist and longtime federal employee, Levi McNutt, who in 1920 became head of the Narcotics Division of the Prohibition Bureau. After Rothstein's murder (among other rackets he controlled was a drug ring), an examination of his papers disclosed McNutt's son and son-in-law were on the mob czar's payroll.

While corruption had occurred under some previous administrations, gangsters could not penetrate the doors of the White House or federal departments except through their local political contacts. For example, a criminal seeking a presidential pardon might have a congressman of the party in power put in a good word with the White House. Under Harding organized crime figures like Rothstein and Remus could reach out directly to a federal commissioner or member of the White House inner circle.

When allegations of corruption began to become public, Jess Smith, a mild-mannered individual who was terrified of guns, shot himself to death. In the summer of 1923 President Harding died of a heart attack in San Francisco after returning from a trip to Alaska. Supposedly he had become ill from eating poisoned fish, although no one else on the trip suffered from it. The probability is that neither man was murdered, but at the time many suspected that they were. Eventually Secretary of the Interior Albert Fall, Attorney General Daugherty, and Director Burns were all indicted—either for accepting bribes or interfering with the Senate investigation of what became known as the "Teapot Dome" scandal.

Strange events continued to occur in the Republican White House during the Prohibition era. In 1930, President Herbert Hoover became convinced that a minor functionary of the Democratic Party in New York City had come into possession of some papers that could seriously damage the president himself. Hoover's top aide, Larry Richey (né Ricci) was a former star Secret Service agent who had been with Hoover since the World War I era, and was well-versed in back-stairs operations. It was Richey who, in 1924, at the time of Teapot Dome, recommended to Attorney General Harlan Fiske Stone that he make J. Edgar Hoover director of the FBI.

This time neither Richey nor Hoover were given the assignment to investigate the case. Instead, the president called on a top Wall Street investment banker, Lewis Strauss, later secretary of commerce under President Eisenhower. Strauss was a naval reserve officer in New York and he arranged for the district intelligence officer, Lieutenant Commander Glenn Howell, who had already led break-ins at Communist headquarters and Japanese consulates, to undertake the investigation. With the help of a former New York City police officer, he made a surreptitious entry into the official's office. Based on Howell's report, the president was assured that the man posed no threat.[5]

*

The 1920 census found that for the first time more Americans lived in urban areas than in rural ones. The consequence of this was that cities became the dominant political and social force in America. As a result both the politics and the culture of the United States would change. Before 1920 political power came from two well-known

---

5. By using ONI rather than the Bureau of Investigation or the United States Secret Service, the president was perhaps hoping that if things went wrong he could raise the claim of national security to shield the matter from public disclosure. It was not the first time military officers had been assigned to conduct domestic investigations for the White House.

thoroughfares: Wall Street and Main Street. The former represented the financial power of the nation which fueled America's great corporations. The latter was the center of life in every small town across the country, the place where the votes came from to elect a president and members of Congress.

The power of Main Street was not distributed evenly. The southern vote was much less powerful than the northern. In Dixie the key issue was how to keep white rule intact and the solution was to vote for the Democratic candidate who had been chosen in white-only primaries. Blacks were discouraged from voting by a poll tax, literacy tests, and in some places, violence. A secondary source of votes in the north came from big city political machines. However, the Republicans who controlled cities like Philadelphia and Cincinnati and on occasion St. Louis, Chicago, Cleveland and Boston, benefited almost as much from the machine vote as the Democrats.

Before 1920, small town Anglo-Saxon Protestants determined who would occupy the White House or control Congress. Post-1920, however, the cities with a large population of immigrants and the children of immigrants, many of them Catholics or Jews from Ireland or eastern and southern Europe, began to turn out sufficient votes to decide elections in states like Massachusetts, New Jersey, New York, Ohio, Michigan, and Illinois. Urban residents were not bound by small-town mores and, in the 1920s, despite Prohibition liquor flowed freely in the cities. In the latter part of the '20s, a symbol of the change in values was the short skirts worn by young flappers that would have gotten them arrested a decade earlier and the cigarettes they openly smoked that would have caused them to be ejected from any decent restaurant. The old order was passing (slowly) and the new order coming on (rapidly).

One of the last successes of the old order, north or south, had been the enactment of prohibition, but its open rejection by the cities spelled its doom. The governor of New York, a Tammany Catholic named Al Smith, served liquor in the Albany mansion and made no secret of his hostility to dry laws. Chicago's millionaire Republican mayor Bill Thompson allowed free reign to bootleggers. Even staid old cities like Boston and Philadelphia were soaking wet.

Prohibition provided the mechanism by which the organized crime gangs would rise to national power. Before the 1920s the gangs of New York had been largely confined to their local turfs and it was the politicians who were the top dogs. Some gangs were led by well-known hoodlums. In the early 20th century the Bowery was ruled by Monk Eastman (né Edward Osterman), leader of a mostly Jewish gang. In the nearby Five Points Paul Kelly (né Paolo Vacharelli) bossed a largely Italian crew. In Hell's Kitchen, the most prominent Irish tough was Owney "The Killer" Madden. Up in Harlem, New York's first Mafia gang was run by brothers-in-law Joe Morello and Ignazio "Lupo" (Wolf) Saietta. The overlord of Manhattan organized crime was not a gangster but Tammany state senator "Big Tim" Sullivan.

In the 1901 election held in the 2nd assembly district on the Lower East Side of Manhattan, Tammany went against its own local leader, Paddy Divver, a saloon keeper and former magistrate, because it wanted to introduce houses of prostitution into the district and Paddy wouldn't go along. So Big Tim put up Tom Foley, a downtown saloon keeper to contest Paddy's leadership post. On Election Day Paul Kelly's Five Points sluggers invaded the 2nd district and blocked the residents from voting. A number of Paddy's boys tried to battle their way through but the Italians were more numerous and used blackjacks. The police stood by passively and Tom Foley emerged victorious. Later Foley would become successor to Sullivan, and his protégé, Al Smith, would be started on his electoral career by winning the legislative seat in the 2nd assembly district.

If the gangs had proven useful in 1901, two years later they disgraced their Tammany overlords. In 1903 the Kelly and Eastman gangs engaged in a gun battle on the Lower East Side in which three men were killed and seven were wounded before a small army of police managed to clear the streets. The affair made headlines and embarrassed Tammany, then in the midst of a mayoralty election in which their reform opponents were blasting them as hoodlums and murderers. Tammany managed to elect their man, Princeton-educated George B. McClellan, Jr., son of the Civil War general and 1864 Democratic presidential candidate. Afterwards both gang leaders were warned by Tim Sullivan that Tammany would not stand for any more front page violence from them.

The next year, Eastman was cruising late at night through midtown Manhattan when he observed an obviously affluent young man drunkenly lurching along while being tailed by two bruisers, whom Monk assumed were about to rob the sucker. Eastman decided to strike first. It was a bad mistake. The young man was a millionaire's son and the two older ones were Pinkerton detectives assigned by the family to guard their wandering boy. The detectives opened fire on Monk who, as he ran away, collided with a policeman and was clubbed unconscious. True to Sullivan's word, Monk spent the next five years in Sing Sing. In 1905 some rivals tried to kill Paul Kelly in his own saloon. In the shootout that followed, Kelly was wounded, his bodyguard was killed, and several other men were hit. Newspapers carried photos of the dead man lying under a picture of "Big Tim." Once again the headlines were blaring and Kelly was ordered to withdraw from the area. Eventually he migrated up to East Harlem and became a leader in the Longshoremen's Union. In 1910, the mafiosos Morello and Saietta were arrested by the federal government for counterfeiting and sentenced to twenty-five and thirty years respectively. Four years later, Owney Madden was sent to Sing Sing for murder.

In 1912 the roof fell in on Tammany and the whole organized crime structure. Lieutenant Charles Becker, who commanded a confidential squad working out of the police commissioner's office, was notorious for shaking down gamblers. When one of them, Herman Rosenthal, began squealing to the Manhattan district attorney about payoffs, he was shot to death outside of a Times Square hotel. During the investigation that followed the police commissioner was fired; the mayor dropped dead; Tammany lost City Hall and the governorship; Tim Sullivan supposedly went insane, escaped from his keepers, and was run over by a train; and Lieutenant Becker was executed at Sing Sing prison. A disaster of that magnitude might well have destroyed the government of a small European state. But Tammany was back in power just four years later, helped by an alliance with the Brooklyn machine. The year after that Al Smith was elected governor. In 1928, despite his Catholic faith and close affiliation with Tammany, he became the Democratic nominee for president. However, his candidacy did not fly on Main Street.

After losing the state house, City Hall, the police department, and their beloved "Big Tim" to avoid similar disasters in the future Tammany bosses decided to make Arnold Rothstein—who was a gambler, not a politician or a killer—the overseer of organized crime under their direction. This would provide them some insulation in the event of trouble. As it turned out, Rothstein became bigger than the politicians. He was so untouchable that though everyone knew he fixed the 1919 "Black Sox" World Series, he was never prosecuted. He operated on a much larger stage than the typical gangster. He was not only involved in gambling, drugs, and bootlegging, he also controlled Wall Street bucket shops. A well-known man about town, he moved in the same circles as tycoons, sports, and entertainment celebrities. He appeared in the Damon Runyon stories as Armand Rosenthal and in *The Great Gatsby* as Meyer Wolfsheim. In 1925 he was a key figure behind the election of Tammany's Jimmy Walker as mayor. Rothstein also trained some of the up and coming Italian gangsters, like Lucky Luciano. Among the lessons he taught Lucky was how to dress like an uptown gentleman rather than a downtown hoodlum. In 1928 Rothstein was murdered in a dispute over a gambling debt.

In 1929, two groups of Italian gangsters engaged in an intramural war and both their leaders, Joe Masseria and Sal Maranzano, were killed. In 1931 the Italian gang leaders agreed to establish five separate mob families, one of them led by Lucky Luciano, who became the premier figure in the New York mob world. Many names were applied to the mobs in New York and other cities. Some reporters called them the Mafia, others the Unione Siciliano, and still others, the Black Hand. Mafia was the most apt. Unione Siciliano was a fraternal organization and many gang leaders were not Sicilians but Neapolitans (like Chicago's famed Al Capone) or Calabrians (such as Albert Anastasia and Frank Costello). The Black Hand was not an organization but a method of extortion in which Italian criminals would send letters to their countrymen demanding that they pay off or be killed. The writers would usually affix to the signature line a black hand. Some "Black

Handers" even sent extortion letters to prominent mafiosos though the payoffs they received were often in lead.[6]

With the passing of men like Tim Sullivan, Tom Foley, and Arnold Rothstein, the Mafia became the rulers of New York City organized crime. Owney Madden, who had been released from prison in 1923, was a top figure in the bootlegging world. However, when the Italians took over he was exiled to the gambling spa of Hot Springs, Arkansas, where he settled into the role of elder statesman. When his mother died he had to obtain special permission from the Mafia to return briefly to New York City to bury her.

As lords of the underworld and powerful political bosses, the Mafia became involved in presidential politics. At the 1932 Democratic National Convention in Chicago, Lucky Luciano and Tammany fixer Jimmy Hines shared a hotel room where they worked for Al Smith's nomination. In another room of the same hotel Frank Costello set up shop to promote the candidacy of Franklin D. Roosevelt. No matter who won the Mafia would hold an IOU. Only the 1933 election of reformer Fiorello LaGuardia as mayor prevented the gangsters from taking over New York City.

Chicago had a similar history. Before 1914 Jim Colosimo was the top boss in the Levee-red light district. However, he was subservient to the political leaders of the first Ward: "Bathhouse John" Coughlin and Mike "Hinkey-dink" Kenna, whose domain included the rich pickings of the Loop business district. Other groups controlled the west-, south-, and northside areas and Mont Tennes ran the racing wire service which made him the most important man in the gambling world. In 1914 Mayor Carter Harrison "the younger" (between the younger and his father "the elder," they served ten terms as mayor), was a polished Southern gentleman educated at Yale. Seeking to clean up his image as a prelude to a possible run for the presidency, he decided to make war on the Levee. Since the district cops there belonged to the politicians and vice lords of the First Ward, Harrison created a special morals squad of detectives to carry out the task. On a summer night in 1914, a shootout erupted on a Levee street between

---

6. In Europe the term was used to denote a Spanish radical group and also a Serbian nationalist group. The later was involved in the assassination of the Archduke Franz Ferdinand at Sarajevo in 1914.

the morals squad, city detectives (who didn't recognize the other cops), and gangsters. When it was over a city detective was dead, two morals detectives were wounded, along with an informer for the squad, a gangster, and several bystanders. The infuriated mayor cleaned out the police command in the Levee area and had the district shut down completely. This angered Colosimo and other dive owners and in the 1915 mayoral election they threw their support to Republican William Hale Thompson, who was victorious.

When Prohibition was introduced, Colosimo, distracted by his new and beautiful young wife, and old-fashioned and set in his ways, declined the appeal of his lieutenant, Johnny Torrio, to get into the bootlegging business on a large scale. So Colosimo was assassinated and Torrio became the top bootlegger in Chicago. Mayor Thompson essentially allowed him to function as overseer of the liquor industry, parceling out territories to other gangs. This arrangement worked fairly well until 1923 when Thompson left City Hall and an all-out gang war broke out, during the course of which Torrio was severely wounded. Afterwards he left Chicago, turning over control to his lieutenant, Al Capone. The mob wars culminated on Valentine's Day 1929, when Capone gunmen killed seven men in a North Side garage. After President Hoover assigned a task force of Treasury agents to "get Capone," Al was sent to prison and never returned to Chicago. His mob continued to operate and from 1933 on were virtual partners of the Chicago political machine.

The same sequence of events happened in other cities. Italian gangsters in Boston, led by Phil Buccola and Joe Lombardo, murdered the leader of the Jewish faction, Charles "King" Solomon, and the top two figures in the Irish Gustin gang, Frankie Wallace and "Dodo" Walsh. From then on the Mafia faction, known as "the office," ran organized crime.

In Detroit, Italians took over the Purple Gang from its original Jewish members who had established the "Jewish Navy" which ferried Canadian liquor across Lake Erie to Cleveland. So the Jewish refugees from Detroit went to Cleveland where their organization, known as the "Jewish boys," managed to exist side-by-side with the mafiosos of the

Mayfield Road gang. Italian gangs also controlled organized crime in Buffalo and Kansas City, whereas Jews ruled Philadelphia.

Beginning in the late 1920s the Italian gangs began to set up a loose national syndicate. In 1928 Cleveland cops raided a Mafia summit meeting being held in the Statler Hilton Hotel, where they seized a number of mob bosses from various cities. In May, 1929, the mobs held an interethnic conclave in Atlantic City, New Jersey. Among the items on the agenda was Al Capone's Valentine's Day massacre in Chicago, which had put a lot of pressure on organized crime nationally. The participants ordered Capone to get the heat off or else. So Al went to Philadelphia, where he allowed himself to be caught carrying an illegal gun, pled guilty, and was sent to jail for a year. Of course it was all a setup. In 1931, after the establishment of the five-family structure in New York City, Lucky Luciano brought his Jewish friend Meyer Lansky to a sitdown in Chicago to brief his Windy City counterparts. Lansky, not being Italian, had to wait outside the room. When they returned to Chicago for a meeting at the Congress Hotel in 1932 Lansky was allowed in, a recognition that, for practical purposes, he was an honorary member of the Mafia. Because Mayor Anton Cermak was feuding with Capone's successor Frank Nitti, Lansky, Luciano, Nitti, and two of Al Capone's cousins were arrested by Chicago detectives as they left the meeting.

Sometimes it is said that any Italian in a Mafia family was more powerful than any Jew. That did not apply to people like Lansky and his longtime friend Bugsy Siegel. The only job they could not have was top boss of a Mafia group, because that was reserved for individuals of southern Italian heritage on both sides of their family.[7] When Siegel was murdered in Los Angeles by Jack Dragna's group, it was not because he was Jewish, but because he had cheated his Mafia bosses back in New York and they ordered him killed. Los Angeles' Jewish Mickey Cohen was shot or shot at on many occasions because of his propensity for pulling crazy stunts that hurt organized crime generally, not his ethnicity.

---

7. The reason for this was that southern Italians placed loyalty to family above all other considerations. In addition, it was easier to trace their backgrounds in Italy in order to ensure that they were trustworthy.

According to many mob sources, the final shape of the national syndicate was put together at a 1934 meeting in New York's Waldorf Astoria Hotel, chaired by Johnny Torrio and Meyer Lansky. After leaving Chicago, Torrio had gone to New York, where he was given a place in the hierarchy of eastern organized crime, while Lansky had come to the fore because of his financial genius and close relationship with Luciano and Costello. From 1934 on, the leaders of the loosely organized national syndicate were the bosses of the five New York mob families and the ones in New Jersey, New England, Buffalo, Cleveland, Chicago, and Detroit (though not always at the same time). Only the New York, Buffalo, and Chicago families had permanent seats.

In the 1930s the northern mobs began expanding into places like Florida and Louisiana, although in the latter they required the permission of Huey Long. During the Depression, the mob sometimes had more money than big corporations, which had been hard-hit. If the national syndicate had existed in 1920, its voice would certainly have been heard in the smoke-filled room at the Republican convention. By the 1940s the mob was playing a significant national role, though its leaders could not be received at the White House but had to work through intermediaries. Hence the mob usually got its way. In one famous New York City standoff between President Roosevelt and Frank Costello, the latter's candidate for a judgeship prevailed over the president's.

Twenty-four years after the 1920 Republican convention, the smoke-filled room scenario was repeated at the 1944 Democratic convention held in Chicago. In 1920, Harding had been picked by bosses, including U.S. senators and men who represented large business interests. In 1944, Truman was picked by machine bosses from various cities who had close ties to the Mafia. In 1945, when he became president, the Missouri gang took up where the Ohio gang had left off. This time the blame for the new administration's scandals did not rest with the various corporate interests they served, but corrupt bosses who did the bidding of murderous criminals.

Chapter 2

New York City: Murder Incorporated

Walter Winchell, a former child vaudeville entertainer, had risen from a New York gossip columnist to a national star of newspapers and radio. A mention in his syndicated column could send a stock zooming up, make a Broadway hit out of a turkey, and turn a supporting actress into a star. An item in Winchell's column or on his radio show was such a mark of prestige that many prominent people paid press agents to get them a mention. Because he was so vicious, other people paid agents to keep them out of the column or off his radio show. He frequently had items like "What blue-blooded patron of the turf is being seen around town with the lead dancer from a Broadway show and does his wife know about it?" Within a short time there would be another Winchell item about the man's wife heading to Reno, the divorce capital of America.

On Sunday night, August 5, 1939, Winchell addressed himself to an unknown person, saying that "if you are listening, a deal can be arranged." Some New York mob watchers figured out that Winchell was talking to Louis "Lepke" Buchalter, a top gangster who had been in hiding for two years from the FBI, Federal Bureau of Narcotics, the Manhattan and Brooklyn district attorneys, and the NYPD for various crimes, ranging from antitrust violations through drug dealing and on up to murder. In the 1930s Lepke[1] frequently employed an organized-

---

1. Yiddish for "Little Louis," the name he was always known by.

crime group of killers that the newspapers dubbed "Murder Incorporated" to carry out hits. Now the growing pressure on the New
York gangs to reveal Lepke's whereabouts was becoming too much for
them to stand. So they looked to cut a deal whereby the fugitive could
surrender and be sentenced in a federal prison, but would not have to
face state murder charges that could put him in the electric chair. It
was feared that if Lepke got a death sentence he would talk and hurt a
lot of important people, not only in the mob world but in politics and
organized labor.

Every top gangster in New York knew that Winchell was in tight
with "Mr. G-man" himself, J. Edgar Hoover. Winchell and he were
frequently seen together at the Stork Club, a glamour spa, founded by
mob money and run by ex-bootlegger Sherman Billingsley. Hoover, an
inveterate horse player, accepted tips from Winchell, though everyone
knew the columnist got his information from organized crime figures
like Frank Costello. Winchell's relationship with Hoover was based on
the directors need to cultivate such a powerful media figure and Winchell's desire for inside information. So some of the boys approached
the columnist to set up a deal. They proposed that Lepke be allowed to
surrender to Hoover. When Winchell broadcast to Lepke on Sunday
night, Hoover was sitting beside him in the studio. Two weeks later,
though, Lepke was still, as they say in New York, "in the wind."
Hoover was furious and told Winchell that the mob was making a fool
out of him and if Lepke did not surrender at once FBI agents would be
ordered to shoot him on sight. Winchell relayed the threats to the mob
and it was agreed that Lepke would surrender on Thursday, August
23rd. That night at 6 p.m., Winchell waited at a Manhattan phone
booth for a call. When the phone rang the person on the other end
instructed him to drive to a theater in suburban Yonkers. When
Winchell got there he received a message to drive back to a Manhattan
drugstore. For a while he sat drinking a Coke at the fountain and then
was joined by a man who ordered Winchell to park at 23rd Street and
Madison Avenue and wait. Shortly after 10 o'clock, Lepke climbed into
Winchell's car. As per arrangement, Hoover was waiting alone in a
government sedan at 28th St. and Fifth Avenue, less than a half a mile
away. Winchell drove Lepke over there and introduced him by saying

"Mr. Hoover this is Lepke." "How do you do" said Hoover, "Glad to meet you, let's go," Lepke replied. At the same tim,e though, he was getting cold feet and thought about bolting the vehicle. But FBI men had moved up along both sides, so it was impossible.

Neither the governor of New York State, the mayor of New York City, the Manhattan or Brooklyn district attorneys were in on the surrender deal. The arrangements were made by a newspaper man and an appointed federal official who in his own Department of Justice ranked below the attorney general and the deputy attorney general. Because Winchell was so prominent and Hoover a law unto himself, the FBI director had agreed on his own to accept Lepke's surrender. However, the case was far from resolved and a few years later it would cast a shadow over the White House.

*

In the 1930s Brooklyn was a place most Americans had heard a lot about but had never visited. Its baseball team was known for having three runners on the same base and its managers for fighting with umpires. In the movies, Brooklyn characters always spoke in a "dees, dos, and dem" accent. Until 1898 it was an independent city (the fourth largest in the United States); then it had been merged with the other boroughs into the modern New York City.[2] Ever since, it had suffered from an inferiority complex vis-à-vis rich and glamorous Manhattan. Still, with its 2,000,000-plus population, the borough carried considerable political weight. Since the merger, three of New York's mayors had been Brooklynites.

Cops regarded Brooklyn as a difficult area to police. It had murderous gangs and produced famous robbers like Willie "The Actor" Sutton. Three of New York's five Mafia families, the Bonnanos, the Profacis, and the Manganos (the latter included his powerful lieutenant, waterfront boss Albert Anastasia), were headquartered in the borough. Two others, one identified with Tommy Lucchese, and the group

---

2. New York boroughs are political subdivisions of the city government. Besides Brooklyn they include the Bronx, Manhattan, Queens, and Staten Island. Their boundaries are coterminous with counties which are political subdivisions of the state government. Bronx and Queens County have the same names as the borough, whereas Brooklyn is Kings, Manhattan is New York, and Staten Island is Richmond.

headed by Charles "Lucky" Luciano (and after 1936, Frank Costello), were based in Manhattan.

By 1939 a pattern of gangland murders in a six-square mile section of northeast Brooklyn, encompassing the neighborhoods of Brownsville, East New York, and Ocean Hill, had drawn the notice of the police. During prohibition the NYPD did not pay too much attention to mob killings. Delving into them was bad for a cop's career. In 1934, the ascension of reformer Fiorello LaGuardia to mayor and Brooklyn's own Lewis Valentine to commissioner shook up the police department. Valentine was a tough cop who defied gangsters and politicians and paid the price for it with frequent transfers to remote precincts.[3]

In response to the homicide pattern, the cops used tactics that would be impossible to employ today because the civil liberties lobby and various advocacy groups would raise a huge protest the moment they were instituted. LaGuardia himself might have been expected to favor restraining the police but he was a complex man. His father was an army bandmaster and Fiorello was raised on a western outpost in Geronimo country. As an adult, he would style himself a cowboy, wear a ten-gallon hat, and claim Prescott, Arizona, as his hometown. As might be expected of a soldier's son, he always expressed patriotic, flag-waving views. During World War I he had quit Congress to become a bomber pilot and saw action on the Austrian front. For the rest of his life he preferred intimates to address him by his military rank of major. As mayor he would lead the police or fire bands in rousing marches. Though his political views were very leftist for his time, he scorned the socialists for their pacifism and the Tammany controlled Democrats for their corruption. So he became a Republican. In Manhattan he cut an odd figure among the social register types who controlled the local GOP.

---

3. Under reform Mayor John P. Mitchel (1914–1917) Lieut. Valentine and his partner Lieut. Floyd Horton worked out of headquarters, making life miserable for corrupt cops. When Tammany came back to power they were both transferred to distant precincts. In 1920, Horton was killed when he interrupted a burglary. Though he managed to write the license number of the getaway car down in his own blood, the police commissioner refused to honor the normal practice of inducting a fallen hero into the police legion of honor. Valentine also suffered. One night he was working the desk in a precinct when his wife called to tell him that their son had suddenly taken ill and was in critical condition. Valentine feared to leave his post because it would give the corrupt city administration an excuse to fire him. While he sat at his desk praying, his relief lieutenant came in several hours early, permitting Valentine to go home and say goodbye to his son just before he died.

Though a labor and defense lawyer, LaGuardia hated hoodlums. Once, when Valentine urged that gangsters be brought into the police station covered in blood, civil libertarians protested to LaGuardia, who supported his commissioner. Another time when lawyers complained to the mayor about their jewel thief clients' faces being battered in, LaGuardia replied "That's just too bad."

The Brooklyn cops began their drive by pulling toughs off the corners and charging them with offenses like vagrancy or loitering. This stopped the sidewalk crap games and broke the gangsters' control of the streets. The cops then went into bars and pool rooms, where hoodlums congregated, dragged them out, and threw them into patrol wagons. On a single day in January 1940, they brought in twenty-two thugs from the Ocean Hill area around Pitkin Avenue. Among those seized were leading hoods like Harry "Happy" Maione, Frank "Dasher" Abandando, and Seymour "Blue Jaw" Magoon. Four blocks south of Pitkin there was a candy store run by a woman called "Midnight Rose" because her place stayed open twenty-four hours a day. There Abandando, Maione, and others could meet with East New York/Brownsville thugs such as Abe "Kid Twist" Reles, Harry "Pittsburgh Phil" Strauss, and Martin "Buggsy" Goldstein.

On January 1, 1940, as the NYPD drive was getting underway, Kings County (Brooklyn) installed a new district attorney named William O'Dwyer. While he owed his job to the Brooklyn machine, actually he got it because of a group of (mostly Manhattan) reformers who comprised an organization known as the Citizens Crime Commission.

In 1935 a runaway Manhattan grand jury defied the Tammany DA and called on Gov. Herbert Lehman to appoint a special prosecutor. The governor offered the post to four stars of the legal world. All of them turned him down and recommended that he appoint a young whiz kid named Thomas Dewey, who had come to New York from Michigan a decade earlier to study law at Columbia and voice in Manhattan conservatories. He had a good baritone, but he proved to be much better as an attorney. He impressed leaders of the field with his skills and in 1931, although only twenty-eight years old, he was appointed chief assistant United States Attorney for the Southern

District of New York. When the U.S. attorney went back to private practice Dewey was named by the district judges to succeed him. As a federal prosecutor he went after crooked cops and gangsters. When the Democrats took over Washington, the Republican Dewey was replaced.

In 1936, as special prosecutor, Dewey managed to convict "Lucky" Luciano on charges of operating a prostitution ring. The judge sentenced "Charlie Lucky" to prison for 30-50 years. Heretofore it had not been an offense that Lucky was suspected of being involved in and the sentence was considered draconian. Some of the prostitutes who were state witnesses later recanted their testimony. The notion that Lucky Luciano would conduct mob business with his lieutenants in his suite at the Waldorf while prostitutes sat around watching was absurd to anyone who knew how gangsters operated. Nevertheless, Luciano was removed to the tough Dannemora prison, along the frozen Canadian border. In 1937, Dewey was elected district attorney of New York County. In 1938 he convicted Tammany district leader Jimmy Hines, the fix man for Manhattan organized crime, who was sent to prison for four to eight years. Dewey's star rose to the top of the local political firmament and he was even discussed as a possible presidential candidate for 1940.

Some key figures in the runaway grand jury that forced Dewey's appointment remained active as a private Crime Commission. In 1939 it brought charges against the Brooklyn district attorney and he was removed by Governor Lehman, who named another Dewey type, John Harlan Amen, to investigate corrupt rackets in that borough. However, Brooklyn was the leading Democratic stronghold outside of the solid South. So Amen could not acquire the political strength to become the Brooklyn district attorney. Instead, the borough machine, led by boss Frank Kelly, selected O'Dwyer.

On the surface O'Dwyer life resembled a Horatio Alger story. Born in Ireland in 1890, he had been sent to a Jesuit training school in Spain. Lacking the vocation, he immigrated to the United States, where he worked at various jobs, such as a longshoreman and bartender. In 1917 he joined the NYPD and was assigned to patrol the streets of a Brooklyn waterfront precinct. One night a drunk, who was threatening his wife with a gun, pointed his weapon at O'Dwyer, who had responded to the scene. The cop fired, killing the man.[4] In 1925, after studying law at night, O'Dwyer quit the force and became a lawyer. He was active in Brooklyn political clubs and Irish social organizations and was eventually named a magistrate, the lowest rung on the city's judicial ladder. Later, he moved up to county judge, where he heard serious cases.

At the end of 1941, a tired Mayor LaGuardia would complete his second term. Since the modern city had been created no mayor had served more than eight years. So the way looked clear for the Democrats to take back City Hall. If, in the two years before the election, the handsome, charming "Bill O" could emulate Dewey by becoming an acclaimed crimefighter, he would probably waltz into the mayoralty. So his office began to work closely with the police anti-gangster drive in Brooklyn.

The cops' tactics started to have an impact. Some of those arrested began worrying about what was coming next. At this point they recalled a basic piece of street wisdom, "He who talks, walks," i.e., hoodlums can cut a deal to mitigate their own sins in return for giving information about other thugs. The first break came when a prisoner in the Rikers Island workhouse, Harry Rudolph, wrote a letter to the district attorney's office saying he would like to talk about a murder case. When questioned, he described the 1933 murder of his pal "Red" Alpert and named "Kid Twist" Reles, "Buggsy" Goldstein, and a lesser hoodlum, "Dukey" Maffetore, as the killers. During the interview Rudolph showed the detectives scars in his stomach where the hoods had shot him. He was taken before a grand jury and the three accused murderers were indicted. A detective captain was ordered to pick them up. After he and his men made a short tour of the area, the captain left a note at a lunch room frequented by the suspects, telling them to be in his office at 8 a.m. the next morning. Normally that was a bad idea, because the wanted men were likely to flee.[5] However, Kid Twist and Buggsy had often been picked up for questioning but rarely charged,

---

4. O'Dwyer always felt bad about the incident. In subsequent years he paid for the schooling of the man's son and later helped him get a job on the police force.
5. As a famous New York detective of the early 20th century, Capt. Mike Fiaschetti, wrote "don't talk about locking someone up, do it." Note in our own time, where O. J. Simpson was put on the honor system to surrender and what followed from that.

so they came in as directed. The lesser hood, Dukey, was collared by police that day.

The three suspects were each kept separated in a different jail. Dukey looked to be the weak link and a detective lieutenant who spoke Italian, which the prisoner was more conversant in than English, started visiting him. At the same time Kid Twist and Buggsy were utilizing covert contacts to offer Rudolph a bribe to forget about them and put the blame on Dukey. The plot was uncovered by a jailhouse stool pigeon from Los Angeles, brought in by the district attorney's office as a spy in another investigation. When Dukey learned what was happening, he talked. Still, that was not enough. In New York, the law does not permit the admission of evidence from an accomplice of the defendant unless it is corroborated by a non-accomplice.[6]

"Kid Twist" was a vicious hoodlum even in the eyes of fellow gangsters. Only five-foot-two, with a squat body and gangly arms, he looked like a miniature monster. His nickname supposedly came from his ability to twist wires around a victim's neck, but it was also the moniker of an early 20th-century New York gangster. Reles was sent to reform school at age thirteen, but he never reformed. Instead he became involved in numerous crimes, was a suspect in at least fourteen murders and when charges were brought against him in others he beat the rap. For example, he stabbed to death a garage attendant who did not retrieve his car quickly enough. He beat the case and three months later, in the same garage, killed another attendant who did not move fast enough. Naturally, Reles again went free.

In those days the electric chair was kept so busy that Sing Sing Prison in nearby Ossining, New York, reserved Thursday night for executions. Frequently, more than one person was dispatched at a single performance. Reles concluded that he had better act quickly to avoid starring in the "Thursday Night Follies." However, he was not going to settle for avoiding a death sentence and then spend years in prison. Instead, he intended to walk totally free. So he made a bold move. He asked to sit down with District Attorney O'Dwyer himself.

---

6. The corroboration necessary in New York State is not required in some other states or the federal system. One reason offered for the New York law is that it is due to the legislature's scrupulous concern for defendants' civil rights. Another reason is that it is designed to keep bribed politicians safe. For example, a bribe-giver's testimony is no good without corroboration. So if a politician just takes the money from the briber, i.e., an accomplice, he is home free.

When he did, Reles told the DA he would make him "the biggest man in the country" by providing information on numerous contract murders, but he wanted an agreement that he would do no time in jail. After some deliberation, O'Dwyer accepted on the grounds that it was better to let one killer go in order to catch many more.

As a result of Reles' testimony, murderers like Maione, Abandando, Goldstein, and Strauss were sent to the electric chair and others, such as Magoon, were given long prison sentences. The round-up of the killers was big news in New York and the nation. The press christened the group "Murder, Inc." Reles did not stop with just providing information on mid-level gangsters. He implicated the man who oversaw all murder contracts in Brooklyn, Albert Anastasia, who was sometimes referred to as the "Lord High Executioner" (from Gilbert and Sullivan's *The Mikado*). When word leaked out that Reles was talking, Anastasia disappeared. Reles also cast a spotlight on the mob's master fixer for Brooklyn, Joe Adonis, a close associate of Boss Frank Kelly. In addition, he revealed that one of the most frequent users of Murder, Inc. was Lepke Buchalter, Czar of Manhattan's garment center, major drug dealer, and controller of a number of unions.

Lepke had an unusual background for a gangster. His family was respectable. One of his brothers was a rabbi, another a pharmacist, and the third a dentist. His sister was head of the English department at a local high school. Lepke, born in 1897, started out early as a burglar. Despite the fact that he only stood five foot seven and was slightly built, he became a garment center slugger in partnership with a hulking childhood friend named Jacob "Gurrah" Shapiro.[7]

Their turf, the garment district of Manhattan, sometimes referred to as "Seventh Avenue," was the place where most of the clothes American's wore were manufactured. Lepke and Gurrah rose to the top of the gangster hierarchy by working both sides of the street. Instead of slugging for the employers or the unions they served both. Seventh Avenue had a unique economic structure. Banks were often reluctant to loan money to small businesses in so chancy a field as fashion, because if a particular line did not find favor with Kansas City

---

7. The nickname came from pushcart peddlers whom young Jake preyed on. When they saw him the peddlers would shout "Gurrah [get away] Jake, gurrah" and like Lepke Buchalter it became his nom de crime.

or Seattle housewives the manufacturer might go broke. Lepke and Gurrah were willing lenders. The condition, though, was the that they would become partners with the borrower. Once in, they could never be gotten rid of and often the manufacturer found himself working for them or pushed out of the business entirely. An owner who objected or complained to the law was likely to be found dead. When employees of shops run by gangsters had their wages cut, the few who dared squawk would be introduced to the mob's favorite grievance mechanism—a lead pipe.

Unions too might acquire unwanted partners or find themselves run by a president or business agent who was a graduate of the Sing Sing school of labor relations. Of course, there were advantages in mob control—a fact overlooked by many theorists. If the owner knew his business, the mob was likely to keep him on and his share of the profits would probably be more than he would have made as an individual entrepreneur. A business under mob control was more likely to get sales orders than a non-mob-owned one. In the Depression, workers were happy to have a job whatever the arrangements.

Lepke was almost an equal with "Lucky" Luciano. In 1931, at Luciano's request, Lepke's gunmen carried out a hit on Salvatore Maranzano, who fancied himself "boss of bosses." Maranzano's had been the last obstacle to Luciano's ascension to power. In 1935, again at the request of Luciano, Lepke's gunmen killed the notorious Jewish gangster, Dutch Schultz (né Arthur Flegenheimer). The popular legend was that Schultz planned to murder special prosecutor Dewey, and Luciano, recognizing that would bring intense heat on organized crime, felt he had to stop him. So he arranged for Lepke's guys to kill the Dutchman. My research suggests that this version is not correct. Rather, it was simply to get rid of an unreliable, fading mob figure, after which Lepke and Luciano could split the Dutchman's holdings.[8]

Dewey also had Lepke in his sights. He started by looking into the 1934 murder of union president Billy Snyder. One night a lieutenant of Lepke's sat down for dinner with Snyder and announced that the mob wished to become partners with him. The idea did not appeal to Billy,

---

8. Schultz was intending to convert to his wife's faith, Catholicism. This raised the possibility that he might try to cleanse himself by confessing his sins to District Attorney Dewey.

so Lepke's messenger whipped out a gun and killed Snyder in front of thirteen witnesses, all of whom told the cops that they had seen nothing. Dewey's investigation then began to look into other garment center killings. In 1936 a trucker named Joe Rosen, whom Lepke put out of business, made noises about going to Dewey and was murdered.

In 1937, Lepke and Gurrah were convicted on a minor federal antitrust violation related to their work in the garment center. This resulted in two-year sentences for each. It was the kind of wrist slap that gangsters could do standing on their heads; instead they decided to disappear. This would allow time for their lawyers to overturn their conviction (which they did initially, thanks to the corrupt chief judge of the United States Circuit Court). Fugitive warrants were issued for the two mob bosses. At the time Dewey was assembling a rackets indictment against them and the Federal Bureau of Narcotics (FBN) was preparing a major case against Lepke and his drug smuggling ring. To Louie, the drug charges appeared to be the most threatening because the FBN was a tough outfit.

In 1930 Harry Anslinger had been named United States Commissioner of Narcotics. Over the next thirty years, under his direction, the FBN became a major force against drug dealers. During World War I Anslinger had been a United States consul in Holland, where he spied on Germany. In the postwar years, as a diplomat, he was peripherally involved in the international aspects of drug trafficking. As FBN Commissioner he came down so hard on drug dealers that the burly, rough-spoken product of a Pennsylvania mining district was sometimes referred to in the underworld as "Asslinger". He constantly preached that a few puffs of marijuana would lead one to addiction and ruination. The 1937 movie *Reefer Madness,* a 1960s camp classic, was produced to carry Anslinger's message to the public.[9]

Lepke knew that a federal narcotics rap would be hard to beat and that conviction would bring a stiff sentence. Gurrah was captured in 1938, but law enforcement's hunt for Buchalter was unsuccessful. When a routine fugitive warrant was issued it had been assigned to the

---

9. Anslinger did not actually arrest marijuana users. Profiting from the example of the Prohibition Bureau's failure, he told his men not to arrest ordinary users or raid the corner drugstore but instead to concentrate on the big shots. Marijuana enforcement was left to the states.

FBI for execution. This placed the ball in the court of FBI director J. Edgar Hoover.

For two years Hoover's G-Men, Anslinger's T-Men, Valentine's New York cops, and Dewey and O'Dwyer's investigators could not find Lepke. It was rumored he had fled the country and was in Europe or Asia. In fact he was living in Brooklyn under the protection of Albert Anastasia.[10] While in hiding, he continued to order hits. In July 1939, Murder, Inc., gunmen killed a respectable businessman named Irving Penn, who resembled a Lepke enemy, Phil Orlovsky. The press headlined the crime and the Mafia family bosses knew that unless Lepke was found the heat on all of them would be intense.

So the mafiosos contacted Walter Winchell and Anastasia personally drove Lepke to meet Winchell. For Hoover the arrest of Lepke was an easy way to get headlines as a mob fighter without actually doing anything and to one-up Dewey, Anslinger, and Valentine, all of whom he disliked.

It was not long before the deal fell apart. In 1940 Lepke was convicted on federal drug trafficking charges and sentenced to fourteen years imprisonment. Dewey then prosecuted him on a state indictment for extortion, which resulted in a sentence of thirty years. In 1941, based on the testimony of Reles and other Murder Incorporated gangsters, Lepke and two of his hit men, Emmanuel "Mendy" Weiss and Lou Capone, were convicted by O'Dwyer's office of the 1936 murder in Brooklyn of Joe Rosen, who had threatened to talk to Dewey. The three defendants were sentenced to death.

*

With numerous convictions, seven death sentences, and the whole world talking about Murder, Incorporated, O'Dwyer was riding high. But the revelations against Anastasia (then in hiding) and major Brooklyn figures like Adonis had the potential to bring down the Brooklyn political organization which had made him.

1941 was an important year in both New York City politics and organized crime. Tom Dewey announced he would not run for reelec-

---

10. A situation which, in my opinion, suggests some law enforcement officials probably knew where Lepke was but, for political or financial reasons, did not arrest him.

tion as Manhattan district attorney. Instead, he would seek the governorship in 1942. Both Tammany and the Republicans agreed to endorse a candidate recommended by Dewey. However, his first list contained three names, all of them Republican. Tammany balked and asked whether there were no Democrats whom Dewey trusted. So he added the name of one of his top assistants, Frank Hogan, who was a registered Democrat. Hogan was chosen and his election in November was the start of his thirty-three-year incumbency as New York County district attorney. Dewey ran successfully for governor the following year.

Mayor Fiorello LaGuardia faced a tough fight for reelection in 1941. In addition, his heart was no longer in his job and he would have preferred Roosevelt to give him a position in the national defense effort. FDR made him director of civil defense, but it was only a part-time position and LaGuardia remained as mayor. The appointment was a symbolic gesture to demonstrate that American cities needed to prepare themselves for possible bombing raids. Roosevelt really wanted LaGuardia to stay as mayor rather than risk him being replaced by an anti-New Deal figure.

With LaGuardia appearing vulnerable, the Brooklyn machine pushed the candidacy of Bill O'Dwyer for the Democratic nomination, arguing that the good publicity he had received in the Murder, Inc., investigation would make him an easy winner. Tammany went along because by 1941 it was much weaker than it ever had been. In the 1920s its favorite son, Governor Al Smith, was considered a serious possibility for the White House. Its wayward son, playboy mayor Jimmy Walker, had been a favorite of the people until various scandals caused him to flee to England. In the 1930s Tammany made major mistakes: it backed Smith for the presidential nomination in 1932 against Roosevelt. With FDR as president and Herbert Lehman as governor, Tammany was starved for patronage. By the end of the decade, Frank Costello would become the de facto boss of the organization.

Demography also hurt Manhattan. In the post-World War I era, the borough began to lose population while the Bronx grew rapidly. The latter contained a mixed Irish, Jewish, and Italian population of about 1,500,000 people who saw their move to the Bronx as a step up in the world. It was said every Jew on Manhattan's lower east side dreamed of someday living in one of the handsome apartment buildings on the Grand Concourse, the Park Avenue of the Bronx.

The boss of Tammany Hall had traditionally assumed precedence over all other Democratic county leaders and Brooklyn held second place. But in the 1930s, Ed Flynn, boss of the Bronx and a strong Roosevelt supporter, was given control of the federal patronage in New York City and named the State's Democratic national committee-man. Flynn also stood well with Gov. Lehman, serving as secretary of state and controlling the state patronage in the city.

As a key lieutenant of President Roosevelt, Flynn even sought to assume the role of world statesman. But he still had to take care of his responsibilities as boss of the Bronx and his county was not immune to organized crime. The "Artichoke King," Ciro Terranova, ran the rackets in the borough's Hunts Point Market. In the 1920s, when Flynn was the sheriff of Bronx County, the area's favorite gangster, Dutch Schultz, acquired a deputy sheriff's badge which permitted him to carry a gun legally. As the foremost New York Democrat, Flynn had to cooperate with Tammany and Frank Kelly's Brooklyn machine, both of which were in bed with mobsters. Counter to FDR's wishes, Flynn threw his support to O'Dwyer. The race was close and only Roosevelt's endorsement of the Republican LaGuardia pulled the mayor through with just 53% of the total vote.

Despite his statesmanlike pose, Flynn also had the usual problems of political bosses. The Bronx superintendent of public works used county employees to install some paving blocks at Flynn's country home. During the war, when Roosevelt nominated Flynn to be United States ambassador to Australia and special envoy to oversee U.S. interests in the southwest Pacific, the newspapers revived the paving blocks scandal and other issues, causing the nomination to be withdrawn.

Where most bosses had very limited educations, Flynn was a successful attorney. Though as Gov. Al Smith once remarked, "Law school is a place where they spend three years teaching you to call a bribe a fee." Some of Flynn's legal income came from individuals seeking favors. Among his clients was Serge Rubenstein, an international swindler. When Rubenstein was murdered in 1955 two Hollywood movies were made about his demise. The title of one, *Death of a Scoundrel*, indicates how he was portrayed.

*

The rise of the New York families to political power in Manhattan and Brooklyn and Flynn's relationship to the White House opened a new era in American politics. The rulers of organized crime, known popularly as the Mafia, were now a national force with almost as much influence in Washington as Wall Street financiers. In 1935, a New York reporter described a meeting of the unknown leaders of New York's mob world that he had supposedly witnessed. He reported that it included three important figures in local and national politics whose names "if revealed would shake every city in the country and topple scores of state and national politicians." In 1933, when a Senate subcommittee chaired by Royal Copeland of New York, held hearings on the crime problem, one of the witnesses, former United States Attorney George Medalie, offered to name four major political figures in league with gangsters. Copeland quickly declined his offer. In later years there were always rumors that Joe Kennedy, Sr., of Boston had been one of the powerful figures behind organized crime. The fact that Lepke could fix a case in the United States Court of Appeals, which ranked just below the U.S. Supreme Court, spoke volumes.

Even Franklin Roosevelt, both as governor of New York and president, sometimes had to operate as a practical politician. In 1930, Manhattan state supreme court justice Joseph Force Crater disappeared, never to be seen again. A major probe of the judiciary was in progress at the time (part of a series of scandals that would send Mayor Walker fleeing to England). While in private practice Crater, as an agent of the court, had authorized the sale of a hotel for $85,000, after which the new owner turned around and sold it for over $2 million. In a letter to his wife, Crater told her to be expecting a substantial sum from the sale.

Just before Governor Franklin Roosevelt appointed Crater to the supreme court, the judge had withdrawn $23,000 from his bank account. Everybody in New York knew that the price of a judgeship was one year's salary, which for a supreme court justice at the time was $22,500. Crater had practiced law in the office of United States senator Robert Wagner, an intimate of Roosevelt's and a powerful figure in Congress. Yet Wagner told investigators that he barely knew Crater. Roosevelt and Wagner were aware that judgeships were bought and with only a few lawyers in his office, Wagner must have at least sensed that Crater was not a paragon of virtue. Though neither FDR nor Wagner profited from Crater's purchase of a judgeship (the payoff likely went to his Tammany district leader in lower Manhattan), they went along with the system.

Even Fiorello LaGuardia had some mob support. In 1933, when he was running for mayor, he accepted the backing of Joe Adonis. Born Doto, Joe was so proud of his good looks that he used the surname "Adonis." After LaGuardia was elected, cops did not bother him much. Back then he could be found in his restaurant, The Italian Kitchen, holding forth with Brooklyn gangsters and politicians. However, in 1937, when Adonis switched his support to LaGuardia's opponent in the mayoralty election (Senator Royal Copeland, the man who did not want to hear testimony about the respectables who were behind organized crime), the NYPD came down so hard on him that he had to establish a new headquarters in Cliffside, New Jersey. Adonis still maintained his power in Brooklyn and his close association with Democratic boss Frank Kelly, but with LaGuardia in City Hall, he had to be more discreet.

LaGuardia disliked Reds and gangsters but the leader of East Harlem, Congressman Vito Marcantonio, protégé of the mayor (some said the son LaGuardia never had)[11] was close to both the Communists and the Mafia. While LaGuardia was mayor, New York cops tread lightly in East Harlem.

Within the mob world, Frank Costello was the city's closest approximation to a boss of bosses, though that title had died out (literally) in 1931 when Salvatore Maranzano was assassinated. When Special Prosecutor Dewey sent Luciano to prison for fifty years, Vito Genovese should have been Lucky's successor, but in 1936 the vicious

---

11. LaGuardia's first wife, and his baby, had died during childbirth.

Vito had to flee to Italy because Dewey was after him on a murder rap. So the more restrained Costello took over the family.

Calabrian-born Francisco Castiglia had come to America with his parents as a child. The family settled in East Harlem where young Frank became involved in a street gang. In 1915, when he was 18, he was given a one-year jail sentence for carrying an illegal gun. During Prohibition he teamed up as a bootlegger with an Irish partner "Big Bill" Dwyer, who became so rich and respectable that he later entertained English Lords at his lavish Florida estate. In later years Costello would also claim Joe Kennedy was his partner.[12]

Frank was not the usual type of gangster. He did not carry a gun or move about surrounded by bodyguards. He lived on fashionable Central Park West with his Jewish wife "Bobby." Childless, the couple doted on their pet dachshunds. Within mob circles, Costello was admired for his ability to acquire important political contacts and to coolly analyze problems. He frowned on murder except as a last resort. Frank came to be known as "the Prime Minister" of New York organized crime, first among equals in the five-family structure and the best connected one. He was also close to his fellow Calabrians, Albert Anastasia and Willie Moretti, the latter the mob boss in northern New Jersey.

In Damon Runyon's short stories about the Broadway crowd, Costello appeared as "Frankie Ferocious" but he was described as a sort of teddy bear. The whole town knew he was the real owner of the city's top nightclub, The Copacabana, and that his friends ranged from Walter Winchell and business executives to stars like Ed Wynn and Jimmy Durante. Nobody associated Frank with the vicious part of organized crime, such as the activities of Murder, Incorporated, or garment center slugging. He projected himself as just a businessman—in fact he owned a number of legitimate ones. Better yet, he like to see himself as a "patron of the turf " just like the society bluebloods that he sat with at the racetrack. Even the *New York Times* referred to him as a "sportsman." The sad thing was that Frank began to believe the story that he had created.

---

12. The younger Kennedys always maintained that although their father might have been involved in the liquor business, he was not partners with Costello.

In 1943 Dist. Atty. Frank Hogan's wiretappers listened in on a conversation between Costello and city magistrate Thomas Aurelio, who thanked Costello for getting him nominated to be a state supreme court justice, a job far above a magistrate. At the time it paid $26,000 a year (which would be at least ten times that amount in today's money). There had been a score of applicants for the post and the leading candidate was a United States congressman who was personally recommended by President Roosevelt. When the nominal head of Tammany, John Kenney, hesitated at giving the nod to Aurelio—because it would mean going against the president of the United States—Costello was heard on the wiretaps saying "are you a man or a mouse". Kenney proved that he was neither man nor mouse but a stooge, by handing the nomination to Aurelio. When the conversation was revealed by Hogan there was a storm of protest and efforts were made to force Aurelio off the ballot, but to no avail. He was elected to the supreme court.[13]

The Murder, Incorporated, investigation threatened the entire hierarchy of New York City organized crime. If Anastasia was charged with murder, his Brooklyn family would be weakened and this might set off a scramble for power with the other Brooklyn mob families like the Bonannos and the Profacis. Anastasia's departure would also remove a strong supporter of Costello's prime ministership. It had taken a great deal of shooting and negotiations to weld together the Five-Family confederation. Luciano and Costello had managed to keep peace among Sicilians, Neapolitans, Calabrians, Brooklynites, Manhattanites, and Bronxites. If the structure dissolved in bloodshed, New York would be back to the murderous gang wars of the Prohibition era.

Shortly after losing the mayoral election, O'Dwyer suffered an embarrassment which would haunt him for the rest of his life. "Kid Twist" Reles and three other mob figures were being held in custody on the sixth floor of the Half Moon Hotel in Coney Island, Brooklyn. On the morning of November 12th, Reles fell or was thrown out of room 623. He landed forty-two feet below, fractured his spine and died

---

13. Where he was regarded as a tough on crime judge. Apparently, Costello had pushed Aurelio's nomination to get an Italian on the bench, not because he expected the judge to be easy on gangsters.

from his injuries. Reles' room was part of a suite that housed other district attorney's witnesses in protective custody. There, behind a steel entrance door, he was guarded by eighteen police officers (six per shift) from O'Dwyer's investigative staff. Supposedly, five of them were on duty at the time Reles went out the window. According to the police report, a guard visited him every fifteen minutes. The report stated that one of the officers checking Reles's room at 7 a.m. noticed him missing, looked out a nearby open window and saw a body on the roof of the bulding adjacent to the hotel. When he went down he found Reles. The police reported that he had fashioned a rope of bedsheets and tied it to himself with some wire that had been left behind on a radiator by an electrician. The rope was only long enough to permit Reles to reach the fifth floor. So the cops theorized that he had attempted to enter room 523 but lost his footing and the wire broke.

There were a number of puzzling aspects to the case. A hotel assistant manager reported hearing a scream about 6:45 a.m. and a draft board official, in a nearby building, said that he looked out at 7:30 a.m. and saw a body on the roof. According to him he alerted the hotel manager. Yet if the detectives' report was correct the police had already discovered the body.

Four theories of Reles's death were canvassed. (1) He committed suicide. If that were the case, why would he have needed to tie ropes around himself rather than just jump out the window. (2) Reles was attempting to escape. Arguing against this was that the gangsters behind Murder, Incorporated, would have sent killers to find him. As a contract killer himself, Reles knew that the reach of Murder, Inc., extended across the country and that the mobs never gave up the hunt for someone who had doublecrossed them. (3) Reles, who was supposedly something of a joker, was playing a prank, planning to enter room 523 and then return to 623 to surprise his guards. One who voiced this theory was Capt. Frank Bals, chief of O'Dwyer's investigative staff, for whom the police guards worked. As Bals' later career would demonstrate, he was not a highly regarded commander, so his theory was essentially good only for laughs. (4) Reles was murdered. The five police officers on duty were placed on departmental trial. Surprisingly, O'Dwyer testified on their behalf at the hearing.

The fact that Reles' landed some 20 to 25 feet away from the hotel suggests that he was hurled out the window by someone else rather than having descended under his own power. The popular, though unproven, theory is that Anastasia's mob pals, led by Frank Costello, had paid $100,000 to have Reles put out of the way. Yet the name of the actual killer or killers has never surfaced. The deed might have been performed by one of the other three prisoners in the suite who could move from room to room, one of the guards, or someone from outside who gained entrance to the area. It is doubtful that the policemen as a group conspired to kill Reles, since it would have been extremely difficult to keep the secret. To date, no answer has emerged.[14]

Later O'Dwyer would claim that without Reles there was insufficient evidence to prosecute Anastasia. Legal experts who have studied the case disagree with that view. In fact, O'Dwyer had Reles in custody for nearly two years but never moved to charge Anastasia. O'Dwyer's chief clerk, Jim Moran, a nonlawyer, who was left virtually in command of the district attorney's office when O'Dwyer went off to the army, ordered the wanted notices on Anastasia to be removed. Whereupon the gangster came in from the cold.

Moran had worked with Judge O'Dwyer as a court attaché and then was named chief clerk in the district attorney's office. Later, when O'Dwyer was mayor, he appointed Moran first deputy fire commissioner. Though there was a great status differential between the two men, people who observed them together noted that Moran sometimes appeared to be the boss and O'Dwyer the subordinate. As deputy fire commissioner, Moran was convicted of receiving bribes and given a lengthy prison sentence. O'Dwyer's close relationship with Moran and the latter's demonstrated corruption led many people to suspect that he had been O'Dwyer's virtual partner.

During the Murder, Incorporated, investigation evidence was gathered that Sidney Hillman, head of the Amalgamated Clothing

---

14. As recently as 2005 a woman claimed that a policeman relative of hers had been responsible for the 1941 murder and had also kidnapped Judge Joseph Crater, who disappeared in 1930. A TV station sent a limousine to take me out to the site of the now-closed Half Moon Hotel where several reporters were waiting. I held an informal press conference in which I threw cold water on the story because the names the woman supplied did not match with those of the police officers on the detail. Nor did some of her other claims hold up. However, it was August and news was in short supply. Even the "killer sharks" had failed to appear off the beaches.

Workers, and the American labor leader closest to President Roosevelt, had used the services of Murder, Incorporated, to beat or kill opponents. With so many conflicting relationships, it was difficult to tell the players without a scorecard. The NYPD was run by an incorruptible mayor and police commissioner yet during the 1939 World's Fair, a study by *Fortune* magazine found gambling and vice continued to flourish in New York City. In 1942 special prosecutor Amen charged a number of Brooklyn cops with corruption. Bosses like Ed Flynn and Tammany Hall's John Kenney had to go against the president to satisfy corrupt local forces. A supposedly crusading District Attorney O'Dwyer, who sent Murder, Incorporated, gangsters to the electric chair was later exposed as a man who courted the favor of mob bosses like Costello, Anastasia, and Adonis. Honest men like President Roosevelt and Mayor LaGuardia were required to accept support where they found it and turn their eyes.

In early 1942, Lepke and his two codefendants, convicted in the Rosen murder, were sentenced to death. For the next two years New York State engaged in a struggle with the federal government over their custody. During that time there was press speculation that Lepke could provide information on Sidney Hillman's involvement in the case and, in so doing, implicate the Roosevelt administration. As it turned out the police crackdown on a bunch of Brooklyn gunmen had set off a chain of events that would lead through the corridors of power in New York City and Albany and eventually to the the White House. The whole affair illustrated that what happened in places like Pitkin Avenue in Brooklyn was sometimes linked to what happened on Pennsylvania Avenue in Washington, DC, and that the distance between a mob murder in New York and the White House was not as great as might be thought.

Chapter 3

Chicago: The Legacy of Prohibition

By the beginning of 1929, Chicagoans had experienced nine years of national prohibition and they liked it no better than when it first started. One hour after the law took effect on January 16, 1920, six armed men entered a Chicago railroad switching yard, tied up a watchman, and cleaned out two freight cars of medicinal whiskey worth $100,000. At the same time another gang stole four barrels of grain alcohol from a government warehouse and a third hijacked a truck transporting liquor. Before a month passed the first murder attributed to bootlegging disputes occurred in Chicago. Hundreds more would follow.

Killings were a fact of life in the Windy City. Out of a force of 7,000 police officers, an average of ten cops a year were murdered. (In New York today that would translate to fifty cops killed annually.) In 1927, after a four-year vacation, "Big Bill" Thompson had been elected to a third term as mayor. In 1929 Al Capone, Chicago's top gangster since 1925, was still going strong, but other hoodlums kept disputing his title by firing Tommy guns at him. In one instance Hymie Weiss (né Earl Wajciechowski) sent twelve carloads of gunmen into Al's suburban fiefdom of Cicero to blast away at him. They failed. Three weeks later Capone's machine gunners killed Weiss and one of his lieutenants and wounded three more in broad daylight outside Holy Name Cathedral, seat of the Catholic archdiocese.

Finally, Al decided to kill his principal rivals, the Moran gang, in one fell swoop. On February 14, 1929, Valentine's Day, Capone gangsters staked out a garage on North Clark Street where the Moran gang stored its trucks. They watched as half a dozen men entered but none of them was Moran. So the watchers did not send for the squad of hit men who were on call. Then they spotted a man entering they thought was Moran. In those days hit men frequently togged themselves out in various disguises, such as a deliveryman, so they could get close to their target. This time the hit squad had a foolproof plan. When summoned, they arrived in an open touring car, with a bell on the hood that resembled a Chicago police squad car. In it were three men in plainclothes and two in police uniforms. To a bystander it looked like a police raid.[1] Four of the men entered the garage and proceeded to line up the seven men in it against the wall. Without warning they cut them down with Tommy guns. When police arrived on the scene only one of the seven, Frank Gusenberg, was still alive. A detective who had gone to grade school with Frank questioned him and told him he was dying (a necessity to obtain a legally admissible dying declaration). Despite the fact that Frank's brother Pete was among the slain, he refused to answer any questions and expired at the hospital. George Moran and two of his lieutenants had been late arriving for the meeting.

There had been mass violence in Chicago for years. Every time there was a major strike, ten or twenty people were killed. Seven more dead gangsters on top of the 600 or so who, over the decade, had fallen in the so-called "Beer Wars" would not make much difference. However, this time the White House got involved. Capone had become world famous and was giving the United States a bad name. The Chicago business community was up in arms and a group of key leaders, such as Sears Roebuck chief Julius Rosenwald and utilities magnate Samuel Insull, formed an organization dubbed by newsmen "the secret six." In March 1929 they met with President Hoover in

---

1. Five man detective squads, known as "big squads," were common in Chicago at the time but they did not include any uniformed cops. Apparently none of the Moran gang picked up on that.

Washington and demanded federal intervention in Chicago. They also pledged financial and political support to the federal drive. The president assigned the task of "getting Capone" to the U.S. treasury secretary, who delegated the matter to Elmer Irey, chief of the intelligence section. With the feds on his back, the town became too hot for Capone and he left for a couple of years. When he came back he was indicted for tax evasion, convicted and given an unprecedented eleven-year sentence to federal prison. He would never return, but the Capone gang would become what the Chicagoans called "the syndicate." Allied with the political leaders, it became virtually the co-rulers of the city and its environs. In time the gangsters, through their political allies and hired hands, would have as much access to the White House as the Secret Six.

*

Chicago will forever be identified with Prohibition, thanks to TV and Hollywood dramas. On screen, actors from Paul Muni to Jason Robards have played Al Capone. Robert Stack, Kevin Costner, and others have portrayed the largely fictionalized character of Eliot Ness. So violent was the 1920s political climate in the Windy City that when Mayor William H. Thompson feuded with his fellow Republican, Col. Robert R. McCormick, owner of the most powerful newspaper in the Midwest, the *Chicago Tribune*, both men traveled around town in armor-plated cars accompanied by bodyguards because each feared being assassinated by the other.

At the beginning of Prohibition Johnny Torrio, leader of the Italian-dominated mob, preferred diplomacy to gunplay. With Thompson's blessing Johnny took the lead in parceling out territories to bootlegging groups and maintaining discipline among the rival gangsters. Not only did the mayor favor Torrio, but Johnny also rescued the Republican governor, Len Small. When his Excellency was accused of embezzling funds from a bank where he had been an officer, Johnny's boys managed to persuade the complainants to drop the matter.

In the final analysis, if Torrio couldn't handle a problem with other gangsters, he could always call on Mayor Thompson's police department for assistance. The mayor's choices for police chief (after 1927, commissioner) were usually go-along cops who served for brief periods and then left under a cloud. In 1923, when the Democrats won the mayoralty, Johnny was no longer able to rely on City Hall and the gang wars of Chicago went into high gear. The violence was heightened by the introduction of the Thompson submachine gun, *aka* the "Tommy gun."

In 1925, after Torrio was badly wounded by gangsters avenging the murder of North Side gang chief Dion O'Bannion, he left Chicago and turned his operations over to Capone. Al was much less restrained than Torrio. Though, like Johnny, he had worked for Frankie Yale (Uale) in Brooklyn, when Frankie shorted him on a liquor delivery, Chicago gunmen pursued Yale's car through the streets of New York, finally cornering and killing him. The New York mobs were not upset about the killing, but that Capone had turned it into a circus, thereby sparking bad publicity.[2] In the 1928 municipal primary campaign, Capone's gorillas not only cut loose with their Tommy guns, they tossed so many bombs that it became known as the "the pineapple primary." In one instance they chased a Republican politician through the streets until they caught and killed him. Afterwards a United States senator from Nebraska demanded that President Coolidge send marines to Chicago.

In 1930, with Mayor Thompson back in office, Jake Lingle, one of Colonel McCormick's *Tribune* reporters, was shot dead in broad daylight on a downtown street. Investigation disclosed that the reporter was a collector for Police Commissioner William Russell. The supposed shooter, another Egan Rat, Leo Brothers, received the light sentence of fourteen years. Many Chicagoans believed that he had been paid to take the rap to satisfy public outcry and the honor of the *Tribune*. Brothers was released after serving just eight years.

Thompson's successor as mayor was Democrat Anton "Tony" Cermak, a West Side saloon keeper who served as president of the county board. Cermak had managed to acquire a $2 million fortune on

2, It was Frankie Yale who had been picked up leaving town after the killing of Jim Colosimo. He was picked up again leaving town after the killing of Dion O'Bannion. Police discovered that the machine guns fired in the Yale assassination and the "Valentine massacre" both belonged to Fred "Killer" Burke, of the St. Louis gang, known as Egan's Rats, who was captured when he killed a policeman in Michigan.

an annual salary of $10,000. As mayor, he failed to reach an agreement with Frank Nitti, boss of what Chicagoans were beginning to call "the Syndicate" on how organized crime should be run in the city. The mayor apparently favored giving the franchise to a North Side gangster named Ted Newberry, a member of the old Moran gang. During the conflict a detective who worked personally for Cermak shot and wounded Nitti. At the time Nitti was unarmed and some other detectives present protested their colleague's action. So the gun-wielding cop shot himself in the hand to make the shooting look legitimate. Newberry, suspected of encouraging the cop to shoot Frank, was assassinated by Nitti's gangsters a few weeks later.

Cermak would have been well advised to maintain the security arrangements of his predecessor, Thompson. In January, 1933, while sitting in a car with president-elect Roosevelt in a Florida park, Cermak was fatally wounded by Giuseppe Zangara. He died three weeks after being shot. Nine days later the assassin was electrocuted. The explanation for Zangara's action was that he was a demented man who hated all rulers. Though why he decided to shoot at that particular time and place has never been explained. While no evidence has been found that mobsters recruited Zangara, over the next generation, most people in Chicago believed that the Capone gang had set him up to kill Cermak, as payback for the shooting of Nitti.

Cermak's successor, Ed Kelly, was selected by the county chairman of the Democratic Party, "Boss" Pat Nash. The 57-year-old Kelly had been operating head of the sanitary district, the agency that flushed the contents of the city's toilets out to the lake. Given the duties of a machine mayor, it was not an inappropriate background. Kelly, a tall, burly, loud-talking man from the stockyards district, whose mother had always admonished him to "never drink out of someone else's beer can," was the archetype of a Chicago ward politician. Though he never went past fifth grade, he had learned enough in his work at the sanitary district, combined with his political savvy, to rise to chief engineer, the top job in the agency.

Though Mayor Kelly did not fear assassination from Col. McCormick, the tactic did not go out of Chicago political life. Other politicians too were shot at and sometimes hit. So Kelly surrounded himself with bodyguards he selected from the toughest cops on the force. The chosen men always finished near the top of the police promotion lists, which could be easily manipulated, and in the later years of the Kelly regime a number of police captains owed their rise to the mayor. Some captains spent their working hours having long liquid lunches and or perfecting their golf game. For such taxing work, they could expect to receive, over and above their salary, fifty to a hundred thousand (depression era) dollars a year.

During his long career there was never any doubt about whether Kelly was honest. During his time as sanitary district head, he had been indicted by a grand jury for corruption, but his good friend, Col. McCormick of the *Tribune,* stormed into the jury room and tore up the indictments. Before Kelly could start his mayoralty, the IRS lodged a penalty of $106,000 (1933) dollars on the mayor for not paying taxes on some extra income he had acquired. When Kelly died in 1950, his executor reported his estate was worth $600,000. The mayor's wife complained that a million in cash that she had recently seen in Kelly's safety deposit box was missing.[3] Obviously the mayor had not followed his mother's advice because he apparently drank out of the taxpayers beer cans on a regular basis.

Chicago, the second largest city in the United States, was run differently from New York City. Gotham had five separate counties ruled by five political machines. Chicago and its surrounding county were ruled by one machine, the Cook County Democratic Organization. New York's most powerful county boss could probably deliver a half a million votes, which was not enough to swing the state. The boss of the Cook County machine could deliver nearly three times that number, which was often sufficient to carry Illinois for the Democratic presidential candidate.

In New York City organized crime was controlled by half a dozen mob bosses. Chicago had one. The Five Families of New York only came to control local organized crime in 1931. The Colosimo, Torrio, Capone, Nitti groups had been at the top of the mob world since before 1920. The New York mobs had ties to ostensibly respectable businessman and professionals. In Chicago the mob's key advisors also

---

3. A close confidant of the mayor was suspected of "beating her to the box."

included federal judges. The Chicago and New York police departments were traditionally open to political influence, though, in reform
periods, the NYPD was usually run by tough commissioners. Chicago
had never had a reform administration and its police department had
not experienced the kind of strict regimen that the NYPD endured
under Mayor LaGuardia and Commissioner Valentine. In the 1930s
the NYPD shook off most of the ill effects of prohibition. The
Chicago Police Department remained, in many ways, a Prohibition-era
police force until as late as 1960.

Kelly retained as police commissioner an honest cop named Jim
Allman. But in Chicago the commissioner's writ did not run much
beyond the front door of his office, and sometimes not that far. The
local district stations were controlled by ward bosses. When one of
them shot a police officer who was trying to close down the man's
saloon because it was running after hours, the cop was fired. The
mayor welcomed the ward boss back to the city council with the
remark that he was "a straight shooter." The Council roared with
laughter. The detective bureau was headed by a virtually autonomous
chief. On paper the morals (vice) squad worked directly for the
Commissioner but it was staffed and commanded by members
(through blood or marriage) of two families from the near North Side
42nd Ward, which encompassed the cities principal vice district.

The Cook County state's attorney (prosecutor), whose domain
included all of Chicago and most of its suburbs, was an elective office.
Never was the job held by an individual comparable to New York's
Tom Dewey or Frank Hogan. From 1933 through 1944 the post was
filled by Tom Courtney, a machine politician and a bitter rival of
Mayor Kelly. The state's attorney investigative unit was commanded by
Chicago police captain Dan "Tubbo" Gilbert, who had joined the
force in 1917 after a career as a gunman for labor unions, during which
time he was suspected, but never convicted, of several murders. Dan
also had been a bodyguard for Democratic county chairman George
Brennan, and was always close to Brennan's successor, another west
sider, Pat Nash. Not surprisingly Gilbert's rise to captain was rapid and

over the years he acquired the tag of "America's Richest Cop."[4] Gilbert not only controlled a number of labor unions: organized crime watchers believed that he was actually a member of the ruling circle of "the syndicate." During the twelve years they were together, it was not clear if Gilbert worked for state's attorney Courtney or it was the reverse. Putting Gilbert in the state's attorney's office was a means for the syndicate or Mafia to control the criminal justice system. No matter what the police did, if the state's attorney would not prosecute, the defendant would walk free.

During Kelly's tenure the mob made a couple of attempts to increase its power over city government. In 1935 Dan Gilbert was named chief of the Chicago police uniformed force which encompassed most of the department's personnel, including more detectives than in the central detective bureau. However, the cops and the political bosses closed ranks against Gilbert and after sixty days he returned to the state's attorney's office. When the police department transferred a detective to Gilbert's staff to serve as a spy, Tubbo found out, beat the man senseless, and sent him back to police headquarters. In 1935, when state's attorney Courtney walked out of a South Side restaurant, a bullet flew past his head. Someone was sending him a message. In the general election of that year, Colonel McCormick eased Kelly's worries by putting up an exceptionally weak Republican candidate. Kelly defeated him by 799,000 to 167,000 votes, in a city which four years earlier had been ruled by a Republican mayor.

Government in Chicago often seemed as incomprehensible as the workings of the Byzantine Empire. The police commissioner was an honest man but his word carried no weight with his district captains, chief of detectives, or commander of the vice squad. The state's attorney's chief investigator was a mob factotum. At a higher level Mayor Kelly was a strong supporter of Roosevelt and the New Deal, whereas Kelly's great friend, Col. McCormick, hated the president and all his works.

Perhaps the key to making sense out of the arrangements was the notion of maintaining balance among competing interests. Though

---

4. An undeserved accolade since there were number of American police officials with far higher net worths than Gilbert. In 1937 a San Francisco vice cop was found to have $800,000 in his bank account. In Gilbert's time a downstate Illinois police official was revealed to have $900,000

every union boss in Chicago had a pipeline to City Hall, they were never allowed to get away with rough picketing. When overenthusiastic strikers crossed from protest to violence, police clubs were brought into play. In 1937, striking workers marched on the Republic Steel plant on the city's southeast side. Supposedly they intended to seize the plant and stage a sit down, as was being done elsewhere in the United States at the time. McCormick's *Tribune* and Chicago's business community, nominally Republican but well served by the Democratic machine, would not have liked that. The marchers were met by a line of police who ordered them to halt. When they kept marching, the cops opened fire, killing ten, wounding thirty more and clubbing an unknown number. Kelly supported the cops and no action was taken to discipline them. Vice, gambling, and all-night drinking were a fact of life in a city which still saw itself as a western town. In the 1930s, drug dealing was run by an independent operator, an Irish Colleen named Kitty Gilhooley, until Commissioner Anslinger's FBN sent her to prison.

The machine also had something for everyone. A black man was sent to Congress, becoming the first African American Democrat elected to the House of Representatives in the 20th century. He was also a ward boss and a member of the inner circle of the party organization. In 1940 a black police captain was given command of a district. Not until 1964 did a black captain in New York take charge of a precinct. In a state with a relatively small Jewish population, in 1932 the machine managed to elect a Jewish governor and reelect him four years later. Busy Crawford Avenue was renamed Pulaski Road to please the city's large Polish population and some Polish lawyers were given important judicial posts. Even Republicans could receive a few patronage jobs as long as they rolled over and played dead at election time. Italians held few offices because a name with vowels in it did not attract many votes. However, they were not completely overlooked. A street in downtown Chicago was named for Mussolini's military chief, Marshal Italo Balbo. Even when the United States went to war with Italy, the name was not changed. Blacks could be elected on citywide ballots since their names did not reveal their racial identity. Though, sometimes opponents would mail their pictures to the voters. The reverse of this was that the machine could deliver the black vote to white candidates whose racial views were as extreme as many Southern politicians.[5]

During World War II servicemen regarded Chicago as their favorite city. They could ride public transportation without paying a fare and there was always free food and entertainment available for them. The city operated a servicemen's center that occupied twelve floors of a downtown building and served 10,000 GIs each weeknight and 40,000 on weekends.

The machine also exercised a degree of restraint over the gangsters. Mayor Thompson had been too accommodating to Torrio and Capone, Mayor Cermak had not been accommodating enough to Frank Nitti. Kelly and Nash struck the right note. Vice, gambling, and saloons were allowed to run wide open under mob auspices. In return, the syndicate would provide over 150,000 votes for the machine from the wards controlled by what Chicagoans call "the Westside bloc" (although not all of the gangster-run wards were on the west side). The syndicate also quit pulling off spectacular stunts like the pineapple primary, the Valentine massacre, or the murder of a newspaper reporter.

In the final analysis, a multiethnic and violent city like Chicago could not have been held together without some compromises. On occasions when civic order collapsed, such as in the major strikes between the 1870s and World War I, and the race riot of 1919, blood flowed in the streets, bombs exploded, and troops had to be called out.

Despite the urging of Secretary of the Interior Harold Ickes and Secretary of the Treasury Henry Morgenthau that the president go on the offensive against bosses like Kelly, Chicago was too important an asset to the Democratic administration for the federal government to challenge its corrupt ways. In 1937, when the president decided to make a speech urging that the dictator nations be quarantined, he chose to do it at the opening of the Chicago outer drive. Many of his advisers thought this was a bad idea. Chicago was the heart of the isolationist Midwest where half the population read the Anglophobic

---

5. Once a Black political worker told Congressman Dawson, "I don't know how I can carry my precinct for this [white] candidate because he is against our people." His response was "If you don't know, I will tell you. Next Friday you won't get a paycheck." Somehow the precinct was carried for the white candidate.

Col. McCormick's *Tribune* every day. It was possible that the crowd might boo Roosevelt's speech. However, the Chicago machine turned out a huge number of its patronage employees who cheered lustily for the president. Once, when U.S. Senate Democrats balked at naming FDR's choice for majority leader, the president called Kelly to make sure the two Illinois senators voted the right way. The Senate might have been a gentleman's club where whip cracking was frowned upon, but both gentlemen from Illinois fell into line and Roosevelt's man won by one vote.

In 1940 the Democratic national convention was held in Chicago. FDR was seeking an unprecedented third term but refused to say so. In a climactic moment in the proceedings a chorus of booming voices began chanting "We want Roosevelt, we want Roosevelt". It was Tom Garry, Mayor Kelly's superintendent of sewers, bellowing into a microphone in the basement of the hall. As his voice blared through loudspeakers Kelly's packed galleries took up the chant. Thanks to "the voice from the sewers" Roosevelt swept to the nomination and eventually the election.

At the end of the 1930s, just as in New York, the machine and the mob began to encounter trouble. The first assault came from Treasury agents. William "Billy" Skidmore, known as "Skid," had many affiliations but principally he was a collector for politicians and police brass. Skid was the Renaissance man of Chicago politics. He was a protégé of west side bosses like Pat Nash and early in his career, he had been the Sergeant at Arms of three Democratic presidential conventions. He was also purchasing agent for the party. He and a partner owned a large gambling empire and Skid ran a flourishing bail bond business. He also owned a junkyard which he used as a meeting place where various individuals could come to him with payoffs or requests for favors. As the old song proclaimed, "Oh how the money rolled in."

Under Sheriff Thomas "Blind Tom" O'Brien,[6] Skid had de facto control of the county police force. While much of the county was composed of sleepy suburban towns, it had some hotspots, like Cicero and Calumet City, that were loaded with gamblers, prostitutes, and

---

6. The nickname came from his inability to see gambling or vice in Cook County. O'Brien eventually became leader of the Illinois congressional delegation and a power in the national Democratic Party.

dives that operated in a wilder fashion than in Chicago. With Skidmore running the county police and Gilbert backstopping him in the state's attorney's office, suburban Cook County was practically owned by the syndicate. When journalists or civic reformers complained about conditions in the city, the Chicago politicians would point to the county as being worse. In Chicago, a visiting conventioneer who yelled that he had been robbed in some joint was thrown out. In Cicero, he was carried out unconscious. Some suburban police departments were completely controlled by gangsters. If a local cop was unwilling to go along, it was not unknown for him to be taken for a ride.[7] Chicago gangsters dropped their victims bodies out in the county because they knew no one there would care or have the resources to investigate the case.

In 1939, the feds began looking into Skid's taxes and some inquiring Chicago newspaper men started writing about conditions in the county. In response, the machine employed the usual tactic of firing the County police chief and replacing him with another one pledged to clean things up. Shortly after assuming his post, the new chief went out to have dinner in a quiet corner of a hotel. Acting on a tip, a news photographer came into the dining room and took a picture of the chief and his dinner companion—Billy Skidmore. When the photo appeared on the front page, the chief was fired. Eventually, Skidmore pled guilty to income tax evasion and was sent to prison where he died a few years later. The federal tax authorities were just too much bother for some Chicagoans. They even made Murray "The Camel" Humphreys, a key syndicate figure, pay taxes on the ransom he received from kidnapping a union official. No suitable replacement for Skidmore was ever found and many of those who paid him off lamented his departure. They claimed that in his day they could give him the money and he took care of the politicians and the police. After his time, a suburban gambling joint might have to pay off state troopers, sheriff's deputies, states attorney's investigators, the local town police, and various elected officials.   ↘

---

7. In one incident a young West suburban officer ran afoul of mobsters who pumped six bullets into his back. While lying prone in a car as they were digging his grave, he somehow managed to loosen the brake causing the vehicle to roll down a hill and crash into a fire station. The local newspapers reported his imminent death. However, he survived and, many years later, as a Chicago police lieutenant, worked for the writer. For some reason, he always manifested a great dislike of gangsters.

Even Capt. Gilbert had problems. A payoff list found in a sub-urban gambling joint showed $4000 paid to "Tub." When the *Tribune* printed the list, Gilbert protested that it couldn't be him because he was called Tubbo. Despite the bad publicity, his power was so great he was not forced out of the state's attorney's office.

In 1939, states attorney Courtney challenged Kelly in the mayoral primary but was beaten by a two-to-one margin. However, in 1940 Courtney started to make trouble again. He began to probe vice and gambling in the city. He brought charges before the Civil Service Commission against the captain in command of the morals division and three of his detectives. The head of the commission also doubled as a ward boss and not surprisingly it exonerated the cops. Newspaper pressure forced a further probe and a special investigator ruled that the decision had been wrong. By that time the cops had been promoted and the whole affair was dropped.

In 1942, some old time Irish Prohibition-era gangsters began to revolt against Nitti's syndicate. Back in 1934, one of them, Roger Touhy, had been sentenced to ninety-nine years for kidnapping Jake "The Barber" Factor (brother of Hollywood makeup expert Max Factor). Roger was a member of a family of brothers known as the "Terrible Touhys". He had lost one of his siblings to police bullets and two more to Capone's gunmen. The Factor kidnapping investigation was led by Capt. Gilbert. In later years a federal judge ruled the case had been a frame up to allow Factor to avoid extradition to England where he had been convicted of swindling investors out of millions of pounds.

In October 1942, Touhy and six other men escaped from the Illinois State Penitentiary. They were on the run for a month, then four of them were captured by the FBI and two more were shot to death while resisting arrest. During the time in which Touhy and company were free, mob bosses worried that they might become targets of the vengeful gangster.[8]

Three months after Touhy's escape, Edward "Spike" O'Donnell, a second-tier Chicago gangster, made trouble for the Kelly machine.

---

8. By that time Touhy was no longer so terrible. The leader of the escape crew was Basil "The Owl" Banghart, who during his time on the loose walked around with a loaded shotgun under his coat.

Spike missed the start of Prohibition because he was serving time for robbing a bank in his home neighborhood around the Chicago stockyards. Headstrong and wild, even for a hoodlum, he had neglected to ascertain, or did not care, that the bank was controlled by local politicians. As a result, when he was caught and brought to trial, he was given a stiff sentence.

When Spike was released he led his gang into the bootlegging business, invading territories which belonged to powerful Irish, Italian, or Slavic groups. Normally rivals, the established gentlemen joined forces to repel the intruder. Some of Spike's gang were taken for a ride and O'Donnell himself was wounded a couple of times, forcing his temporary retirement from the bootlegging business.

Over the years, despite receiving a few more bullet wounds, Spike continued his criminal ways. In January 1943, he accosted the Chicago Commissioner of Streets outside the man's City Hall office and demanded a $70,000 commission on some paving contracts that Spike claimed to have set up. When the commissioner refused, O'Donnell beat him so badly that he required several months' hospitalization. When O'Donnell was arrested for the assault, he boasted of his close association with Mayor Kelly and threatened to initiate a scandal that would "blow the lid off of City Hall" if he did not receive his money. O'Donnell had survived many bullet wounds, so this time his assailants machine-gunned him to death in front of his house.

The killing of a well-known hoodlum was always manna for Chicago's sensationalist newspapers, which had recently feasted on Touhy's escape, so Spike's passing received considerable mention. Some reporters even mused over who could have ordered the murder. Rival gangsters might not have cared much if Spike blew the whistle on city officials, but the officials definitely would have. Certainly the mayor did not shed too many tears over Spike's passing. Could members of the city's political machine have arranged for Mr. O'Donnell's demise? Such things were known to happen in Chicago. A state official under indictment once told the press he would not go down alone. The words were hardly out of his mouth when he was shot dead. A lawyer who said he had collected graft for a police captain was killed the next night by a fusillade of shots.

No sooner had Chicago digested the Touhy and O'Donnell's cases, when a bombshell hit. Most of the top leadership of the Chicago syndicate were indicted for shaking down Hollywood movie studios. The mob's Hollywood debacle grew out of the depression. In the 1930s two minor Chicago hoodlums, a pimp named Willie Bioff and George Browne, business agent for the local stagehands union, set up a petty racket. They extorted $20,000 from the head of Paramount's Balban and Katz theater chain to not press for restoration of a 20% pay cut their members had absorbed. To celebrate, they treated themselves to a fancy dinner at a mob-operated upscale restaurant. Their lavish spending drew the attention of some big-time gangsters. So, shortly afterward the two were commanded to appear at a meeting in the home of Frank Nitti, whose nickname, "The Enforcer," evoked fear even among tough guys. When someone balked at agreeing to one of Nitti's requests, he would ask the man how his wife would look in black. After the sit down with the enforcer and his lieutenants, Bioff's and Browne's union became the property of the mob. However, Nitti arranged with Lepke Buchalter—then virtually coequal with lucky Luciano—to line up eastern locals to support Browne for president of the International Association of Theater and Stage Employees (IATSE). When the new union head, Browne, threatened to strike movie houses unless two operators were assigned to projection booths, the Hollywood studios caved in and began making annual payments to the union in the $100 to $150,000 range. In return, the mob helped the studio moguls beat off strikes by employees whose pay had been cut 50%. This led to a takeover of all twenty-seven Hollywood craft unions by IATSE.

The next step in the scenario was the usual one in industrial racketeering. The gangsters sought to become partners with the management of Hollywood. Bioff would later estimate that the mob had about 20% of Hollywood and was on the way to getting half. However, they overreached. The movie industry was the fifth-largest in the United States and a vital fabric of American life. Soon rumbles were heard from Hollywood personalities and investigative journalists. Studio executives were questioned by IRS agents. With so much writing talent available to them, the moguls had a story fashioned which portrayed them as helpless victims preyed on by vicious gang-sters. It didn't work. The federal government convicted Joe Schenck, boss of 20th Century Fox (brother of Nick Schenck, the head of Loews, which included MGM) of tax evasion. After just a month in prison, Joe Schenck, used to the lavish lifestyle of a movie mogul, could no longer stand it so he made a deal with the government and informed on Bioff and Browne, who were sentenced to prison them-selves.

While the two hoodlums quietly served their sentence, mobsters began threatening anyone who might talk about the role of Nitti and company. A Chicago nightlife queen who was the girlfriend of a minor gangster, jailed for his part in the plot, was murdered and Bioff and Browne were warned that if they cut a deal with the government their families would be killed. The tactic proved to be counterproductive. The two men opened up to federal prosecutors. This led to the indict-ment of Nitti, and a half a dozen of his top lieutenants.

At a stormy meeting in Nitti's suburban home the boss became so angry that he ordered his first lieutenant, Paul Ricca, and such key figures as Charles "Cherry Nose" Gioe, Louis "Little New York" Campagna, Phil D'Andrea, and the mob's Hollywood overseer, Johnny Roselli, out of the house. He then went off to a nearby railroad yard and, in front of shocked observers, shot himself in the head.[9]

The government was wise enough to bring the case in New York where a few of the payoffs from Schenck had taken place, rather than in Los Angeles, where the movie industry was located and a great deal of criminal activity had occurred, or Chicago, the mob's headquarters. If the case had been tried in either of those locations the fix would likely have produced an acquittal. The case had been made by Treasury intelligence agents led by Elmer Irey, the same crew that had brought down Capone. Their big boss, Treasury Secretary Morgenthau, brother-in-law of New York governor Lehman and close friend of FDR, was not a man to play ball with gangsters or corrupt politicians. In addition the case was prosecuted by a sharp and incorruptible assistant U.S. attorney named Boris Kostelanetz. brother of the music

---

9. The claustrophobic Nitti, who had been jailed earlier in his career, swore he would never go back. He shot himself publicly to squelch any speculation that his colleagues had killed him for trying to cut a deal with law enforcement.

impresario, Andre, and brother-in-law of opera diva Lilly Pons. Kostelanetz was untouchable by politicians or gangsters and any attempt to do so would have backfired. The principal appellate judge in the case was Learned Hand, a towering figure in American jurisprudence who was generally regarded as the greatest judge never to sit on the United States Supreme Court. No politician would have dared to approach him

In 1944 the Chicago bosses were convicted and given ten-year sentences. Left leaderless, the mob was run by a group of lesser individuals such as Charlie Fischetti, whose basic qualification was that he was Al Capone's cousin; Tony Accardo, a rising star but not yet a top figure; and Llewelyn Murray "The Camel" Humphreys, the syndicate's Secretary of Labor. At the time, none carried the prestige of their predecessors, although Accardo would eventually become the long-time boss of the Chicago mob.

In 1943, 80-year-old political boss Pat Nash died. Unlike Nash, Kelly was not respected by various factions of the party. Some of the Irish ward bosses thought that the mayor was too accommodating to the Slavic and Jewish leaders. The latter groups thought he was not accommodating enough. The mayor did not evoke much love from either the public or his subordinates. To add to his unpopularity, Kelly had moved out of his Southside home to swanky North Lake Shore Drive and his attempts to pose as an intellectual by discussing books and plays was considered pretentious by his supporters.[10]

In 1939, after beating Courtney in the primary, Kelly faced Republican Dwight Green, former prosecutor of Al Capone, in the mayoral election. Green lost by only 185,000 votes, or the about the number supplied by the gang-controlled wards. The next year Green was elected governor. In 1942, the Republicans made large gains in the congressional elections. The first Republican was elected to the United States Senate from Illinois since the 1920s. Had Kelly faced a strong Republican in 1943, he might have lost. However, Col. McCormick

---

10. The man who was elected mayor in 1955, eight years after Kelly left office, Richard J. Daley, may have learned from Kelly's mistakes. Though Daley remained mayor until his death twenty-two years later, he never moved from his modest house in the stockyards district. Nor did he attempt to pose as an intellectual. Some people even suspected that he occasionally dropped a grammatical error into his speeches to show that he was just one of the boys. In private conversations with business leaders, his grammar was flawless.

chose the party's nominee by declaring in the *Tribune* that it would be Roger Faherty, an unknown lawyer. The Republican state committee only learned of the nomination by reading the *Tribune,* but they had to go along with the powerful McCormick. The novice candidate started badly by saying that he did not have "the slightest idea what the issues will be." He then boasted of being a close personal friend of Mayor Kelly. This gave the Republican committee, led by Gov. Green, the nerve to reject the *Tribune's* candidate. Instead they substituted a little-known state official, George McKibbin. When his name was announced, one reporter said, "Oh I remember him. He's the guy the Republicans send out for coffee at their meetings." Against such a weak opponent, Kelly won by only 148,000 votes (again the syndicate provided the margin of victory for the mayor).

Despite his reelection, Kelly was not out of danger. The county committee named him chairman as replacement for Nash, but it also had the power to remove him, thereby reducing Kelly to a figurehead mayor. The 1943 race riots in New York and Detroit had caused Chicagoans of both races to fear what might happen in their city. In Detroit, twenty-five of the thirty-four people killed were black and of those, twenty-two were felled by police bullets. The events of Memorial Day, 1937, when the police had shot down forty strikers, were not forgotten and one could only imagine what might happen in the midst of a full-fledged race riot.

Shortly after the municipal election, mob killings again made news. An Irish sub-boss and a low-level gambler whom he was drinking with were shot to death. The gambler had recently been released from the srmy under a rule that allowed older GIs to be discharged if they had an essential occupation to return to. The newspapers were quick to ascertain that the dead man's essential occupation had been dealing cards in one of the joints owned by a well-known gambler.[11] A few months later another Irish gambler, thought to have been responsible for the death of the first gangster and his companion, was himself gunned down.

---

11. Full disclosure: the deceased man's employer was the writer's father. Though only of elementary school age, I attended both men's wakes. Louie, the gambler, was buried in his uniform with an American flag draped over him.

In 1944 another mob murder occurred in the powerful 24th Ward. One of its leaders, Ben Zuckerman, *aka* "Zucky the bookie" who controlled local gambling, was murdered. When Zucky's gambling partner heard the news, he dropped dead. The 24th Ward was one of the two or three most powerful in the city and its gangsters ranked high in the organized crime world. Later, another 24th Ward gangster died of a heart attack while in the county jail awaiting electrocution for murder.

A grand jury impaneled by District Attorney Courtney put the heat on gamblers and corrupt police officials, though as long as Captain Gilbert was chief investigator for Courtney, it was hard to take anything the latter did seriously. In 1944, with organized crime in disarray, Kelly feared Courtney might try to indict him for failing to suppress gambling. In his panic the mayor had nine police captains fired over conditions in their districts. Since the captains were virtually given their districts by ward bosses this made many of the mayor's colleagues unhappy. A ward boss who couldn't control the local cops was, for practical purposes, no boss at all. Finally, Kelly decided to back Courtney's unsuccessful 1944 campaign for governor against Dwight Green.[12] Eventually, the captains were restored to duty but various troubles were piling up for everyone in the world of Chicago organized crime.

Kelly knew that unless there was a friendly Democrat in the White House in 1945, he was liable to be targeted by the IRS or the Department of Justice, possibly even removed by his fellow bosses. With FDR or someone Kelly could rely on as president, his colleagues were not likely to remove him and the government would not indict him. The course for Kelly was obvious: make sure that a supportive figure occupied the White House and, as host of the 1944 Democratic convention, he was in a good position to make sure that happened.

---

12. For some reason Courtney did not get the usual number of votes in the machine-controlled wards and he suffered a narrow loss in the gubernatorial race. Usually precinct workers who performed poorly were fired from their patronage jobs. However, the mayor took no action against them. This led many to believe that Courtney had been knifed by the organization. Of course, Col. McCormick was delighted that his man retained the governorship. Courtney, who had been shot at in 1935 and "knifed" in 1944, disappeared from public life. Captain Gilbert continued as chief investigator for the state's attorney's office.

Chapter 4

Kansas City:
Uncle Tom and His Henchmen

At 7 o'clock on the hot Saturday morning of June 17, 1933, Kansas City's Union Station was already filling up with people. For some it would be the most memorable day of their lives. The drama began when four men alighted from a train. Joe Lackey and Frank Smith were special agents of the United States Department of Justice's Bureau of Investigation. Otto Reed was the chief of police of McAlester, Oklahoma, and the fourth was their prisoner, Frank Nash, an escapee from the federal penitentiary at Leavenworth, Kansas, where he had been serving time for bank robbery. Meeting the party was the local Bureau of Investigation special agent in charge, Reed Vetterli, Special Agent Frank Caffrey, and Kansas City detectives Frank Hermanson and Bill Grooms. Though the train was scheduled for an hour's lay-over before proceeding to Leavenworth, the lawmen had no intention of waiting. To avoid a possible rescue attempt by Nash's underworld friends, they were going to drive him the thirty miles to the prison.

Until two days earlier, Nash had been living openly in the gangster-friendly resort town of Hot Springs, Arkansas. Then the three lawmen had seized him, tossed him into their car, and raced out of town one jump ahead of the local police. If the Hot Springs cops had been able to intervene, they would have freed Nash. As it was, the local chief of detectives sent out a kidnapping alarm, even though he was aware of the true facts. Twenty miles east of Hot Springs, the lawmen's car was stopped at a sheriff's roadblock set up in response to the alarm. After a tense discussion, the agents were allowed to proceed. They were stopped again in Little Rock. In each instance, news of their whereabouts was relayed back to Hot Springs. When the bureau agents contacted their superior in Oklahoma City, concerned that they might not make it out of Arkansas alive, he ordered them to board a train at Fort Smith and proceed to Kansas City, where additional lawmen would assist them. While they waited on the Fort Smith platform, an Associated Press reporter spoke to them and filed a story mentioning their destination.

So at Union Station, the lawmen's plan was that Agent Caffrey would use his own Chevrolet (the bureau did not supply its employees with cars) to haul Nash to Leavenworth while the other feds and Chief Reed rode shotgun and the Kansas City detectives followed along in a tail car. In the station parking lot, as Nash was hustled into the front seat of Caffrey's car, Reed, Lackey, and Smith piled into the back. Vetterli, Caffrey, and Detectives Grooms and Hermanson were standing alongside the vehicle, when suddenly someone yelled, "Hands up, up." Then another person yelled "Let 'em have it." Simultaneously, Grooms drew his revolver and fired at a man pointing a Tommy gun at them. Immediately there was a burst of shots. Nash's rescuers had opened fire, killing the two detectives, Chief Reed, Agent Caffrey, and the man they had come to rescue, Frank Nash. SAC Vetterli and Agent Lackey were wounded.

A Kansas City police officer who was attracted by the shooting came out of the station and began firing at the fleeing hoodlums. Supposedly one of them stumbled as though he had been hit. The event, dubbed by the press as the "Kansas City Massacre," stunned the nation and led to the enactment of laws enhancing the authority of the bureau and making a number of crimes federal offenses.

Under Director J. Edgar Hoover what became known, after 1935, as the FBI would lead the war on the gun-crazy robbers who were terrorizing large sections of the country. Hoover, who over a decade earlier had been de facto leader of the war against the "Red Menace" was now charged with combating America's "public enemies." Before the Kansas City Massacre, bureau agents did not normally carry guns or have full powers of arrest. When an apprehension was necessary, agents had to get help from the local police. This led to ludicrous incidents where cops burst through the front door, guns drawn, while the feds stood in the back with brickbats waiting to slug the wanted man if he came out. Less than a year after Kansas City, the G-men, as they came to be called, would be wielding machine guns against the nation's "public enemies."

In the early 1930s, when the midwest and southwest were swept by a wave of spectacular robberies and kidnappings, the popular explanation for this outbreak was that the end of Prohibition and the onset of the Depression caused many bootleggers to turn to violent crime. It was not a profile that fit hoodlums such as John Dillinger of Indiana, Clyde Barrow of Texas, or Charles "Pretty Boy" Floyd of Oklahoma. All three had been in trouble with the law since their youth and had served time in prison.

The real threat came because of the new tactics that criminals employed. Gangs using high-powered automobiles could move rapidly from state to state so that within a few hours of pulling a holdup in Indiana, they could be in Iowa. Faced with this type of operation, classic police detective methods were of little value. It did no good for cops to talk to local informants or raid known gangster hangouts, and municipal police did not have the resources to send their investigators roaming throughout the country. In instances where police encountered gangs in the actual commission of a crime, the cops were usually at a disadvantage. The robbers had machine guns and the element of surprise. Whereas the cops, armed with revolvers, did not know whether a bank alarm was genuine or set off by accident. Thus the robbers left a trail of dead lawmen from Texas to Ohio, some of them virtually cut in half by Tommy gun bullets.

The roving criminals also had a network of fellow crooks they could use for assistance and certain cities where the local police would turn a blind eye to gangsters hiding out. The midwestern gangster network ran through three key cities, Chicago, Illinois; St. Paul, Minnesota; and Kansas City, Missouri. The three were linked in some manner with every kidnapping that occurred, either as the site of the crime, the hideout of the kidnappers or the place where the ransom was paid.

The basic mistake Nash's captors had made was to stop off in Kansas City at all. The town was run by one of the most corrupt political bosses in the country, Tom Pendergast, and an integral part of his organization were members of the local Mafia. Under the Pendergast machine, Kansas City was not only gangster friendly, it was full of gambling joints, bordellos, and drugs. In 1934 a young reporter named Edward R. Murrow wrote, "If you want to see some sin, forget about Paris and go to Kansas City. With the possible exception of such renowned centers as Singapore and Port Said, Kansas City probably has the greatest sin industry in the world." Twelfth Street, in the downtown area, contained blocks of gambling joints while 13th and 14th streets were lined with houses of prostitution. On the plus side KC had some of the best jazz music in the country, featuring big time artists like Count Basie. None of the places ever closed. An upscale businessman's restaurant, the Chesterfield, featured luncheon served by waitresses wearing nothing but high-heeled shoes. Commissioner Anslinger's Bureau of Narcotics rated Kansas City as a major center of the drug trade. Elmer Irey, the head of U.S. Treasury enforcement, describing local law enforcement said:

> You could buy all the morphine and heroin you could lift in Kansas City and the man who wanted to keep his job as a police Capt. had better keep his prostitute file correct and up to the minute so Tom's machine would be certain that no girl practiced her ancient art without paying full tribute.

Pendergast had grown up in St. Joseph, Missouri, the son of Irish Catholic immigrants from Tipperary. In 1882, when Tom was ten years old, Bob Ford killed Jesse James in St. Joe. Pendergast developed into a burly, young man, exceptionally handy with his powerful fists. In 1890 he moved to Kansas City where his older brother Jim ran a saloon in the West Bottom section along the Missouri River. Brother Jim also served as alderman of the tough First Ward from 1892 until his death in 1911. Tom started out as a precinct captain responsible for getting out the votes and dealing with rival factions, usually by using force. He received a patronage job as assistant county marshal, then became the superintendent of streets of Kansas City. After Jim's death, Tom was elected to represent the First Ward in the city council.

Tom was not a hearty backslapping politician. When he met with people he was businesslike and never took his cat eyes off of a visitor. Strangely, for such a tough man, he feared to go out at night lest he be assassinated. By the 1920s he was the boss of the Jackson County Democratic machine. By 1930 he was the acknowledged leader of the party in western Missouri. His machine had a phenomenal ability to get out votes. Sometimes the total number cast exceeded the number of people living in the election district. One reason was that Boss Tom could count on 50,000 ghosts that existed only on the registration rolls. With so many voters, real and false, he was sometimes able to swing statewide elections.

Pendergast was assisted by three key lieutenants. One was Henry McElroy. In 1926, when reformers forced the city manager system on Kansas City as a means of ending control by corrupt politicians, Pendergast designated McElroy to serve as manager. He would hold the job for the next thirteen years. The second key lieutenant was Harry Truman, presiding judge of the county (an administrative post, not a judicial one). Truman, originally from Independence, Missouri, had opened a haberdashery store in Kansas City after returning from World War I, in which he served as an artillery captain in France. When he and his partner went bankrupt, a wartime friend, Jim Pendergast, nephew of Tom, recommended Truman to the boss as a man who would be loyal. The fact that Truman was a Protestant from a farming background, was also a plus because it balanced the Irish Catholic, urban element in the machine. In addition, Truman had good contacts among war veterans and possessed kinfolk in the Jackson County area. So the machine elected him a judge for the eastern district.

In 1924 the machine lost an election and Truman was out of a job. This presented a problem for him. Even in the prosperous 1920s, the bankrupt store owner was not what could be called a "go getter." So, he took a minor position selling memberships in the local automobile club. In 1926 he was returned to office as presiding judge of the entire county.

The third member of the triumvirate was Johnny Lazia, who was the leader of the Italian mob, which had succeeded to control of the First Ward. Johnny was an alum of the Missouri State penitentiary, where he had been sentenced to twelve years for robbery. Given his connections, he got out after only eight months. Where gang bosses like Capone or Luciano rarely smiled, Johnny told jokes and, with his wire-rim glasses, spats, gloves and a cane, he could have been mistaken for a vaudeville comedian. It was Johnny, though, who directed the heavy work that needed to be done, including murder, to keep the machine in power. In 1932, when Pendergast managed to get the Kansas City police department transferred from state control to the city, Lazia became de facto police chief. He even had an office in head-quarters and when people called the chief, Johnny was liable to answer. One of Lazia's first acts as police overseer was to secure the appoint-ment of sixty ex-convicts as Kansas City cops.

With McElroy running the city government, Truman the county government, and Lazia the police and the rackets, things went smoothly for the Pendergast machine until the Kansas City Massacre. The affair had come about because Frank "Jelly" Nash was a popular fellow in the midwestern underworld. A real old-time desperado, as a young man he had held up trains on horseback. Later he served prison terms in Oklahoma for murder and robbery but invariably managed to be pardoned. In the 1920s he was sentenced to the federal penitentiary in Leavenworth, Kansas. There he became a model prisoner, was appointed a trustee, and allowed to work outside the walls. In effect, a career, violent criminal was put on his honor not to escape. Of course, trustee jobs were often given to inmates favored by politicians or the mob. In October 1930, he walked away from a work detail and dis-appeared.

Nash did not go to Kansas City because that was too close to Leavenworth. At first he hid out in Chicago where he frequented Doc Staci's Tavern. Though he had a wife in Oklahoma, he met and married one of the barmaids, a girl named Frances. The newlyweds went on a long honeymoon to Hot Springs, Arkansas. The famous resort town was another community where gangsters went unmolested. It was run by a big time New York prohibition era boss, Owney "The Killer" Madden. After the Mafia took over New York, Madden had been exiled to Hot Springs, where he married a local girl and became an elder statesman of American organized crime.

In Hot Springs, Nash frequented the White Front poolroom run by a fugitive con man named Richard Galatis, who was in solid with the local chief of detectives. So nobody was about to bother him or Nash. For a fugitive with a price on his head, Nash was careless. He wore a hairpiece to cover up his bald dome but he frequently called attention to himself by becoming the life of the party. He had a pleasant voice and would sometimes engage in impromptu sing-alongs with nightclub bands. On occasion he would even grab the baton away from the conductor and lead the musicians. Galatis warned him to stop showing off but he persisted. Hot Springs was a resort town frequented by many visitors and it was likely one of them who notified the FBI where Jelly Nash could be found.[1]

When the two Bureau agents and Chief Reed, who knew Nash by sight from his Oklahoma days, went to the White Front they spotted their man. So they took him down fast and sped off. A few years later, when Lucky Luciano was sojourning in Hot Springs to avoid Tom Dewey's investigators, the local cops refused to turn Lucky over to New York detectives. Finally, the governor of Arkansas had to send state troopers with machine guns into the Hot Springs jail to take Lucky out.

As the lawmen made their way to Kansas City, calls were going back and forth from Hot Springs to Nash's various friends in Chicago and Missouri. Eventually, Mrs. Nash and Galatis were put in touch with Verne Miller in Kansas City, who was also a fugitive. When he had returned from World War I, a decorated hero, the folks in his South Dakota county elected him sheriff. A crack shot, and, despite his small frame, a tough and fearless man, he was a popular sheriff.

---

1. There have been stories that in 1932 Nash was running with a crowd of Chicago bank robbers led by Tommy "Red" Holden, who in the 1950s would be the first man put on the FBI's ten most wanted list. Some accounts suggest that the bureau may have learned of Nash's whereabouts after Holden's group was arrested. Since in later years I was acquainted with Holden's friends, I doubt very much that they would tell detectives the time of day.

Women also fell for him because his charming manner and courteous demeanor won their hearts. He would not allow a man to use vulgarity anywhere in the vicinity of a lady. Shutting up some drunken stranger in a bar is not always the easiest thing to do. But when Verne Miller fixed his steely gray eyes on a loudmouth and told him to "cut it out," there was something about his manner that made men obey.

Miller had a great liking for money and his sheriff days ended when he was sent to prison for embezzling county funds. When he was released, he began smuggling liquor across the Canadian border into the United States. This led him to hook up with Detroit's Purple Gang, who were major liquor importers. The Purples had started out as a Jewish group but by the time Miller arrived they were mostly Italian mafiosos. His skill with a gun led some of the Midwestern mobs to use him as a hit man.

Miller, always gallant to the ladies, told Mrs. Nash he would rescue her husband. Since it was known that there would be a group of lawmen at the Union Station, Miller asked Johnny Lazia for help and he recommended some out-of-town gunsels who frequently sheltered in Kansas City. "Pretty Boy" Floyd and Adam Richetti were stickup men who had served prison time. Charlie Floyd, from the hills of Oklahoma, had acquired his nickname from the Kansas City prostitutes because they thought he was so good-looking. He too was known as a handy man with a gun who cut a wide swath across the Midwest. Floyd was suspected of being part of a gang that, in 1932, had killed six lawmen in a gun battle near Springfield, Missouri.[2] He also was thought to have killed a federal agent in Kansas City and was definitely known to have murdered two brothers there because they objected to him romancing one of their wives. Floyd wounded a police officer in Ohio who was trying to arrest him for the robbery of a Kentucky bank and he gunned down a deputy sheriff in Oklahoma.

Richetti and Floyd had arrived in Kansas City the day before the massacre in their usual colorful fashion. A sheriff in Bolivar, Missouri, had spotted the two of them in a garage, but they got the drop on him and made him drive them out of town in his car. After a while they

---

2. At the time it was common to attribute every unsolved bank robbery or cop killing in Oklahoma, Kansas, and Missouri to Floyd. Later, it was determined he had not been involved in the Springfield massacre.

abandoned the lawman's car, which by that time every cop in the area was looking for, hijacked a motorist and made him drive them and the sheriff to Kansas City. They must've been feeling pretty good because they released both of their prisoners unharmed. On the morning of the 17th, toting Tommy guns, Miller, Floyd, and Richetti journeyed to the Union Station intending to overawe the G-men and Kansas City cops without a fight. Reputedly, Floyd had once managed to disarm five deputy sheriffs who had been staked out to arrest him.

The Kansas City detectives, Grooms and Hermanson, were normally assigned to patrol the downtown area, keeping special watch for bank robbers. As part of their equipment they had two submachine guns. They were what was called in many cities with similar details a heavy weapons squad. Because someone, possibly one of Lazia's ex-con cops, had removed the machine guns from their car before the morning of the 17th they were not available when needed. When Grooms drew his revolver and fired, Nash had time to yell out, "Don't kill me," but it was too late. He and four lawmen were shot to death.

Director Hoover poured agents into Kansas City By tracing phone calls made from Hot Springs, Joplin, Missouri, and Chicago, they thus identified the killers. Verne Miller fled to Chicago where he was tracked down by the FBI but escaped in a flurry of gunfire. He then sought shelter with the Purple Gang in Detroit. But he brought too much federal heat in his wake and one day his body was found on a highway. The Detroit mob was not about to battle the federal government to save some itinerant gunman who was not a made member of their organization.[3] "Pretty Boy" and Richetti made their way to Ohio. There Floyd was killed by FBI agents (from the same unit that had eliminated Dillinger in Chicago), and local police. Richetti was captured, returned to Missouri and executed in the state penitentiary's gas chamber. The individuals who helped set up the massacre with their phone calling were convicted in federal court. The men involved were given sentences in the three-to-four-year range and the women were put on probation. No case could be made against Johnny Lazia.

Initially the Kansas City Police Department claimed the crime had been committed by out-of-town criminals and had nothing to do with

---

3. Some accounts suggest that Miller may have been murdered because he shot an organized crime killer.

them, so they would not even investigate it. This, despite the fact that two of their own officers were killed and that somehow their dead cops' machine guns had been taken from their police car before the affair. Such was Pendergast's power that no one in the Kansas City machine was held to account for the four dead lawmen.

So bold were local criminals that, in 1933, they kidnapped city manager McElroy's 25-year-old daughter Mary. Johnny Lazia quickly collected $30,000 from gamblers to pay the ransom. One of the kidnapper's became the first man to be executed under the federal anti-kidnapping statute known as the "Lindbergh law," passed after the abduction and murder of Col. Charles Lindbergh's son. The second kidnapper was spared when Mary testified that she had fallen in love with him.

By 1933 Pendergast, operating out a modest three-room office on Main Street, was clearly the most powerful politician in Missouri. The previous year he had elected one of his men as governor. People began referring to the state government in Jefferson City as "Uncle Tom's cabin." In 1934 a senate seat was up. The incumbent was a Republican and a prohibitionist, neither label popular at the time. The other senator was from eastern Missouri. So the nominee had to be from the western part of the state. Two individuals declared for the job, but they were not Pendergast men. In sorting possible candidates the boss' eye fell on his faithful lieutenant, Harry Truman, who was often referred to as "Tom's office boy." Truman himself had hoped to be elected county collector, a fee office that provided an income of $30,000 a year. To his credit, Truman had not taken bribes and as a result he had little money and, approaching 50, no real security. The collector job, paying three times the salary of a senator, would provide both. Some of the machine supporters objected to him as a senator because they thought he was too little-known to make a good candidate and, given his limited education and business failure, was not up to the job.

The 1934 election year started off with the Kansas City municipal primary in March. A group of reformers from various factions set out to defeat the Pendergast machine. To combat them, Johnny Lazia dispatched carloads of gunmen to discourage dissidents from voting. In addition gamblers and prostitutes poured out to cast ballots along with the 50,000 ghosts. Regarding the latter, boss Tom ruled that, "every cemetery must do its duty." Before the day ended, four people had been killed and about 200 assaulted. The Pendergast machine was victorious.

Johnny Lazia had managed to steer clear of an indictment in the Kansas City Massacre. But he could not escape the U.S. Treasury. In 1933, he was convicted of evading $50,000 in federal income tax. Pendergast wrote to Postmaster General and Democratic National Chairman, Jim Farley,

> Now Jim, Lazia is one of my chief lieutenants and I am more sincerely interested in his welfare than anything you might be able to do for me now or in the future…. I wish you would use your utmost endeavor to bring about a settlement of this matter.

Despite this Lazia was sentenced to prison. In June 1934, while out on appeal, he was shot in front of his apartment building. As he lay dying in the hospital, he moaned "Who would want to kill me?" In fact, the killer was a minor St. Louis gunman named Jack Gregory, whom Lazia had brought in to provide some additional firepower in the voter suppression drive. Jack decided he liked the atmosphere of Kansas City and asked for a piece of the action. Lazia ordered him to leave town. Instead, Jack killed Johnny. Lazia's gang quickly grabbed Gregory and stuffed him into an apartment building furnace while he was still alive.

Otto Higgins, a former journalist, suspected of committing murders, was appointed director of police. Lazia's lieutenant, Charles Corolla, took over the mob. And a hit man named Charlie Gargotta occupied the number two spot. The Mafia went on. Later in the decade Harry Anslinger would break up a huge Kansas City narcotic operation and send Corolla to jail, after which he would be deported to his native Sicily.

With the help of ghost voters, prostitutes, gamblers and gunmen, Truman bested his two opponents in the primary and went on to win the general election. In Washington he was lightly regarded and became known as "the senator from Pendergast." In Kansas City the United States attorney's office and the FBI began probing corruption and voter fraud. By the late '30s a large number of election officials were being sent to jail. Sen. Truman took to the floor of the chamber to complain that "a Jackson County Missouri Democrat has as much chance of a fair trial in the federal district court of western Missouri as a Jew would have in a Hitler court or a Trotsky follower before Stalin. Indictments have been wholesale. Convictions have been a foregone conclusion. Verdicts have been directed."

The cause of Pendergast's own fall was his addiction to gambling on a large scale. He bought a stable of horses and every morning he would shut himself up with a personal tout (of very limited acumen) and plan the bets he would make all over the country. Soon he was losing $1 million a year. To make up his losses he pressed his lieutenants to bring in more money. Again it was treasury agents who struck.

At the time they were bringing charges against individuals who failed to pay taxes on money they received from shady deals. Eventually the trail led to Pendergast, who had initially turned down a bribe of $200,000 in an insurance case because it was too small. He demanded and received $500,000. Faced with the overwhelming evidence against him, he pled guilty and was sent to Leavenworth Penitentiary. His city manager, Henry McElroy, and Police Director Higgins were also sent to prison. Mary McElroy committed suicide. When officials at Leavenworth released Pendergast's mug shot to the press, Truman wrote a harsh and threatening letter to the director of the United States Bureau of Prisons.

In 1939 the state reclaimed control of the police department and installed an FBI agent as chief. The new man, Lear B. Reed, had led the investigation of the Pendergast machine. Reed, who comported himself like a gunslinger, rather than a button-down G-man, was in some respects the right person to bring order to Kansas City. When gangsters shot at him he shot right back. When people came to his office to offer him a bribe he knocked their teeth out and as they fled through his front door, he warned them that the next time he would use his blackjack. Reed, a former captain of marines, had had a turbulent career in the FBI. In St. Louis he had been indicted for manslaughter after shooting a bystander during a hunt for a fugitive. In 1941 he was pressured to resign as chief in Kansas City.

After his release from prison, Pendergast was forbidden by the conditions of his parole to participate in politics for five years. So he turned over control of the remnants of his organization to his nephew Jim. Though badly damaged, the Kansas City machine was not dead and its gangster allies continue to operate. During the Murder Incorporated investigation in New York, some of the suspects fled to Kansas City to hide out.

The fall of Pendergast appeared to spell the end of Senator Truman, who was up for reelection in 1940. His first hurdle would come in the primary. The incumbent governor, Lloyd Stark, decided to oppose Truman in the primary. The senator's relationship with FDR, never good, was at its lowest ebb. Truman was angry because he generally received little respect from the White House, which saw him as no more than Pendergast's stooge. Steve Early, the president's secretary, told Truman that if he would not run, FDR would appoint him to the Interstate Commerce Commission where he would have lifetime tenure and a salary 50% above the $10,000 per year he made as a senator. When Truman did decide to run for reelection he could not even find a successful businessman to serve in the all-important job of campaign finance chairman. So he chose Harry Vaughn, who like Truman himself was a reserve artillery colonel. At the time Vaughn was selling loose-leaf notebook equipment in Illinois and was flat broke. But at least he could use the title of colonel on official stationary.

Despite an early lack of support, Truman benefited from the fact that Stark, a wealthy apple grower who came from a town near St. Louis, proved to be an uninspiring campaigner. Stark also did not have the support of the state's senior senator Bennett Clark because it would have meant two eastern Missourians in the Senate. That could have led to Bennett failing to receive the western Missouri vote when he ran for reelection. Truman was also helped by the fact that a third candidate jumped into the race. Maurice Milligan had been the United States attorney who led the prosecution of the Pendergast machine. Another weak campaigner, his presence meant that the anti-Pendergast vote would go to him and not to Stark. In addition Truman picked up the support of the powerful railroad brotherhood unions who liked him because, as a member of the Senate interstate commerce committee, he had been very supportive on their issues.

The most important addition to Truman's forces was a 37-year-old St. Louis lawyer, Robert Hannegan. The young Irish-American was a typical machine political boss of the type Truman had gotten along with so well in Kansas City. Big, broad shouldered Hannegan, the son of a St. Louis Police Department chief of detectives, had been a four letterman in college and later played professional football and baseball. As a young politician he took over the 21st Ward and in three months converted it from Republican to Democratic. By 1940 he controlled one-third of the city's wards. Hannegan was a shifty character. He started out supporting Stark but then went over to Truman. The reason for Hannegan's switch was that he feared a doublecross by Stark. The governor had originally been a Pendergast ally but when the machine faltered he had jumped ship while Truman stayed loyal.

The primary race involved the usual skullduggery and brokered deals typical of Missouri politics. Truman emerged the victor in a close race, winning by 7,976 votes. Hannegan's eight wards had provided him a margin of 8,411. Had Hannegan not backed him, Truman would have lost and most likely returned to farming in western Missouri.

In Kansas City, the fall of Pendergast and the conviction of Charles Corolla on drug charges hurt the mob, but it continued to operate. The new mob boss of the city was Charles Binaggio, and like his predecessors his tentacles reached into the police department. Despite the fact that it had been brought under state control, it was not too difficult to persuade a governor to appoint someone to the four-man board of commissioners who would be tolerant of vice and gambling. Even many respectable people in Kansas City felt that such activities were necessary to attract visitors.

*

After Commissioner Anslinger's FBN agents nailed Charlie Corolla, the Kansas City drug ring went right on. The new head of it was Nick Impostato, who had left Sicily in the 1920s. After arriving in Kansas City he became a hit man for Johnny Lazia, then settled in as a drug kingpin. In 1943, a secret meeting was held in a Kansas City hotel room that was bugged by the FBN. Among those attending was the drug boss of St. Louis, Tony Lopipare, and dealers from Tampa, Florida. The purpose was to determine who was informing on the group. None of the participants guessed that it was one of their own, the long-time Kansas City drug dealer Carl Caramussa. Facing federal charges, Caramussa had decided to turn government witness. When he eventually told his story on the stand, his Mafia boss made such threatening gestures that U.S. marshals ejected him from the court-room. The defendants were convicted and, as a reward, Caramussa was released. He changed his name and relocated to Chicago.

Moving to Chicago, a vital link with Kansas City organized crime, was a bad decision. One day, Caramussa came out of his house to find a flat tire on his car. His family, anxious to pile in and go to a party, waited on the porch while he changed it. He probably forgot that flattening tires was a classic way to set up a hit on an intended victim, i.e., it froze him at a particular location where he would be concen-trating on the problem with his vehicle. A car drove by with a shotgun poking out the window and blew Caramussa's head off before the eyes of his family. Naturally the murder was not solved. If anyone doubted that the narcotics distributors had a network reaching from Sicily through Pendergast's Kansas City to Kelly's Chicago, the murder of Caramussa should have changed their mind.

St. Louis also became a link between Kansas City and Chicago. Until the mid-1920s the most powerful gang in "the mound city" was Egan's Rats, formed early in the century by a ward boss named Tom Egan and state senator Tom Kenny. The members were robbers, thugs, and election-day sluggers. By the time of World War I, under the leadership of Tom Egan's brother Willie, the gang possessed enough political contacts to reach into President Wilson's White House and secure a commutation of sentence for a gang lieutenant imprisoned for interstate theft. The ungrateful prisoner, Max Green-berg, then switched his allegiance to the Rats' leading rivals, the Hogan gang, a group led by Edward "Jellyroll" Hogan, another member of the state legislature. In the early '20s, the gangs battled for supremacy. Over two years, twenty-three men were shot, including Willie Egan.

One time the president of the St. Louis board of police commissioners and a Catholic priest brought the two gangs together to make peace. Such sit downs were almost never successful. The St. Louis one led to a short-term truce, after which Egan Rats, shooting at Hoganites, killed two innocent bystanders, one of them a state legislator. A Rat leader explained that the shooting simply arose from "boyish high spirits." In the mid-1920s the Rats pulled off a series of spectacular robberies which led many of them to receive twenty-five years in federal prison. At the same time, the man who had succeeded Willie Egan as leader was machine-gunned to death.

Rat alums were in great demand by the other gangs. As noted earlier, Fred Burke (or least his machine guns) was involved in the murder of Frankie Yale in New York and the massacre of the seven Moran gang members on Valentine's Day in Chicago. Leo Brothers was convicted of killing Chicago *Tribune* reporter Jake Lingle, though it was generally believed he was paid to take the rap.

The carnage in St. Louis was minor compared to the violence in East St. Louis across the Mississippi River in Illinois. There, for over thirty years, a war raged between the Shelton and Birger gangs. Both sides used tanks and bombing planes to carry out attacks on the other. It was a classic family feud of the type known in the mountain districts of the South.[4] The violence in Missouri and southern Illinois some- times made Chicago look tame. In such an environment, corrupt poli- tics was almost inevitable.

Robert Hannegan continued his sharp political wheeler-dealer ways in St. Louis. In 1941, when he and his partner, Mayor Bernard Dick- mann, attempted to steal the gubernatorial election from the successful Republican candidate, Hannegan called upon help from the Hogan gang. As a result of that fiasco Hannegan's political career crashed.

---

4. As late as the 1950s there was a standing bounty on the Shelton's which often lead amateurs to "take a shot" at winning the prize. Some succeeded, others were killed trying. The Republican vote counting in Madison and St. Clair counties that surrounded East St. Louis, usually offset the "errors" in tallying votes in Democratic Chicago. Illinois authorities generally ignored the strife in East St. Louis as a Missouri problem while Missouri authorities pointed to the fact that it was carried on out of their jurisdiction in Illinois. Only on occasions when the conflict was so bloody that the National Guard had to be called out, did Illinois officials take any action.

Luckily for him, Sen. Truman was able to secure his appointment as district collector of internal revenue, then United States Commissioner of Internal Revenue and finally, along with the support of Ed Kelly of Chicago and Ed Flynn of New York, Hannegan was made national chairman of the Democratic Party.

In retrospect it is difficult to understand how a twenty-year member of the Kansas City machine like Harry Truman could have been unaware of the nature of the organization he fronted for. During his time Kansas City was one of the worst sin cities in America, a capital of drugs and prostitution and its police force was run by gangsters. Even Chicago was not as bad. There, drugs were not a significant part of the local criminal scene and, although no one had any trouble locating prostitutes, certain limits applied. Always the shadow of the powerful Catholic church hung over the Windy City and a politician defied the cardinal at his peril.

The truth is that Harry Truman owed his career to one of the most vicious and corrupt organizations in American history. He can hardly claim that he was unaware the facts in the Kansas City Massacre or the killings in the 1934 Democratic primary. Yet, he willingly accepted the support of gamblers, prostitutes, and Mafia gunmen. During that period, he himself was never accused of accepting a bribe, though he kept relatives on government payrolls and arranged a loan of public funds to another relative who defaulted on repayment. Not until the rise to power of the big-city bosses and their mobster allies, especially the Mafia, could a man with his affiliations have become president of the United States.

Chapter 5

Corruption Everywhere:
The Real Governor of California;
Crump of Tennessee; the Detroit Ring;
and New Jersey's "I Am the Law" Hague

The United States has had many political bosses. But few could qualify as dictators because there were always countervailing forces to them. The most famous American boss, Tweed of New York City, ended up fleeing the country and after his capture, died in prison. The longest-serving Tammany boss, George Murphy, held the job for twenty-two years. But he only controlled New York's City Hall for six years, the rest of the time he had to share power with the Brooklyn machine which supplied the mayors, or sit on the sidelines while a reform administration governed. Sometimes Murphy faced rebellions within his own ranks. Richard J. Daley of Chicago served nearly twenty-two years as mayor but he was not considered tyrannical by most Chicago citizens. Where Tweed and Murphy, at the height of their power, did not hold elective office, Daley had to face the voters six times and always won by a large margin. Boston's James Michael Curley was elected mayor four times, but none of his terms was consecutive and he spent a portion of his last one in prison. Huey Long, who came close to being a true American dictator, dominated Louisiana for a decade until an assassin's bullet ended his reign. Still, Long always faced opposition from the New Orleans city government and the U.S. government which sent some of his lieutenants to prison. It is likely had Huey lived, he would have been jailed for income tax evasion, since he was high on FDR's enemies list.

Around the time of World War II, California was not the political colossus it would become later in the century. Though Los Angeles was growing by leaps and bounds, San Francisco, with its great port linking America to Asia, was still the most important city. Until 1938, the City of Angels was run by Mayor Frank Shaw, whose administration was shot through with corruption. Shaw's brother acted as his bagman and the LAPD was for sale. The police intelligence squad under Captain Earl Kynette operated as the mayor's personal gestapo. The real political power in the city was held by the anti-labor *Los Angeles Times* and the business community it represented. In 1911, Union terrorists had blown up the *Times* building, killing twenty-one people. So powerful was the business community that they had their own intelligence squad that operated out of a downtown office building under the command of the famous Captain William "Red" Hynes. His nickname did not come from the color of his hair but because of his hard line, anti-Communist views. The red squad broke into offices of leftist organizations and dispersed radical meetings. Hynes told his troops, "If trouble starts I want to see the Reds on the floor not you."

A second powerful element in the city was the Protestant ministers who appealed to the many Los Angeles residents who had come from the South or the Midwest. Some ministers had the same power as Catholic bishops did in other cities. In the organized crime world, Guy McAfee, a former L.A. police captain, was the top gambling figure. His nickname, "The Whistler, "came from his practice of warning gamblers in advance of raids by calling them up and whistling the tune, "Listen to the Mockingbird."

When Los Angeles reform forces, led by a restauranteur named Clifford Clinton, began complaining about gambling and vice, Clinton himself became disaster prone. Trick motorcyclists and stuntmen were always running into or falling under his car. Eventually his house was bombed. Many suspected that behind his troubles was the hand of

Kynette's intelligence squad. To fight fire with fire, Clinton's organization, the Citizens Independent Vice Investigating Commission (CIVIC) hired Harry Raymond as a private investigator. Formerly an LAPD detective, the police chief of Venice, California, and San Diego, as well as a district attorney's investigator, he was frequently fired over various vice scandals. On January 3, 1938, a bomb wired to Raymond's car exploded, giving him twelve dozen shrapnel wounds. The resulting investigation led to the conviction and imprisonment of Captain Kynette.

The episode was too much for the public and, in a recall election, Shaw was ousted and a judge named Fletcher Bowron replaced him as mayor. Under Bowron both the intelligence and Red squads were abolished and the LAPD undertook a limited crackdown on gambling operations. McAfee and other gamblers began to relocate to the then dust-blown desert town of Las Vegas, Nevada.

In 1937, the New York mob sent Ben "Bugsy" Siegel to look after their interests in Los Angeles. Though not welcomed by the local Mafia leader, Jack Dragna, or the flamboyant Jewish gangster Mickey Cohen, the local hoodlums had to submit to rule from the east. Following Siegel's murder in 1947, protected vice and gambling continued until the police department was cleaned up once and for all in 1950.

Up the coast in San Francisco, organized crime had been run for years by the McDonough brothers. As the city's leading criminal attorney, Jake Ehrlich, described them:

> From their grubby little office at Clay and Kearny Streets, close enough to the Hall of Justice for the chief to wince if Pete McDonough raised his voice in anger, these Argus-eyed, squid-handed brothers supervised the many-splendored nightlife of San Francisco. They kept an eye on the nightly take of every hustling girl... and had the drawings on any burglary, con game or safe blowing that happened *before* it happened or it *didn't* happen.
>
> The McDonough's had lawyers and court room fixes in all price categories for sale. They created judges and uncreated them.... They bankrolled madams and assigned territories to bootleggers. They provided protection for pimps, dice hustlers, bookmakers, pickpockets, after-hours

operations, lamsters and every stripe of fast-money specialists.... and... oh yes, they provided bail bonds.

The other powerful force in the city was the business community, particularly the shipping interests.

In 1934 Harry Bridges' longshoreman's union led a massive strike up and down the West Coast. In the emergency the San Francisco police were given carte blanche to break the strike and the state militia was called out to assist. Amidst some shooting, the strike was broken, but labor unions had a powerful influence in the city and they sought revenge. In 1935, an IRS official casually noted at a luncheon that San Francisco police officers were paying income tax. This was unusual since local government employees were not required to pay federal tax on their salaries at the time. A grand jury was impaneled to look into the matter and Edward Atherton, a Los Angeles private detective and former FBI man, was given $100,000 to conduct an investigation. His report identified 135 houses of prostitution, estimating the payoffs from gambling and prostitution at $1 million annually. He accused the McDonough brothers of "being the Fountainhead of corruption" and named a number of police officers as receiving payoffs. Criminal lawyer Jake Ehrlich, who represented the police fraternal organizations, immediately disputed the accusations in the report. He said the take was at least 4 million and there were at least 300 houses of prostitution in the city. In short, he argued that the whole thing was a political charade.

In 1943, a prominent shipping magnate, Roger Dearborn Lapham, was elected mayor. Though the McDonough's had not survived the Atherton investigation, the police and organized crime continued to operate as in the past. The one favorable thing that could be said about San Francisco's arrangements was that they kept the national Mafia out of the city.

Ultimately the real power in California was not the city administrations of Los Angeles, San Francisco, or the various local power blocs; it was a relatively obscure private citizen. In the period from 1943 to 1952, when Earl Warren was governor of California, he was deemed a strong and honest governor. He was also a law and order zealot, who in one instance raided offshore gambling ships in what the California courts called a "an act of piracy."[1] During Warren's administration the most important political figure in the state was a lobbyist named Artie Samish. Although he never ran for office or held a government job, he was the ruler of the state capital. He often boasted "I'm the governor of the legislature, to hell with the governor of the state." No matter which party was in power he could always name the speaker of the house and the committee chairman. Anyone who wanted to get a bill through the legislature had to go to "Samish Alley," a four-room suite in a Sacramento hotel and pay court to Artie. One element of his power was, as he put it, "I've got the damnedest gestapo you ever saw." His chief clients were gamblers and liquor distributors. In his hometown of San Francisco he shared an office suite with a bookie and casino owner from Chicago. In Los Angeles he was often seen in the company of Mickey Cohen. Frank Costello of New York admitted that Samish was a good friend.

Samish managed to elect his own man, Fred Howser, as attorney general of California Howser immediately had his representatives making the rounds demanding payoffs and announcing that the AG's office would take control of gambling in the state. That caper blew up after a shooting outside of a Hollywood nightclub in which one of Howser's detectives, serving as Mickey Cohen's bodyguard, was badly wounded. Samish's downfall came in the early '50s via the usual problem: tax delinquencies. The Justice Department prosecuted him on criminal grounds and not only was he ordered to pay $70,000 in taxes and $40,000 in fines, he also received a sentence of three years in jail.

*

The oddest political machine in the country was the one in Memphis, Tennessee, run by boss Ed Crump. "Boss Ed" had grown up in Mississippi and was a 19-year-old hick when he arrived in Memphis in 1893. In 1902 he married a local society belle and began to rise in both business and politics. In 1907 he was appointed commissioner of police and fire of the city of Memphis. In 1910 he was elected to the

---

1. As chief justice of the United States he switched his criminal justice philosophy entirely. Possibly he had an epiphany but he also knew that he was not really qualified for the post and, to avoid criticism from legal scholars, he adopted the advanced views of Ivy League law schools.

first of his three two-year terms as mayor. Following his office holding career, he chose to work behind the scenes and run the city through mayors he controlled.

During a time when the South was governed by Jim Crow laws and it was worth the life of a black man to try to cast a ballot, African American voters were a bulwark of Crump's machine. As a result the black population of Memphis received many benefits from the city.

Not content with just running Memphis, Crump extended his machine across Tennessee where he made another strange alliance for the time. He linked up with the Republicans who were powerful in eastern Tennessee but weak in the central and western parts of the state. People looking for favors in the Volunteer State learned that the man to see was Boss Crump.

In one demonstration of his power Crump told a congressman whom he wanted to make the mayor, to stay in Washington and not run for the office. Instead, Crump himself filed for the job. Though he did no campaigning and made no speeches he was overwhelmingly elected mayor of Memphis. Ten minutes after taking the oath of office, Crump resigned and handed over his post to the vice mayor. He then headed off to the Sugar Bowl in New Orleans. The next day the city commission named the Washington congressman as mayor. So in less than twenty-four hours Memphis had four mayors. Nobody cared; they all knew the real one was Crump. Despite the fact Memphis had a figurehead mayor and some country singer or similar person sitting in the governor's mansion, everything flowed back to Boss Crump. Like other Democratic chiefs he also maintained a close relationship with the New Deal administration in Washington.

As has often been used as a plot line in movies about Southern politics, Crump had an unusual personal situation. He was very close to a woman named Georgia Tann, whom he protected from law enforcement officials. Miss Tann would occasionally travel across the United States placing babies, many of them stolen, with new adoptive parents.

Whatever their excesses, men like Samish and Crump provided a certain rationality and continuity in government. In California, despite the division between north and south, Samish could ensure that the wheels turned in Sacramento. In Tennessee, where some people were still fighting the Civil War, his alliance with the eastern section Republicans enabled him to exercise power and get things done in the state capital in Nashville.

*

Detroit's organized crime set up was not like that in San Francisco or Memphis. There was no behind the scenes group of fixers like the McDonoughs or a powerful boss like Crump. In the 1940s, its criminal rulers included the mayor, superintendent of police, and the local prosecutor who were allied with gamblers.

Throughout the 1930s, the real issue in Detroit was the automobile manufacturers versus the United Autoworkers (UAW). The most aggressive leader of the former group was Henry Ford, who strongly resisted unionization of his workforce. Ford's point man in the fight against the UAW was his security chief Harry Bennett, an ex-boxer, who directed a force of 3,000 guards and detectives. Not only did Bennett's men keep union organizers out of the Ford facilities, they prowled Detroit looking for employees who might be consorting with UAW officials.

The most feared group in Detroit was the Mafia-controlled Purple Gang. In 1930, when the Purples were involved in a citywide gang war, eleven murders were recorded. One of them received national attention. A radio reporter led a campaign to recall Detroit mayor Charles Bowles. On the night that the mayor was successfully recalled, the radio reporter, broadcasting from a victory rally at a downtown hotel, was shot to death. Bennett frequently used the Purples to assist his own forces. In 1932, a group of Communist-led "hunger marchers" attempted to march into the Ford headquarters in the suburb of Dearborn. During the fighting, Bennett was felled by a brick bat, whereupon the police and Ford security men opened fire, killing four and wounding twenty of the demonstrators. In 1937, when UAW organizers attempted to distribute leaflets on Ford property, union head Walter Reuther and some of his lieutenants were beaten by Ford men and their gangster allies while newsreel cameras recorded the scene. The so-called "battle of the overpass" became a famous symbol of the 1930s. During the course of the difficulties one clever young Teamster organizer, James Hoffa, cut a deal with the Purple Gang to occasionally help the IBT. Finally, under pressure from Roosevelt's National Labor Relations Board, Ford was compelled to recognize the union and to disband Bennett's security force.

In 1939 a woman who was having an affair with a small-time numbers operator, Bill McBride, became depressed because he was seeing other women. So she sent letters to Detroit newspapers detailing McBride's bribes to police officers, especially naming a lieutenant who commanded a local police district. Then she killed herself and her daughter. At first the county prosecutor responded by saying he lacked the resources to investigate her charges. However, a reform group, the Detroit Citizens League, intervened in the case. It petitioned a local circuit judge, Homer Ferguson, to start grand jury proceedings. Under an unusual Michigan law, he could form a one-man grand jury consisting of himself. Working with a small staff of lawyers and investigators, Ferguson began a full-fledged probe of the local criminal justice agencies. The first person he interviewed was the commander of the district that had been cited in the dead woman's letter. When he found the man was lying, Ferguson immediately sent him to jail for five days. Eventually, a police lieutenant who was a collector for the city administration talked. The probe eventually led to the mayor, police superintendent, and prosecutor being sent to prison. Ferguson himself was elected to the United States Senate in 1942. However, the demise of the police-run ring did nothing to injure the Purple Gang.

*

America's most powerful boss was Frank "I am the law" Hague, born in the tough Irish "Horseshoe" section of Jersey City in 1876. At twenty-one he began his career as a constable and then moved to a deputy sheriff's post. In that capacity, in 1904, he journeyed to Boston and committed perjury in the criminal trial of a burglar friend. Though he was indicted by the Commonwealth of Massachusetts, New Jersey refused to extradite him. By 1910 he was a power in Jersey politics, and to head him off the boss of Newark brought forth Princeton president Woodrow Wilson to run for governor. Once in office, though, Wilson disowned his supporters in favor of Hague, then switched back again, outsmarting both bosses. Hague retaliated by ordering State Treasurer Edward "Teddy" Edwards, a Jersey City bank president, to dock Wilson's pay every time the governor left the state to campaign for president.

In 1913, New Jersey reform elements forced adoption of a commission form of government. As a result Hague, the corrupt cop, was elected public safety commissioner of Jersey City. He immediately began putting policemen on trial for various offenses and abolished their union. On occasion he would fine cops, though he would frequently turn around and give the forfeited money to the officer's wife. He also formed a 100-man spy squad to keep an eye on both police and citizens. Because of the good publicity he received from his supposed reform activities he was elected mayor in 1917. He would remain in the post for thirty years.

Owing to his absolute power over the police Hague was able to suppress all dissent. Anyone wishing to speak or distribute literature was required to obtain a permit and the mayor's opponents were refused. If they persisted they were slugged and frequently expelled from the state. A police lieutenant sat in the Jersey City Western Union office reading all incoming telegrams in order to ferret out any "plots" against Hague. The boss also had spies in banks and post offices. Reds were his special bête noire. Hague claimed he could always identify the Bolsheviks. They were the ones who complained about their civil rights being violated.

When high status, non-Communist protesters, such as distinguished Republican lawyers, tried to hold a meeting in Jersey City, a marching band would circle the area playing loud enough to drown out the speakers. When the local newspaper, the *Jersey Journal,* dared to criticize Hague, he ordered that any city or county employee seen reading the paper would be fired. Cops and firemen then went door to door distributing leaflets describing how the *Journal* lied and solicited subscriptions to a rival paper. Theater owners were forced to withdraw their advertising, on pain of being harassed by city inspectors. The city council even changed the name of Journal Square to Veterans Square. The paper finally ran up the white flag and became supporters of Hague. In a magnanimous gesture, the boss restored the name of Journal Square.

In 1932 Hague backed Al Smith at the Democratic national convention but afterward he quickly switched to FDR and obtained control of federal patronage and various New Deal welfare programs in New Jersey. Despite his rough methods, the voters liked Hague. He provided jobs, new buildings, and excellent free medical care for his constituents. A favorite technique of his to increase police efficiency was to put in false calls for assistance and if officers did not arrive quickly they got a tongue lashing from the mayor, sometimes accompanied by kicks and blows. Some of his illegal acts won him public acclaim. Once during a coal strike, Hague's cops halted a train of coal cars passing through Jersey City and commandeered the contents for his constituents. When railroad lawyers asked the mayor under what law he had acted, he replied "the law of the nightstick." Attacking Reds and vice made him popular with the American Legion and the Catholic church. Prostitution was not permitted except in roadhouses outside of town in rural Hudson County. A teetotaler, every year Hague would take his staff to New York City for a big dinner at a leading restaurant. After the meal he would leave. Only then could his boys order drinks. For all his fearsome persona, Hague, like Pendergast, feared assassination and would not go out in the daytime, preferring to make his rounds at night.

Hague required city employees to kick back 3% of their salary; however, since Jersey City paid some of the highest salaries in the country, the deal was probably a wash. Towards the end of his career he privately admitted a net worth of about $8 million, though his critics estimated it might be ten times that amount. Public opinion mattered little to him. When Hague's 34-year-old son was finally admitted to the bar, after failing the exam twice, the boss had him appointed to the highest court of the state.

Hague's activity contravened many federal laws but the Roosevelt administration did not move against him. Even though Hague had to hand over $60,000 in payment for tax "irregularities," no criminal indictment was sought. By the 1930s, the press generally referred to the boss as Frank "I am the law" Hague, though the statement was taken out of context and the situation in which he made it had been a credible one for the mayor. In trying to get a state official to issue working papers for two truant boys rather than send them to reform school, he had countered the official's protests that the law forbade it by saying, "I am the law, do it."

Although officially Hague was only the mayor of New Jersey's second-largest city, no one could run for governor or senator unless they received his blessing. The Hudson County vote was so large that it frequently decided state elections. In one contest a Republican candidate for governor carried New Jersey's other twenty counties by a total of 84,000 votes but lost Hudson County by 129,000. In one Jersey City precinct, 433 Democratic votes were recorded and only one Republican. Yet at the primary election earlier in the year, 103 Republican votes had been cast. With his power to stuff ballot boxes and his own private gestapo, Hague operated more like a czar than a politician.

*

The state that Hague ran for so many years had an unusual configuration. South Jersey was part of the Philadelphia metropolitan area and the north was an extension of New York City. Thus, New Jersey had a confused identity. Yet, it was a vital part of the northeast corridor that ran between Boston and Washington, and contained the country's largest, most traveled roadway. Its east-west railroads linked New York City to America's heartland.

Even though New Jersey was a boss-dominated state, it could boast of one of the best law enforcement agencies in the United States. The New Jersey State Police were a spit-and-polish outfit, who looked like marines. Their commander was a West Point graduate and the force was hard to enter and easy to be thrown out of. It was modeled after the first state police force created in 1905 in Pennsylvania whose longtime leader was a Philadelphia aristocrat who had served as a cavalry officer in the Spanish-American War. The Pennsylvania troopers were assigned to patrol the strife-torn coal and iron mining districts and were seen by many as pro-management. Some Pennsylvania folks admiringly called the troopers the "Black Hussars" while the United Mine Workers labeled them "Cossacks."

In 1921, when New Jersey proposed to create a similar force, it was expected that Hague's man Teddy Edwards, then the governor, would appoint a Hague crony, Lieutenant Thomas Broadhurst of the Hudson County police, as superintendent of the new force. Instead he named a Newark resident, army captain H. Norman Schwarzkopf, who had been a war-time comrade of the governor's son, Irving. To satisfy the unions, the state police were forbidden to interfere in labor-management disputes. Instead they patrolled the highways (initially on horseback in the underdeveloped south and motorcycle in the built-up north), provided assistance to small local police departments and stood ready to assert the power of the state when necessary. In retrospect, it is doubtful that Edwards would have gone against Hague in the appointment of a superintendent. Just as Hague recognized the social welfare needs of his constituents, he realized that there had to be reliable police force to maintain law and order in the state and, if well-run, it would be a good advertisement for New Jersey. As in Pennsylvania, the troopers went through a tough boot camp, resided in barracks and were forbidden to marry in their first two years of service. Hague had no complaints about the Jersey troopers. Though Schwarzkopf's men were sharp patrol officers, they lacked criminal investigative skills, as demonstrated in the 1932 Lindbergh kidnapping case. So they frequently worked with New Jersey municipal detectives including Inspector (later chief) Harry Walsh of the Jersey City police, who was a special favorite of Hague's. So close was the relationship that one year Walsh received the state police medal of honor.

Hague was not popular with some of FDR's cabinet. Secretary of Interior Harold Ickes hated all corrupt bosses. The postmaster general and the attorney general, on occasion, wanted Hague indicted for such things as opening mail. Treasury Secretary Henry Morgenthau would have liked to go after Hague but instead targeted the Republican boss of Atlantic City, Enoch "Nucky" Johnson, whose boardwalk community ran wide open. To prove that Nucky was not paying his proper income taxes, Treasury agents searched laundry records to find out how many towels were being received from the city's houses of prostitution. Through that they could calculate the number of patrons and determine that the bordello owners were not paying taxes on their full income. When the feds questioned the owners they confessed to paying a portion of their income to Nucky. So he was indicted for underreporting his income. When Johnson was convicted, his empire collapsed. By late 1930s Hague was the leading political boss of the country and was much respected by his peers.

Hague was smart enough not to let the Mafia grow too big in New Jersey, in which case as in New York and Chicago he would have had to share power with them. After the fall of Nucky Johnson there was not as much mob activity in South Jersey. Newark was the principal center of organized crime in the state. In the 1920s the key mobsters there were Ruggerio "Richie the Boot" Boiardo, who was boss of the First Ward and his rival was Abner "Longy" Zwillman, who ran the Third Ward. During a war between the two, "The Boot" was hit by thirteen slugs. According to legend, they "would have torn his guts out" but were stopped by the "Boot's" $5,000 diamond belt buckle. Finally, Boiardo and Zwillman reached an agreement to divide the spoils. From the '30s on, Boiardo ran the Newark numbers racket for New York's Genovese family.

From the late '30s through the 1940s anyone who dropped into Duke's Bar in Cliffside, New Jersey, could see Joe Adonis, Willie Moretti, or Longy Zwillman hanging around. Willie was a transplanted New Yorker and a lieutenant to Frank Costello. It was Moretti who made the career of a skinny singer who performed in one of his nightclubs. The young man, Frank Sinatra, came from Hoboken, New Jersey, where his mother was a worker in Frank Hague's machine and his father owed his job as a fire lieutenant to that connection. From there Sinatra became the band singer for orchestra leader Tommy Dorsey. When his career caught fire Dorsey insisted on holding him to a one-sided contract. Not until Moretti made Dorsey an offer he could not refuse—the offer being a promise not to pull the trigger on the gun Willie had shoved into Tommy's mouth in return for Sinatra being released from his contract—did Frank win his freedom. Adonis still possessed great power in Brooklyn but he spent time in New Jersey because after supporting Mayor LaGuardia's opponent in the 1937 election, he could not maintain too high a profile in New York. Zwillman was known for his actions during the time that the Lindbergh baby was kidnapped. Back then he mobilized the underworld to find the child. The reason was not compassion but the fact that the police were stopping so many vehicles on the highways that Longy's beer trucks could not get through.

None of these Mafia heavy hitters ever challenged Hague. With his own Jersey City/Hudson County cops and the ability to have whoever was governor assign the state police to assist Hague's forces, the gangsters would have been outgunned and, in a state where the boss controlled the court system, those who were not killed would have landed in prison.

While Mayor Kelly, Bob Hannegan, and Ed Flynn took the lead in selecting a candidate for vice president at the 1944 convention, they could not have prevailed without Hague's assent. Frank, who hated Communists, would have never supported lefist Vice President Henry Wallace but, unlike Flynn or Kelly, Hague was confident he could carry New Jersey for whomever the bosses settled upon and no other element in the state could oppose him, much less push him out of the leadership. In New York Costello and Adonis may have told Tammany and the Brooklyn machine what to do; the Chicago mob was demanding that its leadership be let out of federal prison; and Mayor Kelly faced a possible revolt from his fellow members of the county committee. In New Jersey, the man known as "I am the law" did not even fear President Roosevelt. Despite the advice of his cabinet members, the president never allowed the Department of Justice to move against Hague because he needed Frank more than Frank needed him.

By the 1940s, organized crime, whether of the Mafia variety or home-grown, played a major role in the nation's big cities and a number of states. Nowhere did the mobs have to fear law enforcement, except federal tax collectors. Even then, those who were well enough connected only faced civil penalties. The only notable exception was the Chicago syndicate: it got so big for its britches and tried to take over Hollywood, the fifth largest industry in the United States.

This could be written off as the recklessness of Chicago syndicate leaders, such as had been on display at the Valentine massacre.

The wise men of the bar (and sometimes the bench) told the gang leaders to pay enough taxes to prevent being prosecuted and don't mess with the big boys like Standard Oil, U.S. Steel, or Wall Street. At least the Chicago mob could take credit for not being involved in the Republic Steel massacre. The blame for that lay with Mayor Kelly who, having weighed the political calculations, decided that it was more advantageous to allow the police to take a hard line. In 1944, the mobs would demonstrate that they could play a significant role in the naming of a new president as long as they did not display their hand too openly.

Chapter 6

1944—Year of Decision:
Clear It with Sidney

On July 15, 1944, a hot Saturday afternoon, a special train pulled into the 51st Street freight yard on Chicago's South Side for a layover on its journey from the east coast to California. It was the most important train in the world because it carried a person identified in railroad telegraphers' messages as "POTUS," meaning president of the United States.[1] The president's private car, the *Ferdinand Magellan*, was one of a group of coaches named for explorers that a manufacturer had turned out fifteen years earlier. However, when it was acquired for the president it had been extensively remodeled. It now weighed 285,000 pounds, or twice the weight of a regular car. So even a sizable charge of dynamite would not derail it. The armor plate was 5/8 of an inch thick, including sides, roof, floor, ends of the car, and doors. The window glass was three inches thick and could stop any bullet. The car itself was air and water tight.

---

1. A few years earlier the most important train in the world was probably Adolf Hitler's curiously named *Amerika*. But by July, 1944, with the Russians approaching Germany's eastern frontier and the Allies the western border, Hitler was on his last legs. Later in the month, German officers would set off a bomb at his headquarters, although it failed to kill him.

Normally the train was preceded by an advance locomotive to take the shock if explosives were planted on the track, and when the *Magellan* was stopped, a contingent of police or soldiers guarded it. Today there was no advance engine, cops, or troops. A decision had been made to keep secret the fact that the president was out of Washington and on the way to California where he would board a cruiser to take him to Hawaii for a meeting with his top Pacific-area military commanders, Gen. MacArthur and Adm. Nimitz.

Of course, the president was not without guards. In wartime it was difficult for an unauthorized person to enter a rail yard without being challenged. If someone had charged towards the president's car, Secret Service men would have cut him down with machine gun fire. On this afternoon, two individuals were allowed to board the *Magellan*. One was the chairman of the Democratic National Committee, Robert Hannegan, and the other was Chicago mayor, Ed Kelly, host of the presidential nominating convention that would open in four days. They were there to ascertain who the president really favored for the vice presidential nomination among the four he had already expressed support for.

In March, the bosses had learned how seriously ill the president was. FDR had undergone a physical examination at Bethesda Naval Hospital. There a cardiologist diagnosed him with a heart problem so severe that he probably did not have long to live. While Roosevelt had suffered from stomach disorders, bronchitis, and general physical fatigue, the White House physician, Adm. Ross McIntyre, an ear, nose and throat specialist, had either not discovered his condition or concealed the true facts.

Strangely, while insiders knew the situation, the president did not. According to Roosevelt's daughter Anna, not only did he expect to serve a fourth term, but was already planning to run for a fifth. As his enemies said, as long as Roosevelt lived he would run "again and again and again." The fact that the president was unaware of the situation was probably due to the reluctance of subordinates to tell their boss things he did not want to hear. The one person who might have been able to give him the true facts was Mrs. Roosevelt, but she and the president had been estranged for many years. Thus, while party leaders approached the selection of the vice presidential nominee as equivalent to naming the next president, FDR himself saw it in terms of which candidate would add the greatest strength to the ticket or, conversely, lose the fewest votes.

The bosses whom Hannegan and Kelly represented wanted a president who would treat them like the barons that they were, allowing them complete control over their own bailiwicks. This meant that U.S. judges, attorneys, and other appointed federal officers in their cities and states would generally be chosen from people the local political machine approved of. In addition, they didn't want to be personally bothered by U.S. officials such as tax collectors, G-men or T-men. On this score Roosevelt had done well by them. When Mayor Kelly and other officials had made minor errors in their tax returns, like neglecting to report a million or more dollars of their earnings, the government had allowed them to settle the matter by coming up with a portion of the taxes that were due. Under Roosevelt, Tom Pendergast had been the only Democratic boss who had been sent to prison for tax evasion and that was largely due to his own recklessness because of the need to cover his monumental gambling losses.

If Vice President Henry Wallace became president he would not likely shelter the bosses from legal trouble or permit them to control all federal appointments in their bailiwicks. If Roosevelt's Republican opponent, Tom Dewey, were elected not only would the patronage dry up, but Dewey might revert to his racket-busting days and send a few bosses and their mob allies to jail, as he had done with Tammany's Jimmy Hines and gangster Lucky Luciano.

The bosses were agreed that Wallace's re-nomination would be a disaster. A wealthy, farmer/businessman from Iowa, he had served as Roosevelt's secretary of agriculture from 1933 through 1940. His father, Henry Wallace, Sr., a Republican, had filled the same post in the 1920s. At the 1940 convention, Roosevelt had forced the nomination of Wallace for VP on the delegates because he hoped it would help him carry the agricultural states of the Midwest. As VP, he had been aloof and somewhat arrogant. He showed no interest in the work of the Senate over which he presided and did not try to make friends with Democratic leaders, instead he espoused various ultraliberal causes. He also displayed an avid interest in spiritualism. To his adversaries he was both a Commie and a kook. His name was anathema to Southern leaders and city bosses alike, the two groups that had dominated the Democratic Party from the Civil War through the 1920s. However, in the 1930s the New Deal had attracted support from newly empowered organized labor and many liberals who shared Wallace's ideas.

Some of Roosevelt's advisers, like campaign treasurer and California oilman Ed Pauley, conspired with the president's military aide Maj. Gen. Edwin "Pa" Watson to keep Wallace supporters out of the Oval Office and to ensure that Wallace's enemies got full access. Watson also saw to it that the many leading Democrats were informed of Wallace's mystical leanings. For example, the vice president was interested in the ideas of people like the Russian mystic Nicholas Roerich. In some of his letters Wallace had referred to Roerich as the "guru" and said he saw visions of the guru in his morning meditations. Wallace often spoke of "the dark ones," and "dugpas" and beseeched the blessings of "the great ones." Some of his letters passed into the hands of third parties, so the White House engaged prominent New York attorney Morris Ernst to retrieve them and turn them over to Pa Watson, who locked them up in the White House safe. Another count against Wallace was that Mrs. Roosevelt was ardently for him. Almost invariably whatever Eleanor was for, Franklin was against.

*

The bosses knew they did not want Wallace; however, they had yet to unite on a candidate. While Flynn and Kelly, assisted by Hannegan, took the lead in the search, they realized they had to present a united front. In some places this meant winning mob support. There was no doubt that in New York Frank Costello was the senior partner in Tammany and Adonis equal to Frank Kelly in Brooklyn. Every major Democratic politician in the city had to seek Costello's blessing. In 1942, District Attorney William O'Dwyer of Brooklyn was commissioned a major in the army and assigned to investigate fraud in war contracts. While supposedly performing his duties, he found time to meet with Costello in the latter's plush apartment on ritzy Central Park

West. Also present were O'Dwyer's alter ego, Jim Moran, some organized crime figures, and several Tammany officials, such as the organization secretary Bert Stand. O'Dwyer later explained the purpose of the visit was to investigate fraud in contracts. However, he never made a report to his superiors about it. Obviously, the meeting between the mob boss and the politician was to secure Costello's support when O'Dwyer made another run for mayor in 1945.

Gov. Lehman departed from Albany before his term ended in 1942 and Lieut. Gov. Charles Poletti took over for the last month. Poletti later became United States military governor in the occupied zone of Italy. There he utilized the services of mafiosos, including Vito Genovese. It was Vito's homicidal ways that had driven him to Italy. When he fell in love with a married woman he had her husband strangled to death. While he managed to avoid charges in that murder, Dewey's office began looking into the killing of Ferdinand "The Shadow" Boccia, a gambler who had demanded too large a cut of the proceeds of a crooked gambling game. In 1936, with Dewey on his case, Vito decamped to Italy where he lived under the protection of dictator Mussolini. During the occupation, Genovese went to work for Poletti's U.S. military government which gave him credentials and his own Jeep. Some writers even maintain that he was Poletti's chauffeur. His connections enabled him to run a large black market operation.

When U.S. Criminal Investigation Corps Sgt. Orange Dickey began looking into Genovese's activities, he learned the gangster was wanted for murder in New York City. Dickey brought the matter to the attention of Gov. Poletti and Brig. Gen. William O'Dwyer, the former Brooklyn district attorney, who was in Italy at the time. Both had no interest. With the help of British military police, Dickey arrested Genovese and escorted him back to New York City. Shortly after their arrival the case collapsed when the state's star witness, who was being held in a Brooklyn jail, suddenly died. According to the medical examiner, he had been given "enough poison to kill three horses." As the death of "Kid Twist" Reles had revealed, Brooklyn was a dangerous place for witnesses against gangsters to be held.

Tom Dewey became the governor of New York State on January 1, 1943. By that time he had his eyes set on winning the presidency rather than racket busting. The mob's gambling operation in the upstate town of Saratoga, a spa favored by rich folks, continued to run full blast, though it would have been simple for Dewey to order the state police to shut it down.

From 1942-1944, the biggest question mark for the New York mobs was the fate of Lepke Buchalter, then serving his federal sentence for drug dealing and awaiting execution for the murder in Brooklyn. If the state authorities got custody of him, Lepke might cut a deal to talk about mob crimes in order to avoid execution. Under judicial precedents the federal government was expected to turn over the prisoner to the state authorities so they could administer the death penalty.[2] In November 1942, ten months after their conviction, the New York State Court of Appeals upheld the death sentence for Lepke and his two accomplices. Two months later the United States Supreme Court turned down their appeal. The Brooklyn DA's office (no longer run by O'Dwyer) then requested the United States government to release Lepke to the state. In July, after failing to obtain a satisfactory answer, the DA's office appealed directly to U.S. attorney general Francis Biddle, who ignored the request.

When Dewey became governor of New York, he too began to publicly protest about the feds not turning Lepke over to the state. At the time it seemed likely that Dewey and Roosevelt would be facing each other in the 1944 presidential election. There followed more exchanges between New York State authorities and the feds. After various evasions, stories began appearing in New York and national publications that there was some kind of effort to protect individuals close to the White House from any possible Lepke revelations. The *New York Times* stated, "Knowledge Lepke has of an old murder in-

---

2. The justification for this practice was laid down in a case involving a stickup man named Gerald Chapman. In 1922 he was sentenced to twenty-five years for a $2.4 million robbery of the U.S. mails in New York City. Sent to the federal penitentiary in Atlanta, he escaped twice. While at liberty the second time he killed a policeman during a holdup in New Britain, Connecticut. Chapman fled but he was arrested in Indiana and returned to Connecticut where he was sentenced to death. Connecticut requested that the U.S. government turn over Chapman to them so that the capital sentence could be carried out. Chapman's attorneys argued that he could not be released until he had completed his federal sentence. When Pres. Calvin Coolidge commuted Chapman's sentence to time served, his lawyers argued that a commutation was the same as a pardon which as a gift could be refused. But the United States Supreme Court ruled that a commutation was not a pardon but simply a withdrawal of federal jurisdiction. As Chief Justice William Howard Taft noted, "the penitentiary is no sanctuary" and did not confer "immunity from capital law." Chapman was hanged by the state of Connecticut in 1926.

volving labor leaders said to be close to the present national administration... is said to be one of the factors in the long involved negotiations."

Sidney Hillman, head of the Amalgamated Clothing Workers Union, CIO, and a powerful force in the garment center, was the labor leader closest to the White House. The Lithuanian-born Hillman had come to the United States in 1907 when he was twenty years old and unable to speak English. Seven years later he founded the Clothing Workers Union. In the 1920s, Hillman's union had opposed Gurrah and Lepke's racketeers. But then he reached an agreement with them and from 1932 to 1937 Lepke was paid $350 each week. Sometimes Hillman even engaged in face-to-face meetings with him at the Gov. Clinton Hotel in Manhattan. When necessary, Lepke's men were used to carry out sluggings and murder. One time the Amalgamated paid Lepke a $25,000 bonus for his help in winning a strike. In 1935 when a trucker in the garment district was cut out of a contract by the clothing union he went to see Hillman. When Sidney tried to brush him off, the man grabbed him and said "Listen Mr. Hillman, I know that your hands are full of blood. You've killed plenty of people. I'll be damned if you're going to kill me too." A day later the man was approached by a mob hit man who warned him never to go near Hillman again. Even during the period from 1937 to 1939, when Lepke was hiding out from the law, he still received money from Hillman's Amalgamated.

Hillman was a shrewd opportunist. His views were socialistic and he did not rule out working with Communists. Yet he was soft-spoken and polite in his dealings with employers and his actions were usually more pragmatic than ideological. Secretary of Labor Frances "Ma" Perkins characterized Hillman as a man who was "never loyal to anyone but himself." Juggling Communists, gangsters, New Dealers, and rival labor leaders took its toll on Hillman's health. He always appeared to be under great stress and suffered from periodic nervous breakdowns. Whatever he saw himself as, it was very likely he had broken some criminal laws for which he could've been given a prison sentence, possibly the death penalty.

Finally, state and media pressure on the feds became too great to withstand in an election year and Lepke was transferred from the federal house of detention in New York City to the state prison at Sing Sing. There, he and his codefendants were scheduled to be executed on March 2, 1944. Two days before, Lepke met with New York County district attorney Frank Hogan, a former Dewey assistant. Lepke had also been convicted of racketeering in Manhattan but it was the murder charges in Brooklyn that counted. So it was not clear that Hogan had any role in the case except as Dewey's agent. Some suspected that Lepke made certain statements to Hogan that led the DA to ask Governor Dewey to postpone the execution. Whatever, Lepke was granted a 48-hour stay. However, on March 4, he and his two codefendants were electrocuted.

If Lepke really had information damaging to FDR, why would Dewey not have cut a deal to spare his life in return for his confession, especially if it would help elect him president? Of course, the Democrats could have responded that Lepke, who had been characterized by J. Edgar Hoover as "the most dangerous criminal in America,"[3] was simply telling lies to save his life. It could also have been argued that Roosevelt's connection to Hillman was no more than the president had with other powerful labor bosses, many of whom had checkered pasts.

Dewey also faced problems with his own past. The conviction of Luciano in 1936 was thought by many to have been secured by perjured testimony. In 1942 the Office of Naval Intelligence had cut a deal with Luciano's boys to help protect the New York waterfront from sabotage. One condition of the agreement was that Lucky be transferred from the Siberia-like Dannemora prison to a much more relaxed institution on Long Island where he could easily meet with his lieutenants. Some of the ONI officers involved in the case were former Dewey assistants and they should have been much more skeptical of the mob's claims.

When Dewey became governor in 1943 he could have returned Luciano to Dannemora but he did not. In 1946 he released Luciano on condition that he be deported to Italy. Allegedly this boon was granted for Lucky's services in the war. In 1951 a U.S. Senate investigation

---

3. At the time, any individual arrested under Hoover's personal direction was invariably characterized as the most dangerous criminal in America, or words to that effect.

found no evidence of any help Luciano had provided. As Dewey should have known, Lucky had no intention of remaining in Italy. Shortly after he arrived there he left for Cuba, intending to be smuggled back into the United States. Only the intervention by Commissioner Harry Anslinger of the Federal Bureau of Narcotics prevented this. When his agents found that Luciano was meeting with his lieutenants in Cuba, Anslinger threatened to cut off all medical supplies to that country unless Lucky was deported back to Italy. The Cuban government could do nothing but comply and Luciano remained in Italy until his death in 1962. Governor Dewey, in cop parlance, could not "have stood a frisk." If questions had been raised about Luciano's conviction, it might have prevented Dewey's rise to the White House. Thus he may well have concluded that there was more to lose than gain if he saved Lepke's life.

While there were plenty of candidates for the vice presidential nomination, none was an obvious choice. Except for Texas, no major state had a Democratic governor. In Congress, some able men were advanced in years. In the Senate, Majority Leader Alben Barkley of Kentucky, at 67, was five years older than the president. It was an age that would have been all right for a vice presidential candidate in normal times, since the office was largely a symbolic one. It was not suitable for the man who would probably succeed to the presidency. Sam Rayburn, Speaker of the House, was under siege by an anti-New Deal faction in his home state of Texas and at the time was in such a close fight to retain his seat that he could not even break free to attend the convention.

Among other possibilities was Supreme Court Justice Frank Murphy, former mayor of Detroit and governor of Michigan, and a prominent Catholic layman. In 1944 Americans were not ready for a man of his faith on the national ticket. In 1928, when New York Gov. Al Smith, also a Catholic, had run for president, he was beaten in a landslide, even losing six states in the solidly Democratic South.

In preliminary meetings of party leaders such as Chairman Hannegan and Treasurer Pauley, bosses Flynn of New York, Kelly of Chicago and Postmaster General Frank Walker, several names of possible candidates emerged. The most prominent one was Jimmy

Byrnes, who was wartime domestic "czar," or as the press described him, "assistant president." Byrnes had been born a Catholic but left the church to become an Episcopalian. Thus he was subject to attack from both Catholics and non-Catholics. In addition, as a senator from South Carolina, he espoused the segregationist views of his constituents. Boss Flynn believed that his nomination would cost the party as much as 200,000 African American votes in New York, thereby tilting the state to Gov. Dewey. The same concerns about the black vote ruled out other Southern governors and senators.

Still Byrnes was popular in the South where delegates from Virginia, South Carolina, and Texas were pushing Sen. Harry Byrd of Virginia for president. Byrnes, a practical sort, was also acceptable to party officials and bosses. If FDR passed Byrnes over, it would be hard to explain why a man he had appointed to the Supreme Court in 1941 and then persuaded to leave it in 1942 to run the domestic front, was unfit for the vice presidency.

Another name put forth by Roosevelt himself was William O. Douglas, associate justice of the Supreme Court. Bill Douglas, who was usually togged out in a Western hat, was a left winger from the Pacific Northwest who had blossomed in the east as a Yale law professor, then head of the Securities and Exchange Commission. One reason Roosevelt was attracted to Douglas was that when he was a White House guest he always told the kind of dirty stories the president liked to hear. Roosevelt's daughter, Anna, held a different view. She claimed to have seen Douglas drunk on several occasions and in the company of low companions. Douglas not only resembled Wallace with his liberal views but also in his arrogant, aloof manner toward party leaders. Over his career he would marry four wives, two of them young enough to be his granddaughter. On the court his opinions often seemed motivated by his political views rather than the law. He would include in his opinions philosophical musings, and references to movies and books. When he finally retired in the 1970s he continued to attend the court and seek to participate as a justice. Finally, his brethren had to tell him that he no longer was a member of the United States Supreme Court. In 1944, whenever Douglas's name was mentioned at leadership meetings, the room would fall silent. But because he was recommended by the president himself, he remained in contention.

A third name brought forward by Hannegan and some of the other party leaders was Harry Truman, who as a senator had received good publicity when he chaired a committee investigating fraud and waste in the war effort. Instead of embarrassing the administration he had worked closely with the White House. The drawback was that Truman was a product of the corrupt Pendergast machine, and the presumptive Republican opponent, racket buster Tom Dewey, would surely find Truman's background a worthy target. Still he was an ideal candidate from the bosses' standpoint. He was a man who would follow orders and stay loyal, come hell or high water.

To further complicate matters, Roosevelt had given assurances to Hannegan that he could run with either Truman or Douglas.[4] Roosevelt had also given a letter to Henry Wallace saying that if he were a delegate to the convention he would vote for him, though he added that he was not dictating a nomination but allowing the convention to make its own choice. Some would remark that it was the first endorsement ever meant to kill a candidate. Since the president could not bring himself to say directly to his vice president that he did not want to run with him again, Wallace was actively seeking renomination. His most powerful support came from the Congress of Industrial Organizations (CIO), a broad group of industrial unions that had seceded from the American Federation of Labor (AFL), which was controlled by craft unions. At the convention CIO Pres. Philip Murray and the director of its well-funded political action committee (PAC), Sidney Hillman, led the Wallace forces. Roosevelt managed to send Wallace on a long trip to various parts of Russia so that he was kept out of the country in the run-up to the convention. As the president quipped, "I sent him to Siberia." Douglas, an avid outdoorsman, spent his recess time from the Supreme Court in the Pacific Northwest pursuing his favorite sport of mountain climbing. He would have been better off if he had climbed political mountains in New York, Washington, and

---

4. Some Douglas supporters claimed Roosevelt had named Douglas ahead of Truman, though historians have generally discounted this.

Chicago. Instead he was left waiting to inherit Wallace's followers if there was a deadlock.

Some presidential kingmakers had their own local problems. The whole leadership of the Chicago syndicate faced years in federal prison for the Hollywood shakedown, so the mob expected Mayor Kelly to get the extortionists sprung. The shrewd Kelly's plan was that in the event of a deadlocked convention, he could secure the nomination for Illinois senator Scott W. Lucas. Always in the back of his mind was the dread possibility that a President Douglas or Wallace might not be so eager to free some Chicago gangsters. If that happened, the syndicate might decide the city needed a new mayor and Kelly would go the way of Carter Harrison the younger in 1915.

Then there was shrewd old Frank Hague in New Jersey whom the local Mafia was not strong enough to push out. Hague was no Johnny-come-lately to power like Ed Flynn or Mayor Kelly or a wannabe such as Robert Hannegan. Hague had been around since before World War I and he wanted to still be in power after World War II. If his cops were reading the Jersey City mail, they knew that many local boys, now in uniform, were telling their family and friends that they had never realized how bad Hague's image was nationally, where he was regarded as some sort of Mussolini type. The solution for Hague was an obvious one, but impossible to pull off at the moment. It was to put Generals MacArthur or Eisenhower in the White House and wrap the Democratic Party and its leaders in the Stars & Stripes. Doug or Ike would have chosen to stand astride the global scene which they knew well, and since they probably had never heard of Hudson County or places like it, let the bosses run city hall and the county building. Unfortunately, the generals were still busy fighting the war.

*

On Wednesday, July 18, the convention opened at the Chicago Stadium. The area around the site was a classic example of how politically protected organized crime worked. Madison Street was lined with cheap dives where a chump could expect padded checks, possibly a Mickey Finn, and prostitutes who promised him a night of delight.

Though in the last instance, they might lure him into the hands of thugs who would relieve him of his money and possibly his teeth. If the chump went to the cops he would be brushed off.[5] However, for the duration of the convention the area was flooded with police, and the pimps, whores, and sluggers had been ordered to make themselves scarce.

After the Saturday afternoon conference in the railroad yard, Hannegan and Kelly had left believing that Roosevelt had agreed to accept Jimmy Byrnes. But as they knew from experience, the president often said things and then went back on them. Some observers at the time believed the sickly, worn-out chief of state did not always think clearly. Nevertheless the mayor called Byrnes and informed him that, based on their conversations, Roosevelt wanted him for his vice presidential running mate. Byrnes immediately entrained for Chicago, arriving on Sunday. He was then driven in the car of the city's fire commissioner to Kelly's home on Lakeshore Drive.

As an afterthought, Roosevelt had told Hannegan to "clear" Byrnes' nomination with Sidney Hillman. Later the Republicans would use this phrase as a slogan in the campaign, implying that if Roosevelt were reelected every government proposal would have to be "cleared" with Sidney and his New York (read Communist) friends. When Hillman was contacted he made it clear that he and Phil Murray, as leaders of the Wallace faction, would never accept Byrnes as the nominee. Some party leaders were ready to call Hillman's bluff, pointing out that the old-line AFL had not expressed a preference for Wallace and unions like Dan Tobin's giant International Brotherhood of Teamsters (which was heavily infiltrated by gangsters) would back Roosevelt's decision to the hilt. In the final analysis, unless the CIO supported Dewey it had no place to go. In 1940 John L. Lewis, president of United Mine Workers Union and founder of the CIO, became so estranged from Roosevelt that he publicly endorsed Republican Wendell Willkie. After Willkie's defeat Lewis's star began to decline. Murray and Hillman were nowhere near the stature of Lewis and if

---

5. Of course there were exceptions. Once a Catholic priest lost $170 in a rigged game of chance. When he complained to the cops they not only got his money back they closed the place down.

they had backed the GOP in 1944 they probably would have lost power completely.

At the convention, Hillman was his usual shifty self. At the time he was involved in a struggle back in New York City with liberal union leaders, David Dubinsky of the Garment Workers and Alex Rose of the millinery trades, who were seeking to purge labor's New York State political arm, the American Labor Party, of Communists. In contrast, Hillman was trying to expand their role in the party.[6] True to form, Hillman arranged a private meeting with Truman to tell him that if Wallace could not be nominated the CIO would support him. Hillman did not bother to inform his ally and union superior, Phil Murray, of this.

One of the delegates arriving at the convention was Bert Stand, secretary of Tammany Hall (then under the de facto control of Frank Costello). When Stand was asked whom he was supporting he replied only "Roosevelt" and would not designate a vice presidential candidate. There is no doubt that the New York delegation, including boss Flynn and Stand, was very well aware of Hillman's dealings with Murder Inc. Did the New York political bosses or someone like Frank Costello put pressure on Hillman to abandon Wallace and support Truman? Certainly it was in their character and interest to do so. A Wallace presidency would have made the American Labor Party the most powerful political group in New York City. A Wallace-appointed attorney general might have fired J. Edgar Hoover and started a drive against organized crime and corrupt politicians. The racing wire service, which served as the lifeblood of gambling, was subject to federal laws. The old reliable Mann Act forbidding interstate transportation of females for immoral purposes was also on the books. There was a law against conspiracies to obstruct interstate commerce. Irey's T-men had enough information to file cases against political big shots as well as mob bosses. Without someone like Truman or Byrnes in the White House, the Mafia might have been in a lot of trouble. With one of those two as president, its leaders would probably be safe from federal prosecution.

---

6. The feud was eventually resolved by Dubinsky and Rose leaving the ALP and founding the New York State Liberal Party.

Flynn's memoirs are vague as to why Hillman cozied up to Truman. Stand and Costello were not above threatening Hillman with exposure or worse, if he insisted on supporting Wallace to the bitter end. If Hillman was pressured by forces in New York to support Truman as the second choice, it might explain why he did not reveal this maneuver to Murray, who was the president of the CIO, not Hillman. It probably would not even have required a threat to expose Hillman to bring him into line. Had Flynn, who was Roosevelt's man, gone to the White House and told the president the truth about Hillman and how much damage he could do to the administration, Hillman would've been cast into oblivion.[7]

Mayor Kelly decided to consult Chicago's black congressman William Dawson, on the possibility of Byrnes' nomination. Dawson informed Kelly that Byrnes' presence as VP would not drive blacks away. However, in racial matters Chicago and New York were very different cities, a fact that sometimes eludes people. Chicago's black voters were often treated like plantation hands who took orders. New York's were emancipated and could not be delivered by a single leader. However, if Kelly had stuck to Byrnes, he would have had to break with Flynn and the bosses knew that to split their united front would lead to Wallace's nomination.

On Monday night Byrnes was informed that he would not be nominated for VP and that instead it would be Harry Truman, who at the time was scheduled to nominate Byrnes. The bosses were comfortable with Truman. He was a product of a corrupt political machine and had remained loyal even when boss Tom Pendergast went to jail. Hannegan, the party chairman, had been pushed into high positions by Truman, whom he called "coach." Kelly was close to Hannegan. Hague was on board; the stars were properly aligned.

Despite the machinations of FDR and the bosses, the Wallace forces almost pulled off a coup. Their leadership in the words of Ed Pauley included "a strange mixture of actual Communists, would-be

---

7. Hillman died two years later at the age of 59 and never had a chance to write his autobiography, where he might have explained his actions at the convention. An authorized biography published shortly after his death was essentially a tribute to him with no questions asked, much less answered. Another likely possibility is that Hillman made a personal decision that Wallace could not win and to support him to the bitter end would cost Hillman his position with the White House as it ended up costing Murray his because he stuck with Wallace all the way.

Communists, do-gooders and other hypertension personalities who had jumped on his bandwagon, ruthlessly shoving aside a small core of men and women who were sincere believers in Henry Wallace."

In 1940 a group of liberal Republicans had stampeded the convention in Philadelphia to nominate Wendell Willkie, a Wall Street lawyer who had never held political office. In doing so they beat out the candidacies of Tom Dewey and Senator Robert Taft of Ohio. At the Democratic convention in Chicago in 1896, William Jennings Bryan's speech ending with the phrase "you shall not crucify mankind upon a cross of gold," threw the convention into a frenzy and resulted in the obscure Bryan receiving the nomination.

In 1944, Tom Garry, now known as "the voice of the sewers," because of the way he stampeded the convention in 1940, was again in charge of arrangements and Kelly's people controlled the distribution of tickets, and the entrances to the hall and galleries. The bosses believed they were strong enough to prevent any stampede. But the Wallace activists spotted a chink in Mayor Kelly's armor. The Kelly forces had printed tickets for each session of the convention. However, they printed them all in the same green color, like a dollar bill. To guarantee that no one could storm past the ticket takers, police were stationed at all the entrances and any attempt to form flying wedges would have been stopped—with clubs. But the Wallace forces managed to collect tickets for all the various sessions from their supporters and friends and on the second day of the convention, when President Roosevelt would be nominated, Wallaceites poured into the hall, while the harried ushers only noted the color and not the date and time on the tickets.

On Thursday evening when Roosevelt was nominated, Wallace delivered a stirring seconding speech which energized his supporters. After the balloting FDR addressed the convention by radio from California. When that ended the cry went up—"We want Wallace! We want Wallace!" and his supporters began flooding the aisles, sometimes snatching state signs from delegations that did not support their man. The organist, either by mistake or because someone had slipped him money, began playing over and over the song of Wallace's home state, Iowa. It was a catchy tune, well known in neighboring Illinois, and the crowd picked it up.[8] Pro- and anti-Wallace forces realized that if a vote were taken then, Wallace would probably win. The convention chairman, Senator Sam Jackson of Indiana, was a Wallace supporter but he had been put in his job by Hannegan, who now screamed at him to get back on the platform and bring the convention to order. Ed Pauley sent word to the organist to stop playing and when he didn't hear or didn't pay attention to him, he told an aide to get an ax and cut the organ cable. None could be found. At that point Boss Hague came to the platform and huddled with Hannegan and Kelly. If the convention had been held in Hague's backyard, his marching band would have drowned out the organist and his cops would have cleared the hall. Kelly had always functioned best with a more senior boss like Pat Nash over him. Now Hague played the same role. He told Kelly and Hannegan to adjourn the convention. So Kelly announced that the auditorium "was dangerously overcrowded and that on his authority as mayor he was ordering the hall to be shut down." The mayor of Pittsburgh, boss David Lawrence, moved that the convention be adjourned; Jackson called for a voice vote and declared that the motion had carried. The organist was still playing and with the noise few people actually heard what had happened. The organist was now told to play louder so no shouts of protest could be heard from Wallace supporters. Many of them did not know that the session had ended until they saw people walking out and the lights go dark on the platform. It had been a close call. Because of Kelly's failure to control tickets, Wallace had almost snatched the presidency of the United States.

The next day police checked all tickets carefully and the convention resumed with the bosses in firm control. On the first ballot Wallace got the most votes and Truman was second. On the next ballot the bosses put their plan into operation and all of the states who had supported favorite sons and other candidates switched their votes to Truman. In the end even Iowa, with Wallace sitting as a delegate, voted for Truman.

When Truman's nomination was announced, California delegate Helen Gahagan Douglas, a minor Hollywood actress, wife of star

---

8. The song went "Ioway, Ioway, state of the land, friends on every hand, we're from Ioway, Ioway, that's where the tall corn grows."

Melvyn Douglas and an ultra liberal Wallace supporter, fainted on the floor. She was helped out of the hall, put in the mayor's limousine, and driven by the police chauffeur to her hotel. During the ride she blasted Truman as a member of the corrupt Pendergast gang and as crooked as any of the bosses. When Mayor Kelly left the convention hall with a companion, he was furious when his car was missing. Finally, it returned and Kelly and his friend got in to it. The chauffeur told the mayor about Mrs. Douglas's tirade against Truman. Not until he finished did Kelly introduce his companion—Senator Harry Truman. Not surprisingly the Douglases were not welcome at the Truman White House over the next few years.[9]

During the presidential campaign, the Republicans pushed the "clear it with Sidney" issue. Even before the Democratic convention, Hillman had been attacked by anti-New Deal columnist Westbrook Pegler, then a national figure in American journalism, who disclosed the affiliation of Hillman's Amalgamated Union with racketeers. The mob charge did not register with the average American, who assumed most labor leaders were tied in with gangsters. Connecticut congresswoman Clare Booth Luce, wife of Time, Inc. publisher Henry Luce, noting that the PAC Hillman headed was trying to get her defeated, announced "If my head is to roll it will be a more American head than Sidney Hillman's." It was not a remark likely to appeal to immigrants or first-generation Americans. Mrs. Luce also described how President Truman's wife was the fourth highest paid employee of the United States Senate, calling her "Payroll Bess." (Luce was apparently unaware that Truman's niece, Mary Jane, was also on the payroll and doing virtually nothing to earn her salary.) Since Truman was not the only member of Congress with relatives on the payroll, the country yawned.

President Roosevelt won handily in the electoral college, though his popular vote margin of three million was the lowest he had registered in his four campaigns. One explanation was that the Roosevelt magic was wearing thin. Alternatively, it could be argued that many of the Democratic voters were young people who were away

---

9. In 1950 Helen Gahagan Douglas, then a congresswoman, ran for the United States Senate against another congressman, Richard M. Nixon. Throughout the campaign Nixon railed at her leftist views, dubbing her "the Pink Lady," pink being a term for someone who was nearly a red Communist. The California voters got the message and sent Mrs. Douglas into retirement and Congressman Nixon on the road to the White House.

in service or had moved to other parts of the country to obtain war jobs and were not eligible, or had not bothered, to register to vote in the new locales.

As vice president, Truman was treated in the usual way of his predecessors. He was not taken into the president's inner circle, was told very little and nothing at all involving the secret of the atom bomb. Clearly, FDR did not think he only had a short time to live. Even the president's aides who knew about his condition did not suck up to Truman, because they did not expect that the president would die as soon as he did.

On April 12, 1945, while lunching with his former mistress in the presidential retreat at Warm Springs, Georgia, Roosevelt died of a massive stroke. As a result, Boss Pendergast's "office boy" became the leader of the free world. Pendergast himself had died in December so was unable to offer his services to the new president. Vice president-elect Truman had commandeered an army bomber to fly to the boss' funeral in Missouri.

Chapter 7

The Missouri Gang:
Scandals and Exposure

Nineteen forty-five was a glorious year for America. World War II ended in complete victory for the Allies. It was also glorious for the corrupt political machines and their Mafia allies. An ordinary man who had spent most of his public life as a front for a crooked, mobbed up politician, rose to the highest office in the land. He appointed his political ally Bob Hannegan as postmaster general of the United States, making him the chief dispenser of federal patronage. In New York City, with Frank Costello's support, Bill O'Dwyer advanced his Horatio Alger legend by being elected mayor. Governor Dewey, who was looking forward to another try for the presidency, was about to release Lucky Luciano from prison. Bosses Flynn, Kelly, and Hague were firmly entrenched in their domains. The Chicago syndicate mourned for its leaders who were doing time in a federal prison because of their extortion of Hollywood. However, with the Truman administration in Washington, it would probably not be long before the Chicagoans were back home doing business at the same old stand.

Truman approached the presidency in the spirit of Kansas City politics. He began by firing anyone connected with the prosecution of Boss Pendergast, including the United States attorney in Kansas City,

Maurice Milligan; Treasury Secretary Henry Morgenthau; and the chief of Treasury intelligence, Elmer Irey; in some cases without the usual letter thanking them for their services to the government. When Truman had an aide inform Attorney General Francis Biddle that he too was dismissed, the Philadelphia mainline aristocrat told the emissary that he had been appointed by the president (FDR) and would only accept dismissal when he heard it from the president himself. So Truman reluctantly scheduled a meeting at the White House to tell Biddle that he was no longer wanted. When Truman finished delivering the message Biddle smilingly put his arm around the chief executive and said, "See there, Harry? That wasn't so bad was it?" as though he was addressing a scared little kid who balked at going to the dentist.

Though Truman could summon the courage to oust the attorney general of the United States, he was too frightened to dismiss Biddle's subordinate, FBI director J. Edgar Hoover. In effect, "Give 'em hell Harry" was afraid of the hell that Hoover could give him. Logically Truman should have fired Hoover because the FBI had played a part in jailing Truman's political friends for vote fraud. However, Hoover was very popular with the Congress and many important people. He was also known to be ruthless. He kept confidential files on virtually every one of importance in the country and undoubtedly there was one on Truman containing many interesting items dating back to the president's Kansas City days.

Throughout his administration Truman was not happy with the FBI's emphasis on communist subversion within the government. Yet during his nearly eight years in office he never moved against Hoover, and his various attorneys general always interpreted federal laws to allow the FBI to wiretap and engage in other controversial investigative methods. Ironically, as president, Truman fought a cold war with Russia and a hot war with the Chinese communists. Yet he was denounced by the right, helped on some occasions by leaks from Hoover's FBI, which pictured the president as "soft on communism."

*

Left to his own devices, Truman proceeded to surround himself with incompetents, cronies, and in some instances, crooks. With the war ending, numerous highly decorated, outstanding officers were available to serve as military aides to the president. Instead of choosing one of them, he brought in the Missouri political hack, Colonel Harry Vaughn, who had been his campaign treasurer in the 1940 Senate campaign. Vaughn was essentially a ne'er-do-well, but Truman had him promoted to major general and gave him a place in his inner circle. During the course of the administration, Vaughn was mixed up in several questionable situations, including receiving gifts for doing favors. Alongside the slovenly, unmilitary-looking Vaughn, Truman chose an equally unappealing naval aide, a Missouri lawyer-politician named Jim Vardeman. He was as repellent to officers of the regular navy as Vaughn was to the army brass. The explanation for the two appointments was Truman's lifelong dislike of the American professional military since his World War I days and his own preference for choosing Missouri pals to have around him.

Bob Hannegan's successor as Democratic national chairman was William Boyle, another Missourian, and Truman's aide for personnel matters was Donald Dawson, also from Missouri. Both men were accused of taking payments to help applicants secure loans from the Reconstruction Finance Corporation (RFC). *Time* magazine wrote of the "peculiar Washington species known as influence peddlers," stating that

> The finest specimens claim Missouri as their habitat, have at least a nodding acquaintance with Harry Truman, a much chummier relationship with his aides and can buzz in and out of the White House at will; they also have great fondness for crisp currency.

Twenty years after the fall of the Ohio gang, the Missouri gang brought the same tawdry climate to Washington. Not only did the Truman presidency resemble the Harding presidency, in the Missouri gang cabinet was a reincarnation of Harry Daugherty in the person of Postmaster General Hannegan.

A director of RFC testified later that Dawson had told him to clear all top personnel matters with the White House and the director's telephone log showed 145 calls from Dawson and 150 from Bill Boyle or his office, mostly urging him to see some "very dear friend." At a black-tie dinner in Boyle's honor in the Kansas City Municipal Auditorium, the president praised both Boyle and Hannegan, stating "they are there when you need them, and that's the kind of friends I like to have around me." Present among the diners were several well-known Kansas City gangsters, including the boss racketeer Charlie Binaggio.

Some of the largest scandals of the Truman administration were the ones that involved the Bureau of Internal Revenue. For years, under both Republican and Democratic administrations, it had been a highly respected, though not loved, organization. Its agents brought civil or criminal cases against people like Kelly of Chicago, Hague of New Jersey, Pendergast of Kansas City, and crime lord Al Capone. It even went after movie idol Tom Mix, the John Wayne of his day. It was treasury agents who brought down the Chicago mob in the Hollywood extortion case.

After Senator Truman had managed to install Hannegan in the top job, the agency started to fall apart. A district collector's job began to be viewed as a patronage appointment and the occupants were allowed to maintain their private occupations, such as the practice of law. The district collector in New York was a politician named Joe Nunan, who earned as much as $50,000 in his private law practice in addition to his $10,500 salary as collector. For his faithful service, Nunan was made commissioner of the entire IRS. Under his administration scandals became commonplace. St. Louis collector James Finneran, named to the job by Hannegan, frequently failed to show up for work, instead devoting his time to his law practice. Any well-connected person in St. Louis who had a tax problem could easily get it resolved by the collector. Finneran himself was found to be in arrears on his taxes. The collector in Boston had been appointed despite a previous conviction for larceny and eventually pled guilty to accepting bribes and was sent to prison. The collector in Brooklyn, a close ally of boss Frank Kelly, supplemented his salary with $235,000 earned in his private law practice. In addition, he was known as a man closely associated with gamblers. It was the same in San Francisco. The chief field deputy of the office was indicted for selling worthless stock in a gold mine.

Finally, Commissioner Joe Nunan himself was indicted and sent to prison.

Another St. Louis lawyer who was given a White House job was Clark Clifford, who was named a naval aide to the president but functioned as an assistant counsel. In later years he would become the most influential lawyer in Washington. His ability to move the levers of power would bring him the title "King of the Permanent Washington Government." Clifford would serve as personal attorney for John Kennedy and secretary of defense for Lyndon Johnson. In his later days tall, handsome and white-haired, with a deep voice and a pontifical manner, Clifford fit the image of a statesman, though as authors James Ring Adams and Douglas Frantz have noted, "Washington's unique brand of self-importance transforms all its fixers into statesman." At the end of his career, Clifford's involvement with the corrupt Arab-controlled Bank of Commerce and Credit International (BCCI) led to his own indictment, although he was adjudged too old to stand trial. Current evaluations of Clifford's life rate him as essentially a fixer who got his start in the Truman White House and carried on until the 1990s. His career was another example of the fraud and hypocrisy found in American government at all levels, including the highest.

In 1947, the Truman administration was revealed to be as much a servant of the Mafia as any Chicago ward heeler or Cook County Sheriff of the time. On August 13, Paul Ricca, Louis "Little New York" Campagna, Phil D'Andrea, and Charles "Cherry Nose" Gioe were released on parole. In 1944 the men had been sentenced to ten years in a federal penitentiary as principals in the Hollywood extortion scandal. Ricca Compagna and D'Andrea were incarcerated in Atlanta, Georgia. Gioe was lodged in Leavenworth, Kansas. In the spring of 1945, after the death of President Roosevelt and the dismissal of Attorney General Biddle, Ricca and Campagna expressed a desire to be transferred to Leavenworth. The Atlanta prison officials objected because it was the policy of the federal government not to send all the members of a gang to the same prison because it would give them too much power within the institution. Even though there were many prominent lawyers in Chicago, the two Chicagoans retained the services of Paul Dillon of St. Louis. In 1934, Dillon had served as the campaign manager for Harry Truman when he was a candidate for the U.S. Senate. He had also been the lawyer for John Lazia, the man who ran the Kansas City Mafia.

Dillon visited the assistant director of the Bureau of Prisons in Washington, DC, and introduced himself as a former campaign manager for President Truman. He then made a formal request for Ricca and Campagna to be transferred. In July, the warden of Atlanta directed a letter to officials in the Bureau of Prisons which said "From information received, it is quite evident that money is being paid to obtain the transfer of these men." Nevertheless, Ricca and Campagna were moved to Leavenworth in August, 1945.

Prison regulations only permitted visitors who were either a convict's attorney or a member of his family. Upon arrival Ricca and Campagna were visited by Chicago attorney Eugene Bernstein and another gentleman who introduced himself as attorney Joseph Bulger of Chicago. Actually Bulger was Tony Accardo, boss of the Chicago syndicate who apparently had important face-to-face business to discuss with Ricca and Campagna.

In 1947, as they were completing the third year of their imprisonment, the Hollywood extortionists sought to receive a parole at the earliest possible date. At least two barriers stood before them. The federal government had outstanding income tax claims against Campagna and Ricca amounting to a half million dollars. Secondly, there was a mail fraud indictment still pending against the gangsters. The benevolent Treasury Department, then in the midst of massive internal revenue scandals, decided to settle their half-million dollar debt to the government for $126,000.

Having disposed of the tax claims, Campagna and Ricca sought the dismissal of the indictment for mail fraud. This required the consent of the attorney general of the United States, Tom Clark of Texas. Once again the gangsters went far afield to obtain a lawyer and they selected Maury Hughes of Dallas, Texas, who had been a political associate and personal friend of Attorney General Clark. Hughes later testified before a congressional committee that he was retained on behalf of the gangsters by a mysterious man whose identity he never established. In fact he knew so little about him he could not even remember a telephone number through which he could be located. Hughes secured a dismissal of the indictment.

Now the gangsters faced the final hurdle. Paul Dillon was dispatched to Washington to consult with the Parole Board. Immediately following his visit, representatives of the parole board in Chicago received telephone instructions from Washington headquarters to telegraph approval of the parole plans. They also were required to waive the customary investigations which would've taken several weeks. One week after Dillon's intervention in Washington, Ricca, Campagna, D'Andrea, and Gioe were released on parole.

Newspapers such as the *Chicago Tribune* were outraged and devoted considerable space to the story. A congressional investigation was commenced. Campagna and Gioe were returned to prison but their lawyers instituted new court action to free them. Though a federal appellate court ordered them returned to custody, they were allowed to remain free in Chicago. During the course of the investigation it was revealed that lawyer Bulger was actually Accardo, and both he and Bernstein were indicted. However, they were acquitted. When a congressional committee tried to question the U.S. Parole Board, the members resigned en masse. It was obvious that the parole had been granted because the petitioners' lawyers were close to the president and the attorney general. So because of top-level politics, some of the most dangerous criminals in America had been freed. It was a demonstration of how the Chicago syndicate could work its will on the White House.

The first few years after World War II saw the departure or death of some long, entrenched bosses. In 1947, New Jersey's Frank Hague stepped down as mayor because he knew he could not be reelected. As he had feared, the returning GIs spread the word that Hague was viewed as a national disgrace. As a face-saving gesture his nephew, Frank Hague Eggers, was elected in his place but it was the last hurrah for the Hagues. New men would take over the Hudson County machine. In Tennessee, some returning war veterans went into a rural county courthouse and drove the old boys of the Crump machine out at gunpoint. Though the incident received national publicity it did not presage a trend. A more damaging blow came in 1948 when Congressman Estes Kefauver defeated Crump's man Senator Kenneth J.

McKellar, a long-time power in Washington. At first Crump had dismissed Kefauver as a "pet coon" of various interests. Kefauver shot back that he may be a "pet coon but I am not Mr. Crump's pet coon." He then outfitted his supporters with coonskin caps, a potent symbol in the home state of Davy Crockett.

In early 1947 Mayor Kelly of Chicago was forced out. Even though Colonel McCormick had put up an exceptionally weak Republican candidate. For years Chicago's much criticized school superintendent, William Johnson, had been co-authoring textbooks on a variety of subjects. So brilliant were these works that all of them were adopted for use in Chicago's schools, providing a nice side income for co-author Johnson. He also received an honorary doctorate from the Chicago Teachers College, a part of the city school system which he ran. Some Chicagoans did not believe that their Dr. Johnson was the intellectual equal of his 18th-century English namesake and various educational groups began to protest.

At first Mayor Kelly refused to remove Johnson—even when a bomb exploded under the superintendent's porch. Whether planted by an educational reformer or a disappointed vendor, it was written off as just one of those minor annoyances Chicago officials were expected to endure. However, when the regional accrediting association threatened to disaccredit the Chicago public schools, the parents rose in fury. If that happened their children would probably be unable to get a job or enter college.[1] So, reluctantly Mayor Kelly had to remove the school superintendent and make him president of the city's community college.

Polls showed Kelly could not be reelected, so his fellow bosses dumped him. The only way he could have kept his job was if Franklin Roosevelt were still alive and willing to personally campaign for him. Truman's popularity was such that if he stumped for Kelly it would have lost the mayor votes. Since the ward bosses were not about to turn the city, with its graft and patronage, over to the Republicans, like the Mafia bosses they were so friendly with, they "resolved all doubts in favor of the organization." In mob land that usually meant a funeral.

---

1. As a student at the time, I was not worried. I eventually joined the police department where a high school diploma was not required.

In the political world the ward bosses reasoned that after fifty years at the public trough, including fourteen as mayor, Kelly was rich enough to retire. So he was replaced by an honest, nonpolitical businessman, Martin Kennelly, who served as the front for the Democratic machine. Kennelly had made his fortune in the moving business. His skill at filling space made him ideal to be a figurehead mayor. The party chairmanship went to a west side lawyer named Jake Arvey.[2] Jake was a product of the 24th Ward, whose gamblers played such a role in the local syndicate and whose feuds were usually fought out with guns and bombs.

In postwar Chicago, the syndicate had close relations with a coterie of successful lawyers, many of whom had grown up together on the west side of Chicago. One was Sid Korshak, who had been assigned by the mob to advise the defendants in the Hollywood shakedown case. Korshak began as an errand boy, carrying messages from the mob leaders who met in downtown restaurants such as Henricis and the Saint Hubert's Grill, to big shot lawyers on LaSalle Street and the suite of rooms maintained by Captain Gilbert in the Sherman Hotel. In the postwar era Korshak moved to Los Angeles where he represented the syndicate in Hollywood and in the entertainment and hotel worlds nationally. In this capacity he dealt with many of his boyhood friends who rose to be the leaders of great entertainment corporations.

The leading mob figure in Los Angeles, New York gangster Bugsy Siegel, began to build a hotel and casino in Las Vegas. Unfortunately, he and his girlfriend Virginia Hill played fast and loose with the mobs' money and Bugsy was murdered. However, the eastern bosses realized the potential in Las Vegas and took over its development themselves. Chicago eventually became the leading mob family in Vegas and its designees were the resident overseers of the casinos.

Despite revisionist histories, the Truman administration in its time received low approval ratings in public opinion polls. Even Democrats believed the job of president was over Harry Truman's head. In 1946, after an overwhelming Republican congressional victory, Democratic Senator William Fulbright of Arkansas, a highly respected figure (for

---

2. The removal of Kelly restored the practice of many years where a west sider was county chairman and a south sider was mayor.

whom the Fulbright scholarships are named), urged Truman to resign, and let the Republicans come to power. At the time there was no vice president and the first in line of succession to the presidency was the speaker of the house, a Republican.

Given the scandals in his administration and Truman's own mistakes, it was assumed he would be defeated for re-election in 1948. Southern Democrats were beginning to rebel and if Truman were nominated he could expect a Dixiecrat party in the field with its own presidential candidate. However, his embrace of what came to be known as "the Cold War" made him highly popular with elements of the eastern elite who ruled the Ivy League universities, investment banks, and the diplomatic service. At the end of World War I such people had urged that America replace Great Britain as the dominant power in the world. Instead the United States turned its back on the League of Nations and, while pursuing world economic power, eschewed political dominance.

After World War II Britain and France could no longer police the world or even maintain the balance of power in Europe. Thus America stepped into the vacuum. For a generation after the end of the war, the eastern elite gloried in international policymaking, secret intelligence operations, and the other fun and games that Britain had carried on for so long. Then, when America got bogged down in Vietnam, much of the elite turned its coat and voiced antiwar sentiments. Finally the educated class excused themselves permanently from military service.[3] One does not have to line up with Oliver Stone and the other Cold War revisionists and embrace Joe Stalin to suggest that if Truman had been a man of broader knowledge he might have questioned his advisers about what exactly he was committing to and whether there other ways to achieve the same result.

Truman's aggressive anti-Russian posture made many liberals dissatisfied. In 1948 they rallied behind a newly formed "Progressive Party" that nominated Henry Wallace for president. The Progressives were essentially the old Wallace supporters who felt that their man had been jobbed out of the presidency in 1944 by the big-city bosses.

---

3. It is interesting to speculate that if there were still a draft that took in the upper middle-class, the United States might not have had so many foreign adventures in recent decades.

While the 1948 Democratic and Republican conventions were held in Philadelphia, the Progressives returned to the Chicago Stadium. Even though the party was regarded as a Communist front, the city administration and the cops were polite to the delegates and their friendly sentiments were returned full fold.

Pundits predicted that the Dixiecrats would carry some southern states and that the Progressive Party would receive enough votes to throw key states, like New York, to the Republicans. The GOP again nominated Tom Dewey, who had made a comparatively good showing in 1944, against a wartime president. Dewey was the heavy betting favorite to win the election.[4]

The experts made three mistakes in assessing prospects for the 1948 race: 1. They ignored the fact that Wallace was too identified in the public mind with the Soviet Union and Communism to attract many votes. 2. Tom Dewey, described as "the little man on the wedding cake," was no longer a crusading prosecutor but was regarded as a stiff, and Truman was able to pose as "Give 'em hell Harry," the voice of the common man. 3. The economy was good. Farmers were prosperous, workers had no trouble finding jobs, and the G.I. Bill had enabled returning servicemen to go to college and buy homes. Truman was elected, though without great enthusiasm by the voters.

In 1950, the Korean War broke out. Truman had made a serious miscalculation. He allowed the eastern elite to set the terms of U.S. foreign policy whereby the United States would block communist expansion everywhere, if necessary by military force. Yet, he radically reduced the American military so that the army had less than one-tenth the strength it had possessed five years earlier. In the navy, admirals who disagreed with the cutbacks were forced out. The president had picked Louis Johnson, a Democratic politician from West Virginia, who harbored his own presidential ambitions, to be his secretary of defense. Johnson ruthlessly slashed military budgets. The army filled its top jobs with men who had been staff officers rather than field commanders in World War II; others had once been capable but were now past their best. Senior officers, particularly in the Far East, wanted

---

4. Though at the last moment some Truman money began to come in. The Mafia was always good at picking winners.

to spend the last years of their career leading a comfortable life in the army of occupation in Japan, where it did not appear likely that any difficulties would develop.

As a result of cutbacks in strength, obsolete equipment, poor training and bad leadership, the army was totally unfit to fight the North Koreans. In the early days of the war U.S. troops suffered heavy casualties and were nearly driven into the sea. After American forces made a successful amphibious landing at Inchon, they drove into North Korea, but when the Chinese intervened, the American troops suffered another debacle. So serious was the situation that Truman announced publicly that the United States might use atomic bombs, thereby throwing her European allies into a panic over the prospect of unleashing World War III. During the remaining two years of the war the UN forces were locked in a stalemate. By the end of the president's second term his approval ratings were lower than they later were for Richard Nixon at the time of Watergate or George W. Bush in the last years of his second term. It is likely that in the future Truman will rank among presidents well below his current standing.

Despite the problems of his second term, Truman still was available to help corrupt politicians and mob bosses. In 1946 Bill O'Dwyer became mayor of New York City thanks to Frank Costello. His former chief investigator, Frank Bals, who had presided over the Kid Twist fiasco, was named deputy police commissioner in charge of a special squad to enforce vice and gambling laws. The word was out in the mob world that the Bals squad would collect for City Hall. Between the Mafia and the NYPD, they were able to generate enough bad publicity for Bals that after ninety days his squad was abolished. Jim Moran, whom many believe was the real boss in the O'Dwyer administration, was made first deputy fire commissioner, where he immersed himself in a shakedown scheme involving fire safety inspections.

Under O'Dwyer the police department went back to its pre-LaGuardia days and corruption was rampant. Again the waterfront was a source of problems. In 1947, Bill Keating, one of District Attorney Hogan's assistants, managed to make a case of murder against some top waterfront gangsters. Two of them were sentenced to death, a rare outcome in a mob killing. In the summer of 1949, one of them offered to expose corruption on the waterfront, including payoffs to politicians, in return for commutation of his death sentence. Upon hearing the news Mayor O'Dwyer took to the hospital and declared he would not run for reelection that year. However, the killer did not go through with his threat and was executed in July.[5] Shortly after the gangster's execution, O'Dwyer, pushed by Jim Moran, decided that he would be a candidate and in November was reelected by large margin.

O'Dwyer was finally brought down by a massive police scandal in Brooklyn. Unlike the Murder, Incorporated case and the Reles "suicide," this investigation did not involve murder. Rather it stemmed from the discovery of a gambling ring run by a bookie and an ex-cop who were paying off top police officials. O'Dwyer himself faced indictment, so he sought some face-saving way to leave the United States. President Truman obliged by making him the United States ambassador to Mexico. The mayor held a press conference in which he tearfully declared "my country needs me" and implied that he was being sent south of the border to foil some mysterious Communist plot, which no one in or out of the government seemed to be aware of. After Eisenhower was elected in 1952, O'Dwyer was replaced as ambassador but remained in Mexico as a private citizen until the statute of limitations in New York expired. The spectacle of the president of the United States throwing O'Dwyer a lifeline by giving him an important foreign embassy was just another example of the power of corrupt mobbed-up politicians to receive favors from the White House.

The election to fill O'Dwyer's vacant post was a contest between the president of the city council, Vincent Impellitteri, and Judge Ferdinand Pecora. Impy, as Impellitteri was known, had been an obscure law secretary (glorified clerk) to a judge when he was nominated to run on the ticket with O'Dwyer in 1945 because as an Italian he would complement an Irish candidate for mayor and a Jewish candidate for controller. Impy was also helped to the post by

5. Dewey was still the governor but apparently neither he nor his aides could persuade the man to talk in return for commutation of the death penalty.

mob boss Tommy Lucchese, who controlled the East Harlem area from which Impellitteri came.

When O'Dwyer, as they would say in Brooklyn, "took it on the Arthur Duffy,"[6] Impy surprised everybody and decided to run for the remainder of O'Dwyer's term. His opponent, Judge Pecora, owed his nomination to Tammany Hall. The race was essentially between Impy's overlord, Tommy Lucchese, and the ruler of Tammany, Frank Costello. It was a situation likely to upset the balance of mob power within the Five Families to have a Lucchese man in City Hall replacing a Costello man. During the campaign Frank forgot that he was a gentleman sportsman and sent his gunmen out to help sway the voters. Impellitteri came over as the underdog candidate and was able to run an anti-Tammany campaign, which appealed to voters outside of Manhattan. He was elected to fill the remaining three years of the term. Impy then appointed as police commissioner a former assistant United States attorney, Tom Murphy, who had just prosecuted and convicted Alger Hiss for lying about his Communist affiliations.[7] Later, when Murphy was nominated for a federal judgeship, he had to admit to a Senate committee that he too was a friend of Lucchese, but had been unaware of the man's organized crime involvements. If so, he was the only one in New York public life who was.

*

Given the power of the mobs in America, some public officials and civic reformers thought the postwar years were the time to rein in the Mafia. The 1948 presidential election had given them hope because it appeared that Truman would lose and that Dewey as president might possibly go back to racket busting and even force J. Edgar Hoover to take some action, although that was highly unlikely. If any fact illustrated the power of the Mafia in the American national government it was that presidents and the head of the FBI were both afraid to take on the gangsters. When Truman was reelected it was obvious the

---

6. Arthur Duffy was a noted turn-of-the-century long-distance runner.
7. The case became a cause célèbre for the next forty years. However, the government acquired absolute proof of Hiss' affiliations by breaking code messages from Moscow. Because of national security this could not be revealed by the prosecution. Since the opening of Soviet intelligence files in Moscow, the case for Hiss' innocence has collapsed.

executive branch was not going to do anything. So the reformers began to shift their attention to Congress.

A leading figure in the promotion of a national campaign against the Mafia was Virgil Peterson, a former FBI special agent who had been in charge of several different offices, and, since 1942, head of the Chicago Crime Commission. Peterson came from a little town of 250 people in Iowa. In 1930 he received a law degree from Northwestern University just as the Depression hit, so he joined Hoover's Bureau of Investigation. As crime commission head, Peterson was a man who was so straightlaced and honest that even the Chicago mobsters respected him.[8] In September 1949, speaking on behalf of the American Municipal Association, an organization that represented 10,000 local governments, Peterson called on U.S. attorney general J. Howard McGrath (a former Rhode Island senator and Democratic national chairman who was more politician than law enforcer) to bring the federal government into the fight against organized crime. Peterson cited the activities of Frank Costello as proof "crime and gambling syndicates operate on a countrywide basis." In November, *Newsweek* magazine hit the stands with Costello's picture on the cover. A week later he was on the cover of *Time*. When Peterson addressed the Municipal Association's annual conference in Cleveland in December, he again called for federal assistance to fight against organized crime. The association passed a resolution supporting his ideas and with the *Time* and *Newsweek* cover stories and Peterson's proposals, it looked as though a war on organized crime was in the offing.

In January 1950, Estes Kefauver, the coonskin-wearing freshman Democratic senator from Tennessee, introduced a resolution to authorize a Senate investigation of organized crime's impact on interstate commerce. Truman realized that no good could come to him or the Democratic Party from such an investigation. So he immediately took steps to block the resolution. Attorney General McGrath unexpectedly invited local officials and heads of anti-crime groups like Peterson's to attend the annual conference of U.S. attorneys in Washington in February 1950. Truman himself agreed to address the

---

8. Unlike many so-called reformers, he never took bribes from racketeers, nor did he garner cheap headlines by insulting them.

session. There he advised federal, state, and local prosecutors to cooperate in stamping out organized crime.[9] Peterson characterized the event as "window dressing" to sidetrack demands for a thorough investigation of the mob.

With Truman blocking the way and J. Edgar Hoover also opposed, the Mafia appeared safe. Then, in April, Kansas City mob boss Charles Binaggio and his enforcer Charles Gargotta were gunned down in the First Ward Democratic clubhouse on Truman Boulevard. Pictures of Gargotta's body lying under an enlarged photograph of the president appeared on the front pages of newspapers across the country. With his own photo serving as the public face of organized crime, Truman had to drop his opposition to the Kefauver resolution. In May the Senate approved the appointment of a special committee to investigate organized crime. Senate protocol required that the sponsor of the resolution, Kefauver, be named chairman. So, opposition now switched from obstruction to containment. Some senators did not want an investigation. Among them were Majority Leader Scott Lucas of Illinois, who owed his job to the Chicago political machine. Another was judiciary committee chairman Pat McCarran of Nevada, a state which was propped up by gambling dollars. Former majority leader Alben Barkley, who had been elected vice president with Truman in 1948, carried great weight with his former colleagues and, being loyal to his president, he too sought to contain the investigation. The Democratic leadership chose as one of the other two Democratic senators for the committee Lester Hunt of Wyoming, where the primary crime problem was cattle rustling. It was doubtful that Frank Costello could find Wyoming on a map or spell Cheyenne. The third Democrat named was Herbert O'Conor of Maryland. Baltimore had organized crime but it was loosely constituted and not linked to the Mafia. O'Conor was a smooth, suave individual who could be expected to keep the investigation within safe limits.

On the Republican side, Joseph McCarthy of Wisconsin was eager to be named a member but he was shunted off. Some GOP leaders, angry over Dewey's defeat and the way the mob-affiliated, big-city

---

9. In his speech Truman noted that, though he was "the most important man in the world," he ordered his chauffeur to stop at red lights. Reporters, who followed the president's limousine back to the White House, observed it run through seventeen stoplights.

machines had helped carry states that were thought to be solidly in the Republican column, favored a no-holds barred attack on gangsters and their Democratic allies. However, it was never certain what a wild man like McCarthy would do. The Senate Republicans preferred that he attack Communists rather than Republican bosses in places like Philadelphia where organized crime was strong.

Another Republican who wanted to be a member of the Kefauver committee was Senator Homer Ferguson of Michigan. As a judge in Detroit, he had brought down the mayor, police superintendent, and county prosecutor. Though not a Joe McCarthy-type, Ferguson was another man who might possibly kick over the political traces. Instead the Republican leadership named Alexander Wiley of Wisconsin, who most charitably could be described as not a very forceful figure, and Charles Tobey of New Hampshire, who with his New England preacher manner, excoriated some of the witnesses. Tobey was in a tough reelection fight and in a closely divided Senate the Republican leadership wanted to retain every seat it could. Getting some good publicity would help Tobey to get reelected.

Chosen as chief counsel for the committee was Rudolph Haley, a shrewd New York lawyer with political ambitions. Before the investigation opened, Haley was counseled by Judge Pecora, who had made a great name for himself when he was counsel to a Senate committee investigating Wall Street in the aftermath of the 1929 crash. Back then, J. P. Morgan was the designated villain; now it would be Frank Costello (who had recently supported Pecora for mayor of New York City).

The Kefauver committee knew little about organized crime but it received assistance from Anslinger's Federal Bureau of Narcotics, Virgil Peterson, and other crime commission heads. The committee opened hearings in Washington, DC, with Anslinger and Peterson providing reams of information on the Mafia. Hoover would have nothing to do with the Kefauver probe and in the informal hierarchy of Washington, he outranked the U.S. Senate. Kefauver then took the show on the road. In July, 1950, it held hearings in Miami. The local crime commission head, Dan Sullivan, an ex-FBI agent, provided a great deal of information to the committee, especially documenting the Chicago mob's infiltration of the Sunshine State. When the sheriff of Dade

County (which encompassed the Miami area) testified, he acknowledged that in five years he had managed to parlay his net worth from $2500-$70,000. The sheriff of nearby Broward County admitted that over the previous three years his income had been in excess of $1 million. The committee carried its investigations all the way to the office of Governor Fuller Warren, whose aides had been very helpful to the Chicago mob when it infiltrated Florida. When Warren restored the suspended Miami sheriff to his office, the *Miami Daily Herald* ran an editorial with a black border around it saying, "How lousy, stinking—and obvious—can a governor of Florida be before the people rise up and strike him down?" Of course Florida could be written off as a state that was always known for gambling and vice. In truth, the tourist industry required it. The findings would have no national impact.

After a few other hearings, in October the committee arrived in Chicago. There it opened against the background of two front page murders. One was that of former Chicago police captain Bill Drury, who had been fired from the department for daring to arrest two top mob figures in the investigation of the murder of racing wire boss James Ragen. When called before the grand jury in the Ragen case, Drury and another police captain refused to sign immunity waivers as required of all policemen at that time. So they were dismissed from the force. The killing was never solved, although it was believed to have been carried out by several top members of the Chicago syndicate.

Three hours after Drury's assassination, a Chicago attorney whom he had spoken to the day before was murdered. Over the years Drury had been a colorful, hardcharging cop, tough on gangsters. Yet as a captain (actually an acting captain) in charge of a police district he had been suspended on charges of permitting gambling to flourish in his command. It is generally believed that the reason for his murder was to prevent the exposure of any relationship between the Cook County machine under Arvey and the Chicago mob in which Captain Dan Gilbert was a top figure. Despite Gilbert's background, Arvey had agreed to put him on the ticket for county sheriff. The reason was probably that with Tom Courtney no longer state's attorney, the mob needed a reliable man in charge of law enforcement in the suburban areas of the county.

The Chicago organization, with majority leader Senator Lucas leading the 1950 ticket, was not anxious for Gilbert to testify in public. Luckily for the syndicate, Senator Kefauver behaved in Chicago like a hick from the sticks. He was known as a serial womanizer who hated to sleep by himself, so the mob made sure he was not lonely. According to later findings by *New York Times* investigative reporter Seymour Hersh, mob attorney Sid Korshak arranged for Kefauver to be photographed in a compromising position with a young lady in a room at the Drake Hotel. After the womanizing, Kefauver was shown the photo; he agreed to take Captain Gilbert's testimony in a private session. There Tubbo admitted to a net worth in excess of $300,000, explaining how he had made the money betting illegally on sporting events. He also detailed his successful speculation in the grain market and other business deals, causing Rudy Halley to ask him where he found the time to carry out his law enforcement responsibilities. Just before the election a *Sun-Times* reporter managed to procure (steal) Gilbert's testimony from a stenographic firm used by the committee and splash it on the front pages. Its publication was widely credited with defeating Gilbert and Senator Lucas. It also disgraced party leader Arvey and he was later replaced as county chairman by Richard J. Daley.

The following month the committee journeyed to Los Angeles where LAPD chief Bill Parker testified that an attorney named Sam Rummel was the brains behind Mickey Cohen. After the hearings the committee announced it would return in a few months for another round of hearings and at that time would probably call Rummel. In the interval Rummel was shot to death. When the committee did return, a sheriff's captain, who had been involved with Rummel, was under indictment. When he was called to testify his jaw trembled as he sought to explain why he and fellow police brass had held secret meetings with Mickey Cohen's lawyer.

In Philadelphia the committee heard testimony that in some police districts the numbers operators were paying $100 a week to patrolmen and $1,000 to captains. When the inspector in charge of the vice squad was subpoenaed to testify, he killed himself.

The committee hearings coincided with the arrival of a new force in America—television. Locally televised hearings of the Kefauver committee proved popular in certain cities and the committee members were becoming identifiable. Kefauver came over as a Southern gentleman, fair-minded, courteous to all without being soft. Tobey was an Old Testament prophet, browbeating witnesses he deemed morally deficient. In New Orleans he told the sheriff "Why don't you resign? It seems to me that a man like you... is not worth a damn. I cannot sit and listen to this type of what I call political vermin." The other three senators were reduced to bit players, or as the TV columnists advised their readers, when they are on, that's the time to go to the bathroom. Attorney Halley, with his grating voice, was the hit man who fired questions at witnesses as though he were shooting bullets. Few were prepared for the volume of names, dates, and places that Halley confronted them with. Heretofore, mobsters had been shadowy figures. TV permitted the public, for the first time, to see gangsters, most of whom looked like Hollywood heavies. But instead of being on a movie set they were in the viewers' living rooms. It also showed mayors, police chiefs, and sheriffs, not as crimebusting heroes but mob accomplices. In Kansas City the committee concentrated on the Corallo-Gargano murders but out of deference to President Truman little was said about past political history.

After its road trip, the committee's show was ready for the big time in New York City where the audience would determine whether it was a hit or a flop. The two projected stars of the show were to be Frank Costello and former mayor William O'Dwyer. Costello, still believing that he was just a sportsman, was anxious to testify and set the record straight. O'Dwyer refused to appear for fear that charges would be brought against him. He demanded and was granted legal immunity for the duration of the hearings. It was a telling situation where the recent chief executive of the country's greatest city demanded protection from the law and the Mafia Prime Minister did not.

In New York, seventeen times the normal daytime audience tuned in and the national ratings were twice as high as those for the World

Series. In addition, the evening network news programs showed excerpts from the hearing. When Costello took the stand Halley launched an all out attack on him. Soon Frank became flustered and complained that the TV lights bothered him. So his lawyers asked that the cameras be shut off. As a compromise they showed only his hands. In doing so he came over to the audience as a man with something to hide. Hour after hour for two days the camera was focused on his hands nervously toying with a water glass, papers or his spectacles, all gestures that suggested he was lying. On the third day of his testimony, Costello claimed he was too ill to go on. Kefauver was not about to let the star slip off the stage and he ordered Halley to continue his questioning. Costello claimed that he was too sick to continue and walked out of the hearings, creating a media sensation. He later came back and provided a TV clip that would run for the next six decades. When Tobey asked him, "What have you ever done for your country as a good citizen?" Costello said, "Paid my taxes." The answer brought down the house because everyone knew that the government had evidence that he had not paid them in full.

Other mob bosses had taken the fifth or testified in cities far from their own bailiwicks, thereby mitigating the impact of their appearance and sparing themselves contempt or perjury charges. Frank's fellow gangsters were astonished that their prime minister looked so bad. Joe Adonis, who had taken the Fifth himself, watched the television muttering, "What a sucker, what a sucker."

When O'Dwyer arrived he entered like a man used to dominating a room. His career had largely been based on his ability to expound blather and blarney. He began his testimony with long rambling statements about his Horatio Alger life and his wartime services. Viewers flooded the TV stations demanding that his monologue be cut off. Finally, Halley interrupted with a blistering cross-examination about the death of Kid Twist Reles, the mayor's relationship with Costello, why he had failed to prosecute Anastasia, etc. O'Dwyer grew flustered and his hair became rumpled from wiping his brow. Finally, he completely lost his composure, accusing Senator Tobey of accepting a campaign contribution from New York gamblers. When it was quickly revealed that the ex-mayor was wrong, he had to publicly apologize.

O'Dwyer was exposed to the world as just a squirming, corrupt politician. His long-time comrade, Jim Moran, had not accompanied O'Dwyer to Mexico to fight the Reds. He had remained in New York City where he would be sent to prison for accepting bribes. When it was Moran's turn to testify he tried to con his way through. Instead, he dug himself in even deeper. Urban viewers recognized his type, a blustering, crooked ward heeler. The question in their minds was how could someone like this have become the right-hand man to the leader of the world's greatest city? It was not hard for viewers to figure out the answer.

The hearings were a sensation but there were no immediate results. J. Edgar Hoover had refused to cooperate with the Kefauver committee and no mere mortal like the president, attorney general, or the congressional leadership could make him. At the same Truman fired General MacArthur, a national hero, but he did not dare tangle with Hoover. It was not good for the country that in the seventh year of his presidency, Truman was afraid of Hoover who was himself afraid of the Mafia.

By the end of Truman's presidency in 1953, all of the key figures from the 1944 convention—Flynn, Hague, Hannegan, and Kelly—were either dead or out of power, but their work was still paying dividends for the Mafia. It was becoming obvious that big city mobs would continue in power until America had a president who would proclaim a war on them and see that it was actually carried out.

Chapter 8

The Rise and Fall of the Kennedys

In the late 1950s Jimmy Hoffa became the most famous labor leader in America and held that title until his disappearance in 1975. Even today, whenever his body is supposedly discovered, the story makes news. Part of his appeal was his tough, brash, give or ask no quarter manner. However headstrong Jimmy was, he was also shrewd. In 1957 he was under investigation by the United States Senate select committee probing labor racketeering. When it was time for him to take the stand he met his match in the committee's hard charging chief counsel, Robert "Bobby" Kennedy. From then on no love was lost between the two of them. While Kennedy had the power of the Senate behind him, Jimmy had a secret weapon. John Cye Cheasty, a former Secret Service agent who worked as an investigator for the Senate committee, was on Hoffa's payroll. Unbeknownst to Jimmy, though, Bobby Kennedy had the same secret weapon because Cheasty was a double agent.

On a night in March 1957, Cheasty arranged a rendezvous with Hoffa in Washington's Dupont Circle and gave him a folder containing committee documents. In return Hoffa handed Cheasty $2,000 in crumpled bills while FBI cameras filmed the action. The next night Cheasty passed more documents to Hoffa, though without receiving any money. Hoffa then walked into the lobby of a nearby hotel and was arrested by the FBI while still in possession of the papers. At midnight he was arraigned in the District of Columbia courthouse. As he was led in, he noticed Bobby Kennedy waiting and the two men glared at each other for a few minutes. During a brief discussion, like two school boys, they began arguing about who could do the most push-ups. The young chief counsel, a lawyer who had never tried a case, rashly promised that if the jury failed to convict Hoffa he would personally jump off the Capitol dome. If Bobby had had more legal experience he might have known to temper his remarks. Hoffa and his celebrity lawyer, Edward Bennett Williams, had more secret weapons available. Jimmy was going to win his acquittal by playing what today would be labeled the "race card," a neat trick for a white guy to pull off.

Williams retained as one of his co-counsels an African American female lawyer, who was possibly chosen with an eye toward the eight black jurors. During the trial, an African American community newspaper printed a special edition extolling Hoffa and his lawyers and delivered copies to all the jurors' homes. On the day that Hoffa took the stand, the former heavyweight boxing champion Joe Louis dropped by to put his arms around "my friend Jimmy," in full view of the jurors. Despite what appeared to be solid evidence, Hoffa was acquitted. Edward Bennett Williams immediately announced that he was going out to buy a parachute for Bobby Kennedy to use when he jumped off the Capitol. Williams' skills and the embrace from Joe Louis were given the credit for the acquittal. Though one racketeer in the courtroom was heard to say, "Let the lawyers think they did it." It would not have been the only time in Jimmy's career that his agents bribed a jury.

A shaken Kennedy told his staff that they now had a lot of work to do. He was so obsessed that while driving home one night at 11 p.m. he noticed lights still burning in Hoffa's office, so he went back to his own office to work for several more hours. When Hoffa heard of the incident, he ordered that the lights in his office be left on every night.

The Kennedy-Hoffa feud would continue for over a decade, during which time Bobby Kennedy and President Jack Kennedy were both assassinated. Seven years after Bobby was killed, Hoffa himself was presumably murdered. In retrospect it is hard to discern any winners in this feud.

*

General Eisenhower's landslide victory in the 1952 presidential election ended twenty years of Democratic rule in Washington. With the momentum generated by the Kefauver committee and a president who owed no obligation to corrupt big-city political machines, the individuals and groups who had urged a crackdown on organized crime were hopeful that the incoming administration would follow up with new laws and vigorous enforcement drives to destroy the American Mafia. In this they were disappointed.

Since the Roaring Twenties organized crime had never been without Republican friends. During the period of GOP rule of the nation from 1921 through 1932, the Prohibition Bureau was shot through with corruption. In cities like Philadelphia and Chicago, Republican mayors posed no threat to gangsters. The boss of southern New Jersey, Republican Nucky Johnson of Atlantic City, was one of the most powerful figures in organized crime. Not surprisingly his bailiwick was a favorite meeting ground for mob conclaves. It was at one of these, in 1929, that the bosses ordered Al Capone to step out of the spotlight to cool down the heat from the Valentine massacre. As a result, he went through a choreographed routine where he journeyed to Philadelphia, got himself arrested for carrying a gun and was promptly given a year in jail. The fact that Capone would personally carry a firearm and, instead of fighting the charge with an army of lawyers, would meekly plead guilty, demonstrated that the whole thing was a setup. It was not by chance that the detective who captured him had previously been a guest at Al's Florida estate. Later that detective would become the safety director in charge of the police and fire departments of Philadelphia during the time it was a Republican stronghold.

In 1952 Eisenhower's nomination had been secured by the strong support of Governor Tom Dewey's New York state machine and when the new administration took office Herbert Brownell, a former Dewey campaign manager, was appointed attorney general and was later succeeded by a former Dewey assistant district attorney, William Rogers. Neither man was interested in following up on the Kefauver investigation. Even if they had, they would have found a huge road-block in FBI director J. Edgar Hoover. Brownell himself often told the story of how he came down to work on a Sunday and was refused admittance to the DOJ because he had forgotten his building pass. When he explained that he was the attorney general the security guard declared, "I don't care if you're J. Edgar Hoover himself, you can't get in without a pass." The guard was simply making a realistic assessment of power within the DOJ where attorneys general came and went but Hoover stayed on forever.

All through Eisenhower's first term organized crime was ignored. Behind the scenes, following the Kefauver hearings, Hoover had ordered his field offices to submit reports on Mafia activities. With the help of local cops some useful information was gathered. For example, the San Francisco office received intelligence from police inspectors Frank Ahern and Tom Cahill, who had served as investigators for the Kefauver committee. In 1954 the office submitted a generally accurate report identifying "presumed heads of the mobs" in sixteen American cities. The problem with Hoover was not so much a lack of information but a lack of will. He did not want to tangle with the Mafia families and the mayors, governors, and senators who were their allies. His assessment was right politically but it was wrong in terms of the national interest.[1]

Around the country there were a few changes in the organized crime hierarchy. In New York City the Five Families still flourished, though after the beating he took in front of the Kefauver committee and the tax and contempt of Congress charges that resulted, Frank

---

1. On Hoover's tenure and post-Hoover changes in federal law enforcement, see Appendix II, Federal Law Enforcement from Hoover to Homeland Security.

Costello was no longer the Prime Minister. His rival, Vito Genovese, took advantage of Costello's decline to assert his own claim to primacy. However, his personality was such that he could never be a Prime Minister who had to persuade colleagues. Genovese was also handicapped by the fact that he was heavily involved in narcotics trafficking, which to some of the bosses around the country was a forbidden activity because it would make trouble with their political friends. A senator could front for a mob boss who posed as just a gambler but not for one who peddled drugs to kids.

The most important politician in New York City was Carmine DeSapio, who engineered the election of Robert Wagner as mayor in 1953 and Averill Harriman as governor in 1954. He was not only boss of Tammany Hall but was secretary of state of New York and the Democratic national committeeman for the state. Yet it was an open secret that he had many contacts with gangsters. In the 1950 mayoral election DeSapio had led Frank Costello's forces in their unsuccessful attempt to install Ferdinand Pecora as mayor.

In the South, Carlos Marcello of New Orleans headed the oldest Mafia family in America. In that traditionally corrupt, wide-open city his power was immense. In 1954, when Santo Trafficante, Sr., died (of natural causes), Santo Junior inherited both control of the Tampa family and its extensive holdings in Cuba. Young Santo, known in the underworld as "the man with the green eyes," divided his time between his wife in Florida and his showgirl mistress in Cuba. On the island he was recognized as the most powerful mobster next to Meyer Lansky, the financial wizard of the Mafia.

In the west the Los Angeles mob world was dominated, at least on the front pages, by Mickey Cohen, a Jewish gangster who had arrived in the city in the '40s from Cleveland. Mickey was good for comedy but the Italian faction under Jack Dragna continued in power. Because the Los Angeles Police Department which, unlike other municipal police forces, was constantly on the offensive against organized crime, the local mobs were not as strong as in other cities and they were frequently derided as the "Mickey Mouse Mafia." The real area of growth in the west was Las Vegas, where several of the families, backed by Teamster money, controlled casinos.

In Eisenhower's first term, the mobs operated as though the Kefauver investigation had never happened. In 1957, the first year of Eisenhower's second term, a plague of troubles descended on the Mafia. In Los Angeles the (natural) death of Jack Dragna in 1956 removed the last force that could keep Mickey Cohen from going off the reservation completely. In that year Mickey did an interview with ABC network reporter Mike Wallace in which he called Police Chief William Parker of Los Angeles "alcoholic and sadistic" and blasted the captain of the intelligence division, Jim Hamilton. Parker and Hamilton sued Cohen and the network and collected damages. Mafia bosses usually avoided publicity and now a Jewish gangster on national television had made organized crime look ridiculous as well as menacing. At the same time one of Mickey's enforcers, Johnny Stompanato, was carrying on a torrid romance with screen goddess Lana Turner. When Turner went off to England to make a movie, Stompanato followed her and interfered so much in the production of the film that detectives from Scotland Yard took him into custody, read him an expulsion order from the British government, and placed him on a plane back to the United States. When Lana returned to Hollywood the two continued their tempestuous affair and while the mob heavy was scuffling with Lana in her own house, he was fatally knifed by her 14-year-old daughter, Cheryl. Cohen immediately jumped into the affair with both feet, proclaiming that it was not the daughter but Lana who had murdered his man Johnny. Because of Turner's fame the story became a national sensation.

In Chicago, the leading city of mid-America, though Tony Accardo was the top boss, Paul Ricca, the old Hollywood extortionist, was regarded as the virtual co-boss. In 1953 Richard Daley took over the party chairmanship and two years later was elected mayor. This was the end of the practice of having a Westsider as party chairman and a Southsider as mayor. Daley would fill both jobs and become the strongest political leader Chicago ever had. Unlike Mayors Thompson and Kelly, or bosses like the deposed Jake Arvey, he was not beholden to the mob. On the other hand he did not declare war against it. The mob remained influential politically but it had less access to city government than previously.

In 1957, Accardo decided to voluntarily step aside as boss in favor of Momo Salvatore "Sam" or, as the cops called him, "Mooney" (in the sense of spacey), Giancana. Since Accardo was only fifty and in good health, few people could understand his decision. Most of the crew chiefs did not like the idea. Accardo was considered a tough, smart, and fair boss. On the other hand, Giancana was regarded as not overly bright and prone to recklessness. In 1957, after a local banker was murdered, when the victim's body was examined by cops, they found on it a marker (IOU) from Giancana. The hit man assigned to kill the banker had not searched his victim thoroughly. As a result, Giancana had to answer a lot of questions about his relationship with the dead man. Sam, the product of a violent West Side gang that had flourished in the 1920s, was furious. The hapless hit man (a discharged police officer) was taken for a ride the hard way, chained to the back of a car that sped down gravelly suburban roads. Already nearly dead, he was then shot. When his body was searched all that was found on him was a comb—the message to hit men being, "Comb your victim after you kill him."

It was in New York where the worst difficulties befell the mobs. In May one of Vito Genovese's hit men, Vincent "The Chin" Gigante, later a top boss himself, shot at Frank Costello outside the former Prime Minister's swank apartment building and grazed his head. In that same year Carmine DeSapio alighted from a taxicab leaving $11,200 in crumpled bills behind in an envelope. In an era when cops made $5000 a year, it was a substantial sum. The cab driver turned the money over to the police and the passenger was identified from trip logs. When contacted, DeSapio denied ownership of the bills. Everybody assumed Carmine had the money because he had just taken a bribe. That an obviously corrupt, organized-crime-connected politician like DeSapio could remain in the good graces of supposedly clean officials like Mayor Wagner and Governor Harriman illustrated the continuing importance of mob families in New York politics and the hypocrisy of officeholders who denounced them but benefited from their support.

In October 1957 an assassination team, probably captained by Joey Gallo, leader of a dissident faction in the Profaci family, killed mob boss Albert Anastasia in a Manhattan barbershop. The hit was carried out on the orders of Vito Genovese to help Carlo Gambino become head of Anastasia's family. At about the same time Harry Anslinger's Federal Bureau of Narcotics began to zero in on Genovese. With all that was happening many of the leaders of the national syndicate decided a sit down was needed to address questions such as why bosses were being hit without permission of the national commission and whether it was wise to engage in drug trafficking.

Chicago offered to host the gathering, promising that the meetings would be held in small, west suburban towns where cops were owned by the mob and there would be no interference. The police forces in those communities were frequently used to harass snoopers from other law enforcement agencies when they tried to spy on mob bosses.

Since the greatest power of the Mafia was in the east, it was decided to hold the conclave there. A preliminary meeting was held at an estate in New Jersey. The attendees were scheduled to reassemble a few days later at a rural location in the southern tier of New York near the village of Apalachin, where a local boss, Joe Barbara, had a home. National commission member Stefano Maggadino of Buffalo assured everyone that there would be no police interference.

On November 14, 1957, the meeting no more than got underway when two state troopers accompanied by two U.S. Treasury, Alcohol and Tobacco Tax agents, arrived on the scene, set up a roadblock and seized sixty-three men. Among those taken into custody while attempting to leave Barbara's estate were New York mob heads Vito Genovese, Joe Profaci, and Joe Bonanno (leaders of the families that bore their names), and Anastasia's successor, Carlo Gambino, who would give his own name to the family. Joe Ida, boss of Philadelphia, was also pulled in. Others who got away or were late arriving at the meeting included the fifth New York City boss Tommy Lucchese, Stefano Maggadino, and Joe Zerilli of Detroit.

Among the notable absentees from Apalachin were the mobs' financial guru, Meyer Lansky, and Carlos Marcello of New Orleans, both close allies of Frank Costello. Because of that some people believed that the police raid had been inspired by Lansky in order to embarrass Genovese and other leaders. However, it actually arose from a local situation where the state troopers had been wiretapping Joe

Barbara's calls. When they learned about the planned gathering, they decided to have a look at it.

The fallout from Apalachin was tremendous. The FBI was particularly embarrassed that a meeting of the top mobsters in the country was being held and they knew nothing about it.[2] All over the United States officials who had denied there was a national Mafia were red-faced—no one more so than J. Edgar Hoover. Those, like Anslinger, or Virgil Peterson of the Chicago Crime Commission who had argued that the Mafia was real, were dancing with joy. Given the crisis nature of the situation, Hoover had to make some movement against the mobs. He expanded the number of organized crime investigators in various cities but they were still far too little. For example, in Chicago a list of the top ten mobsters (including some who didn't belong there and omitting others who did) was compiled and one FBI agent was assigned to each man. Five or ten per subject would have been a more realistic allotment. Hoover also ordered a top official of his security intelligence section to examine whether an organization such as the Mafia actually existed. After reading 200 books and numerous reports the official had a breakdown. However, he decided that in fact the Mafia did exist. Hoover printed up twenty-five numbered copies of the report and circulated them to a handful of people. Before the end of the decade, though, he began to cut back on the size of the organized crime squads and he withdrew from circulation the report on the Mafia that his agents had compiled.

Under the Eisenhower administration only three major mob prosecutions took place. None of them was an FBI-initiated case. A special prosecutor appointed by the Department of Justice secured indictments against twenty-seven of the men arrested at Apalachin on charges that they conspired to conceal the purposes of the meeting. Twenty were convicted and sentenced to prison for terms of three to five years. However, the United States Court of Appeals threw their convictions out because there were no laws covering such a meeting and no evidence produced that any existing laws had been broken.

---

2. Both the Buffalo and Albany field offices of the Bureau produced maps showing that Apalachin was in the other's territory.

The second case was made by the Federal Bureau of Narcotics against Vito Genovese. A New York drug dealer named Nelson Cantellops claimed that he had been present during meetings between Genovese and other top figures when they discussed drug trafficking. In 1958, Vito and twenty-three of his gang were indicted. Observers thought that the case, which relied on a single informant, would never hold up. But Cantellops underwent four weeks of questioning by teams of skilled defense lawyers without changing his story and, to everyone's surprise, the defendants were found guilty.

The Genovese drug conviction was always regarded in the same way as Dewey's 1936 prosecution of Lucky Luciano for running a vice ring. Back then the witnesses' stories were highly suspect. Prostitutes claimed they had sat in Lucky's suite at the Waldorf while the boss discussed his operations with lieutenants. In the Genovese case NYPD's top Mafia-fighting detective, Ralph Salerno, declared, "To anyone who understands the protocol and insulation procedures of [the mob] this testimony is almost unbelievable." Whatever the quality of evidence, like the 1936 case, the Genovese conviction removed the top organized crime boss in the city from circulation on a permanent basis. Some believe that Cantellops may have been persuaded to lie by Carlo Gambino and Tommy Lucchese because they feared Genovese was planning to hit them.

In Chicago a private attorney named Richard Ogilvie, who had been appointed to head the midwest office of the Department of Justice's organized crime section, prepared a tax case against Accardo. Tony, who claimed to be a beer salesman, reported an income of $60,000 a year. An investigation disclosed that he was not actually peddling beer. The arrangement was made to provide him with a legitimate income so he could pay taxes and avoid a federal net worth prosecution for not declaring his mob earnings. However, he had taken a $3,000 deduction for the use of his car and since he was not actually selling beer, the deduction was not legitimate, so he was indicted for filing a false tax report. It was a minor charge, but it was all the government could come up with. He was convicted and sentenced to six years in prison, though he remained free while he appealed the verdict. The Circuit Court of Appeals threw out the conviction and ordered a new trial, where he was acquitted. In 1962, when Ogilvie was elected sheriff of Cook County, he chose as his chief investigator Richard Cain (né Scalzitti) a Chicago police detective who doubled as a hit man for Sam Giancana. During Ogilvie's term, Cain was convicted of arranging the burglary of a pharmaceutical warehouse and sent to prison. In 1968, the voters elected Ogilvie governor. The whole Ogilvie relationship with Cain did a great deal to increase the cynicism of police and federal agents. How could a supposed reformer pick a well-known mob hit man to be his chief investigator? How could the voters pick someone so naïve or worse to be governor?[3]

*

The most serious effort against organized crime in the 1950s came about indirectly from a United States Senate probe of the International Brotherhood of Teamsters (IBT). In 1957, a committee headed by John McClellan of Arkansas began an investigation. Its eight members included John F. Kennedy of Massachusetts, at the time still serving his first term in the Senate. It was no secret that Kennedy's father, Wall Street tycoon Joseph, Sr., was planning to make Jack the president. At the 1956 convention that nominated Adlai Stevenson to run in a rematch against Eisenhower, Jack Kennedy was almost nominated for VP, losing out in a close vote to Sen. Kefauver. The defeat was actually a plus for Kennedy because the Democratic ticket had no chance.

Joe Kennedy did not like the idea of Jack serving on a committee that would offend unions. His other son, Robert ("Bobby," or his personal preference, "Bob"), who was named committee counsel, realized it was a very good opportunity to score points with the Southern wing of the party, particularly since Jack's Catholicism posed a barrier to him receiving support from that region of the country when he ran for president. Bobby reasoned that without the (then) Democratic solid South, Jack could never be elected president of the United States and that, by focusing on the Teamsters, the probe would boost Jack's standing with conservative Democrats. In addition it could steer the

---

3. During the 1962 sheriff's race, Ogilvie's Democratic opponent was Roswell Spencer, who had headed a squad of FBI agents investigating organized crime in Chicago. Shortly before the election the word was passed by the mob that Ogilvie was their choice.

investigation away from liberal labor unions like Walter Reuther's United Autoworkers (UAW), who, though not involved with the Mafia, were prone to using violent methods in labor disputes.

During the hearings, Bobby Kennedy continually clashed with Jimmy Hoffa, vice president of the IBT in charge of Midwestern operations and soon to be president of the union. Hoffa was a strange figure on the mid-20th century landscape. Though uneducated, he was able to hold his own in a battle of wits with Harvard graduates like the Kennedy brothers. Only a shade over five feet five, he was a veteran of many vicious battles connected with strikes and labor organizing. Even when his life was threatened, unlike many labor leaders who were always surrounded by armed escorts, Hoffa never carried a gun or used a personal bodyguard. Despite the fact that he had never driven a truck but had only been a freight handler, the "knights of the road" (as drivers were portrayed on screen by Humphrey Bogart, George Raft, and Jimmy Cagney) always gave him their loyalty. While some labor leaders such as Walter Reuther sought out the friendship of the president of the United States and were delighted to be invited to attend seminars at Brookings and other upscale think tanks, Hoffa had never had intellectual pretensions. In 1935 the 22-year-old Hoffa had been made business agent for Detroit Teamsters local 299. He, who reveled in physical confrontation, was useful to the union in its organizing drives. In the 1930s it was common for Detroit employers, like the Ford Motor Company, to employ Mafia goons to break strikes. However, Hoffa persuaded mobsters to remain neutral by cutting a deal to provide tips on where valuable merchandise could be found by hijackers or by leaving trucks unattended, thereby giving thieves a chance to loot the cargos. Jimmy came to the attention of national IBT president Dan Tobin when he was part of a team sent in to battle a dissident Trotskyite Teamster union in Minneapolis. Tobin was a favorite in FDR's White House and to accommodate him the Department of Justice indicted the Minneapolis Teamster leaders for violation of the sedition laws. Their conviction and imprisonment helped pave the way for Hoffa's rise.

In 1949 Hoffa cut a deal with Chicago mobsters like Paul "Red" Dorfman and Joey Glimco to win their support for Teamster organizing drives there and in other parts of the Midwest. In return, he allowed the gangsters to steal from the local Teamsters' funds and to go easy on employers who paid off the mob. Hoffa then began making inroads in the South. Next, he carried out a campaign to take over the east where there was no powerful regional leader, only a number of separate unions, many of them controlled by Mafia figures. His ultimate goal was to become president of the Teamsters International. In New York he enlisted the support of Anthony "Ducks" Corallo and Johnny Dioguardi, capos in the Lucchese crime family. In New Jersey, he made an ally of Tony Provenzano, a capo in the Genovese family, and head of a powerful Teamsters local.

The Senate committee's hearings documented mob influence in the Teamsters and brought to national attention that a new and more powerful vehicle was available for Mafia exploitation than the big city political machines. The mob now played a big role in a union that by calling a nationwide trucking strike could paralyze the economy.

The hearings illustrated that Hoffa and the IBT had powerful friends among the Republicans. Dan Tobin's successor as Teamster head, Dave Beck of the West Coast, had switched the union affiliation to the Republican Party. GOP members of the investigating committee, such as Karl Mundt of South Dakota and Barry Goldwater of Arizona, constantly favored the IBT, throwing softball questions to Hoffa and seeking to rein in committee counsel Robert Kennedy. During an earlier probe of the IBT led by a Kansas Republican congressman, Hoffa had retained the services of a former Kansas Republican governor. Shortly afterwards the investigation was quietly dropped. Another IBT ally was Senator George Bender, a Republican from Ohio. As a congressman Bender had opened an investigation into the IBT. He started out by blasting the Teamsters, but when they agreed to support him in his (successful) race to fill a Senate vacancy, he shut down the hearing. After his Senate service, Hoffa placed Bender on the IBT payroll at $5,000 a month (in 1950s dollars) to investigate corruption. His principal activity consisted of sending form letters to every Teamster local asking if they had a corruption problem. Not surprisingly, none replied in the affirmative. Bender later told the Senate he had not uncovered a single instance of racketeering. By the beginning of 1960, the Republican Department of Justice had prepared an indictment against Jimmy Hoffa for racketeering activities in the Teamsters union. However, the GOP candidate for the presidency, Vice President Richard Nixon, used his influence to have the indictment withheld. Not until after the election was it released.

After the committee hearings, Hoffa consolidated his power within the Teamsters and when Dave Beck was convicted of committing crimes, Hoffa assumed the presidency of the IBT. The Kennedys, basking in the good publicity and the legends created by their PR people, opened their campaign for the presidential nomination. In the 1960 general election Hoffa's IBT was one of the few unions to back Nixon.

*

The Kennedy patriarch, Joseph, Sr., took charge of his son's campaign. He had risen from being the son of Pat Kennedy, a Boston Ward boss, to son-in-law to the city's mayor, John "Honey Fitz" Fitzgerald. Then he made the big leap to become a major Wall Street financier. His career was not without rough spots. While proud of his family and his Catholic religion, he was a notorious womanizer, who maintained a long-term relationship with movie siren Gloria Swanson. During Prohibition he was engaged in illegal liquor trafficking. As a result he rubbed elbows with gangsters. Frank Costello would always claim that Kennedy was heavily involved in organized crime. Some mobsters referred to him as "Meyer Lansky with a Harvard degree." In 1938 FDR appointed Joe ambassador to Britain. There, he was regarded by the host government as sympathetic to the Nazis. In 1940 he advised President Roosevelt that Britain would lose the war and the United States should make the best of the situation. Kennedy's eldest son, Joseph, Jr., who had been groomed by his father for the presidency, was killed while serving as a navy pilot. So his brother Jack inherited the duty of fulfilling his father's hopes, though he himself had been badly injured while serving as a PT boat skipper, and was in delicate health. With his father's money and political influence behind him, Jack had advanced from a congressman to United States senator.

Joe Kennedy was an astute political operative, but during the 1960s primaries he made a major mistake: he enlisted the support of Frank Sinatra, who was well known to be closely associated with Mafia figures. Frank's mob contacts ranged from New York to California, and with his "Rat Pack" buddies, like Dean Martin and Sammy Davis, he practically owned Las Vegas. Another Rat Packer was movie actor Peter Lawford, Joe Kennedy's son-in-law.

It was Sinatra who persuaded Atlantic City gambler and convicted white slaver, Paul "Skinny" D'Amato, to use his influence with West Virginia sheriffs, who were powerful figures in the state, on behalf of Kennedy's campaign. Sheriffs who visited Skinny's nightclub in Atlantic City were always comped for food, liquor, and ladies. With "Skinny's" political clout and Joe's money, Jack carried heavily Protestant West Virginia, causing his rival, Senator Hubert Humphrey, to drop out of the race

Joe also sought to ensure that the Chicago mob would not knife Jack at the polls. So he had Sinatra approach mob boss Sam Giancana. Sinatra supposedly assured Giancana that Kennedy's election would not see any stepped-up activity against organized crime—in fact it would be just the opposite. Though Joe Kennedy, owner of the huge Merchandise Mart in Chicago, had installed another son-in-law, Robert Sargent Shriver, to head it, he did not understand Illinois politics circa 1960. Mayor Daley was a strong supporter of Jack Kennedy and a more powerful figure locally than Sam Giancana.

Unlike most party bosses, Dick Daley had a first-class brain and, though a lawyer, his forte was financial management. Under Governor Adlai Stevenson he had been the director of revenue for the state, a post where incoming dollars often stuck to the hands of the man who was director. No such charge was ever made against Daley. Chicago executives who dealt with the mayor on financial matters found him their equal in knowledge and some averred that he could easily have been chief financial officer of a major corporation. Where Kelly frequently faced revolts from fellow Ward bosses, Daley never did. None of them ever thought of themselves as equal, much less superior, to the mayor. It was inconceivable that they would ever try to oust Daley as they did Kelly.

If Sam Giancana had attempted to intervene against Kennedy in the 1960 election, he would have faced opposition within the mob by leaders who feared retaliation from Daley. Ward politicians of the Westside bloc who did not deliver votes to Kennedy would have been fired from their government jobs and stripped of patronage. If necessary the police department would have pulled out all stops to ensure that the mob did not interfere with the election. As far back as the 1920s Al Capone's brother was shot dead by a squad of Chicago detectives during one Election Day struggle. In another incident, one of Capone's top lieutenants was shot and killed in the backseat of a squad car while in police custody. As long as the Kennedy forces had Mayor Daley on their side, there was no need to placate Giancana.[4] All that Sinatra's sit down with him ultimately produced was a bitter feeling by Sam that he had been double crossed by the Kennedy patriarch, a man whose hands he believed were no cleaner than his own.

Since the Kefauver investigation it was obvious that the national Mafia could never be defeated except by a president who carried out a full-fledged anti-gangster campaign. This would require the appointment of an attorney general who was strong enough to run the program, and if necessary to bring J. Edgar Hoover to heel. President Kennedy's appointment of his thirty-four-year-old brother Robert to be attorney general shocked even the Democrats. Bobby (or "Booby" as Jimmy Hoffa referred to him), had never tried a case, yet he was going to direct the largest law firm in the world. Jack managed to defuse some of the criticism by quipping, "I just wanted to give him a little legal practice before he becomes a lawyer." As attorney general, Robert Kennedy immediately began an all-out drive against mobsters using whatever means were available. Joey Aiuppa of Chicago was jailed for shooting migratory birds. Carlos Marcello of New Orleans,

---

4. There were always limitations on both sides in the relationship between the political machine and the gangsters. The Mafia could not dictate to the county committee whom to endorse for president. During Kelly's time, it did have influence on nominations for state and local offices. Under Daley the balance tilted back in favor of the machine. For example, Daley would never have put somebody like Dan Gilbert on the county ticket. Instead, he selected a candidate for sheriff who was a well-known criminologist and professorial lecturer at the University of Chicago. Unfortunately, in office, the man proved more disastrous than Gilbert. He charged a suspect with a double murder, although Chicago detectives (including the writer) who were also working the case, saw no real evidence against the man. The sheriff ignored their views. Within forty-eight hours the state's attorney dropped all charges. The attempt to, in effect, frame an innocent man only increased the belief of many police officials that there was nothing of value that could be learned in a classroom and that if anybody needed their ethics improved, it was the academic sheriff.

Albert Anastasia. "Lord High Executioner" of New York's Murder Incorporated, a group of contract killers available to carry out hits.

The dead body of Abe "Kid Twist" Reles. A key witness in the Murder Incorporated case, he was pushed or jumped out of the window of a hotel where he was being held under police guard.

Brooklyn District Attorney William O'Dwyer. After receiving the blessing of New York's top mob boss, Frank Costello, O'Dwyer was elected mayor.

FBI Director J Edgar Hoover receives the National
Security Medal from President Dwight Eisenhower
on May 27, 1955, as Vice President Richard Nixon and
others look on.

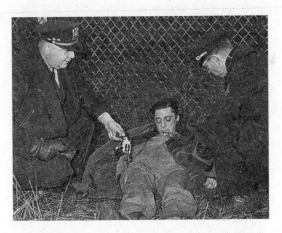

The body of Frank Nitti, Al Capone's successor as boss
of the Chicago Mafia. In 1943, when he was indicted
with his lieutenants for extorting money from Hollywood,
Nitti shot himself.

Missouri Senator Harry Truman *(left)* and Kansas City political boss Tom Pendergast *(wearing hat)*. Truman remained loyal to him even after Pendergast was sent to federal prison.

Kansas City Mafia boss Johnny Lazia
(left) and his enforcer, Charles Gargotta.
Lazia, like Truman, was one of Boss
Pendergast's principal lieutenants.

The Kansas City Union Station Massacre. In 1933 gangsters killed
four lawmen, including an FBI agent, in an unsuccessful attempt
to free a prisoner from their custody.

Frank "I am the law" Hague, czar of New Jersey,
shaking hands with President Franklin Roosevelt.

Robert Hannegan, Democratic national chairman, presiding over the 1944 party convention where
he played a key role in securing the vice presidential nomination for Truman.

Sidney Hillman *(left)*, head of the CIO political action committee, with Philip Murray and John L. Lewis *(right)*. President Roosevelt told aides to "Clear it [Truman's nomination] with Sidney."

Vice President Truman (left) and Mayor Ed Kelly of Chicago *(center)* in 1945. Kelly, boss of the Democratic Party in Illinois, played a major role in securing the nomination for Truman.

Anthony "Tony" Accardo. After the bosses of the Chicago mob were imprisoned for extorting Hollywood, Accardo took over the leadership.

Charles Gargotta. When Gargotta was shot to death in Kansas City, photographs of his body, lying under a picture of President Truman, appeared in newspapers all over the country.

Frank Costello *(standing, right)*, Prime Minister of the New York Mafia, looks wary as he prepares to submit to questioning by a Senate Committee. Chairman Estes Kefauver is seated at left.

President John F. Kennedy with Frank Sinatra at the 1961 Inaugural Ball. The President's father, Joe Kennedy, made the mistake of asking Sinatra to enlist mob support for Jack's presidential bid.

Sam Giancana, boss of the Chicago Mafia, who had supported JFK for president, was furious at being a prime target of the Kennedys' federal drive against organized crime.

Judith Campbell Exner, pictured with her husband, actor William Campbell, was the girlfriend of Sam Giancana and President John F. Kennedy at the same time.

Jimmy Hoffa *(wearing raincoat)*, president of the International Brotherhood of Teamsters, entering the federal prison at Lewisburg, Pennsylvania, in 1967 to begin serving a 13-year sentence.

President Richard Nixon *(right)* with Frank Fitzsimmons, acting head of the IBT. Nixon's Justice Department paroled Hoffa under terms that permitted Fitzsimmons to continue in office.

Jackie Presser at a union convention. Presser was simultaneously a corrupt president of the IBT, close ally of the Mafia, top-level FBI informant, and a favorite of President Reagan.

Louis "Lepke" Buchalter. A key figure in Murder Incorporated. Eventually he went to the electric chair rather than reveal information about President Roosevelt's favorite labor leader, Sidney Hillman.

Paris Riot, 1934. After the French public believed that swindler Serge Stavisky was murdered to cover up political corruption, mobs attempted to storm the Parliament building.

Sir Basil Zaharoff, the mystery man of Europe. Over several decades he manipulated governments of various countries. Here he is in a British dress uniform about to become a knight.

who was not a U.S. citizen, was forcibly seized by federal officers while making a quarterly visit to the local U.S. immigration office. The agents arrested him, handcuffed him, and took him to a border patrol airplane that flew him to Guatemala and dropped him off. There, local officials escorted him to a village just over the border in El Salvador, where he was arrested by soldiers. After five days in custody he was released— still clad in a silk suit and alligator shoes—in a remote mountain area of Honduras. Marcello walked seventeen miles to the nearest village and during his journey fell several times, breaking two ribs. He would later claim that some of the locals seem to be getting ready to rob or kill him. Finally, he was picked up by a military plane provided by Dominican Republic dictator Rafael Trujillo, and eventually arrived in Miami—where he was arrested for illegal entry into the United States.

Kennedy appointed a "Get Hoffa" squad under the direction of Walter Sheridan, an ex-FBI agent and former chief investigator for the McClellan committee. Sheridan, a non-lawyer, was put in charge of a staff of twenty attorneys who were supplemented by thirty investigators, including FBI agents. Soon, thirteen grand juries across the country were busy scrutinizing the Teamsters union and its leaders. When the suppressed federal indictment against Jimmy Hoffa was returned, just before Robert Kennedy took office, he jumped on it. The gist of the charges was that Hoffa and another union official had incorporated a truck-leasing corporation in their wives' names and over the years the firm, Test Fleet, had received money from a Detroit car hauling company that employed union drivers. Under the Landrum-Griffin Act, union officers were forbidden to accept money from employers they were negotiating with. Next, some of Jimmy's associates were indicted in Chicago on charges of making fraudulent loans from the Central States Pension Fund.

*

Bobby Kennedy made a major mistake by treating J. Edgar Hoover as a lackey. Hoover had been friendly with Joe Kennedy, Sr., and during the Roosevelt administration the FBI did virtually anything the president had asked it to do. Had the Kennedys flattered Hoover and given him the credit for results against the mob, the old director might have gone along with the program. However, with the arrogance or inexperience of youth, Bobby ignored advice from the older generation. When House Speaker Sam Rayburn proposed Sarah Hughes to be appointed a federal judge in Texas, Bobby Kennedy turned her down because she was "too old," prompting Rayburn to remark, "Everybody looks too old to you, sonny." President Kennedy needed "Mr. Sam's" support, so he made the appointment.[5]

The Kennedys might also have benefited from Hoover's advice in personal affairs. He would have certainly kept them away from relying on gangsters like Giancana and the Sinatra-Marilyn Monroe crowd. Joe Kennedy, Sr., suffered a stroke just before Jack was inaugurated so he was not available to counsel his sons. If he had been in good health he might have been able to improve the relationship with Hoover. Instead, Robert Kennedy treated Hoover in a peremptory manner, circumventing the FBI chain of command when he wanted to get information from subordinates. He even compelled Hoover to put a phone from the attorney general's office on his desk and answer it personally when Kennedy called.

The Kennedys were always prone to place themselves in harm's way. Volumes have been written trying to explain the behavior of various members of the family. Perhaps it is simply that many rich and privileged people do not believe that laws or rules of conduct apply to them. Through Sinatra John Kennedy had been introduced to a woman named Judith Campbell (later Judith Campbell Exner), ex-wife of a minor Hollywood star, with whom he quickly developed a close relationship. In his first year in office she made seventy phone calls to the White House. At the same time she was carrying on with, of all people, Sam Giancana. Naturally, Hoover learned about it. After the Kennedy fiasco at the Bay of Pigs, Robert Kennedy apparently did not have enough to do as attorney general, so he took charge of eliminating Fidel Castro as head of the Cuban government. His agents began lining up mafiosos with Cuban connections who would hit Castro. This too involved members of Sam Giancana's circle, such as

---

5. It was Judge Hughes who swore in Lyndon Johnson in Dallas after President Kennedy's assassination.

Johnny Roselli, the Mafia's man in Hollywood and Las Vegas.[6] Naturally, the plot became known to Hoover and provided him with the leverage to exert influence over the president and the attorney general. He could embarrass the president by citing his relationship with a gangster's girlfriend and revealing Bobby's role in a plot to kill the head of another country. Instead of leaking information to the press or Congress, Hoover went to the Kennedys and informed them that his agents had picked up the various pieces of information. One result of this was that he obtained the written authorization of Attorney General Kennedy to tap the phones of civil rights leader Martin Luther King.[7] Although when it was eventually revealed, Robert Kennedy would claim it was just to show Hoover that King was not influenced by Communists. It is more likely that he feared that if Hoover's request was rejected, knowledge of the Campbell and Castro affairs might get out.

Bobby Kennedy's constant spurring on of the troops and making direct contact with subordinate FBI agents led to other embarrassments. In 1963, on the orders of the attorney general, the Chicago FBI office set up a lockstep surveillance of Giancana. When Sam was chauffeured around town, an FBI car kept on his tail, and on the golf course a foursome of G-men would tee off right after his party. It was a silly harassment, likely to lead to a judicial decision limiting surveillance efforts. When Sam sued, and the local special agent in charge of the Chicago office was called to testify, Kennedy ordered him not to

---

6. Allegedly Bobby Kennedy was not immediately aware that those in the U.S. government trying to remove Castro were using Chicago gangsters and, when he learned about it, he was supposedly furious. That the attorney general of the United States, who was directing the operation, did not know about the Chicago mob involvements was either an example of how badly the anti-Castro efforts were managed or a case of a high official employing plausible deniability for the dirty work carried on by his subordinates.

7. Electronic eavesdropping—or in FBI jargon, ELSURs (electronic surveillance)—was a controversial subject. Wiretapping of phones had been outlawed by the 1934 Telecommunications Act. Planting a bug usually required trespassing onto private property, and the Supreme Court had declared that unlawful. However, the FBI had been permitted, in certain circumstances, such as national security investigations, to do both, although the fruits of such efforts had to be kept in-house and could not be used as courtroom evidence. Agents involved in wiretapping the mob were ordered not to carry credentials. They were forbidden to tell anyone, including the police, that they were FBI men; if they got caught, the Bureau would disavow them. They were also open to prosecution under state law, and could even be shot as burglars. The administration should either have gotten the laws changed or stopped flaunting them. Instead, they gave orders to FBI agents to break the law, which set a bad example and would eventually come back to haunt the government. With Southern Democrats and Northern Republicans effectively in control of the Congress, it should not have been hard to change the law. Given the president's power of appointment, had JFK not been killed, he could have created a majority of justices sympathetic to national security concerns.

answer questions. As a result, the SAC was held in contempt and fined $500. This made Hoover furious. In addition, the federal prosecutor in Chicago was unable to respond adequately to Giancana's lawsuit, for fear that during court proceedings Sam might blurt out what he knew about the plot against Castro and the president's relationship with Judith Campbell. Giancana obtained a federal court order requiring the FBI tails to remain several cars and several foursomes behind the gangsters.

On November 22, 1963, the Kennedy dynasty, as people were already calling it, came tumbling down. The president was shot and killed while traveling in a motorcade in Dallas, Texas. The incident would become the greatest murder mystery in American history and remain so up to the present.[8]

The assassination brought to an end Bobby Kennedy's influence and eventually he resigned in order to run, successfully, for U.S. senator from New York. Before leaving he had the satisfaction of seeing Jimmy Hoffa convicted of jury tampering and loan fraud. Hoffa was sentenced to eight years on the former charge and five years on the latter, for a total of thirteen. Sam Giancana was eventually jailed on a contempt of court charge for refusing to answer questions posed to him by a grand jury after he was given immunity. He was held in jail for nine months until the grand jury session ended. The Chicago mob, tired of his antics and the federal pressure he had brought down on all of them, passed word through Tony Accardo that Giancana should step down. So in 1966 he and his pal, ex-Chicago cop Dick Cain, went off to Mexico for an extended stay.

*

Lyndon Johnson, like Truman, was an accidental president who reached the office because of the death of the elected president. In Truman's case he was too inconsequential to have ever become president on his own. LBJ had been a powerful majority leader of the United States Senate and was a candidate for the presidential nomina-

---

8. For a further discussion of the Kennedy assassination, see Appendix III, 11-22-63: The Shadow of Murder Over the White House.

tion in 1960, though it is doubtful that even a deadlocked convention would have turned to him. As Teddy White observed in his book, *The Making of the President 1960,* Johnson was too Southern—too "cornball"—in his manner and speech to attract northern voters. Texas was also a segregated state, and that fact alone might have cost him support, particularly among liberal and black voters. In 1960, the country had not elected a southern president for over 100 years.[9]

In office Johnson vigorously pushed civil rights measures, which, as a Texas senator, he had not generally supported. The son of a small landowner, Johnson acquired great wealth in his career though he never held other than political jobs that paid modest salaries. When pressed, he would explain his wealth as coming from his wife Claudia "Lady Bird" Taylor's family, and wise investments over the years.

During his career, Johnson was accused of various improprieties, including stealing the 1948 primary election for senator from Texas. Supposedly, he managed to defeat his opponent by eighty-seven votes—and then go on to win the general election which sent him to the United States Senate. Yet many accounts picture him as having obtained fraudulent votes. After the lead changed hands several times, he was finally provided with the winning margin by corrupt political bosses in some south Texas counties.

Johnson was close to three individuals who either were sent to prison or had to resign their position over charges of impropriety. The first was his protégé, the Senate majority secretary, Bobby Baker. In 1963, when Johnson was vice president, Baker was jailed for obtaining defense contracts for people who had done business with a private firm that he ran. Another close ally in the 1950s had been Billy Sol Estes, who in 1963 was tried for various commercial frauds and was sentenced to twenty-four years in prison; he served eight years. At the time, many Washington observers believed Jack Kennedy was going to use the Baker and Estes scandals to remove Johnson from the 1964

9. Woodrow Wilson was born and raised in Virginia but his career was made in the North, notably as a professor and president of Princeton University and governor of New Jersey. At the 1912 Democratic convention, where he was nominated for president, many Southern delegates initially supported Oscar Underwood of Alabama or James "Champ" Clark of Missouri.

ticket. In addition, prosecutors might very well have brought criminal charges against him.[10]

Another of Johnson's close confidant's was Supreme Court justice Abe Fortas, who had represented him in the ballot fraud case in Texas. Fortas had been one of those "starry-eyed New Dealers" who had come to Washington in the 1930s to do good and stayed to do well. Their knowledge of the bureaucracy and their inside contacts made them ideal to represent corporate interests in the capital. Often, they became the biggest fixers in Washington. Fortas was a name partner in one of D.C.'s most powerful law firms.[11]

Johnson persuaded Supreme Court justice Arthur Goldberg, who held the "Jewish seat" on the court, to resign by painting a picture whereby he would become ambassador to the United Nations, make peace in Vietnam, and then move on to the White House himself. How a slick lawyer like Goldberg, whose career had been made as counsel to the United Steelworkers Union in Chicago, fell for that is hard to explain. With the "Jewish seat" open, Fortas was nominated to fill it. As a Supreme Court justice he continued to sit in on, even chair, White House policy meetings. The president's plan to make him chief justice failed when it was revealed that Fortas had taken a huge fee from private interests for delivering an academic lecture. Next it was learned that he had agreed to accept a lifetime annuity from an individual who was facing securities fraud charges and was hoping to get a presidential pardon. To avoid impeachment, Fortas was forced to resign. As a mark of his disgrace, the powerful Washington law firm, where he had once been a major figure, refused to accept him back.

Johnson himself moved to quickly dismantle anti-organized crime programs and later actively blocked efforts to combat the mobs. One

---

10. For a discussion of theories about the Kennedy assassination, including some that attribute it to LBJ's fear of dismissal and disgrace, see Appendix III, 11-22-63: The Shadow of Murder Over the White House.
11. One of the most annoying things about such people as Fortas was that their offices were full of pictures from their New Deal days and they made sure to tell everybody what great heroes they had been. When a government agency was making things difficult for some fat cat, the old New Dealers would casually remind the federal investigators that they had powerful friends, including the head of the agency that the investigator represented. Sometimes they would drop hints that if the young official played ball, after he left government he might have a job in their offices. If none of those ploys was successful, they would call the agency head and complain about the "smart young punk" who had been in to talk to them. Frequently, the agency head was a fellow fixer who was temporarily in government service. From a historical perspective it would be useful to determine how many of these "starry-eyed New Dealers" went to Washington during the Depression because they badly needed a job, whereas in normal times would have been working on Wall Street or some similar place.

reason for his hostility toward a federal probe of organized crime was that it could hurt the Democrats and thereby damage Johnson himself. Another reason was that it was a signature issue of Bobby Kennedy's, whom Johnson hated and feared. He rightly suspected that in 1968 Kennedy was likely to oppose him for the Democratic presidential nomination.

During the months that Kennedy continued as Johnson's attorney general, J. Edgar Hoover was able to deal directly with the White House and ignore Bobby's orders. G. Robert Blakey, one of Kennedy's mob prosecutors, who would later become the country's top organized crime expert, has related how the Department of Justice quickly reverted to its "lackadaisical pre-Kennedy days" and cut back on significant portions of the government's anti-mob drive. In 1965, Edward Bennett Williams sued the FBI over electronic eavesdropping in Las Vegas. When he won his case Johnson ordered the practice to stop and across the country bugs were turned off. It is not clear that the administration had to abandon electronic surveillance. It could have argued that the activities of the Mafia constituted a clear and present danger to national security, citing, for example, the Teamsters ability to paralyze transportation. By 1965 the American Mafia was far more of a threat to the United States than some old line Communists. Another justification for the eavesdropping might have been to determine whether the Mafia had any role in the assassination of the president. Certainly that would have constituted a national security matter. Sitting justices of the Supreme Court Tom Clark and Byron White had been attorney general and deputy attorney general of the United States, respectively, and as such they had authorized eavesdropping in national security investigations. Thus the Supreme Court might well have upheld the practice. But not even a halfhearted attempt to save the bugs was made. Years later the FBI would admit to Congress that after the departure of the Kennedys, "the steam went out of the drive against organized crime."

Following the 1964 election, when Barry Goldwater had scored points against Johnson by protesting about crime in the streets, the president decided to appoint a commission to investigate crime and criminal justice. The purpose was to defuse the issue so that it would not be harmful in 1968 when Johnson planned to run for another term. He appointed a number of leading figures, making sure that it included men who would see that the commission did not criticize his administration. The chairman was Attorney General Nicholas Katzenbach and another member was Johnson's close confidant, Texas lawyer Leon Jaworski. The commission formed task forces to investigate police, courts, corrections, juvenile delinquency, narcotics, and alcoholism. It did not create one on organized crime. Johnson had seen the harm that the Kefauver committee had caused to the Democratic Party and to some of its leaders and he had no intention of repeating that mistake. However, eighteen months into the commissions hearings, under pressure from the commission's deputy director, Henry Ruth, a Philadelphia lawyer, and commission member Lewis Powell, president of the American Bar Association and later associate justice of the United States Supreme Court, Johnson provided a mere $30,000 for a task force to look into the subject. It was headed by Charles Rogovin, who had been chief assistant district attorney of Philadelphia. There he had approached the local mob problem in an innovative way. Instead of proceeding on a case-by-case basis, he installed a staff of detectives in a location away from the district attorney's office, and set them to work collecting basic intelligence.

In 1967, the commission issued an overview report supplemented by individual reports from each task force. The organized crime one recommended that the government legalize electronic eavesdropping. Everyone in the mob-fighting field realized that without it, there would never be any major cases made. Johnson's aides attempted to block the proposals from being included in the full commission report but were unsuccessful. The president then told the commission he would not accept their report because of the task force recommendations. They countered by telling him that they would notify TV networks that they were going to deliver it by throwing it over the White House fence. Finally, Johnson had to accept the report with the electronic eavesdropping in it.

The Johnson administration was a happy time for the Mafia. The president dismantled the government's anti-mobster operations and sought to block an organized crime task force from being formed. If Barry Goldwater had won in 1964 there would have been no change in the status quo either. In the 1950s, when Goldwater was rising in Arizona politics, he developed a friendship with a Phoenix man named Nelson, who was actually Willie Bioff, the small-time Chicago gangster who had been the syndicate's lead man in the Hollywood extortion case and had gone to prison for it. While there he cut a deal with the government to testify against the Chicago syndicate leaders. He spent nine and a half days on the stand being cross-examined by lawyers. When he was asked why he had lied in the previous trial and was now telling the truth, his reply was, "I'm just a no good, uncouth person." As the convicted defendants were led out of the trial in the district court, "Little New York" Campagna warned Bioff "we can wait a long time."

After his release from prison Bioff took his wife's name of Nelson and, with the $6.5 million he had saved from his illicit earnings, he went off to Phoenix, Arizona. So friendly was he with Goldwater, that when the latter would fly his plane to Las Vegas where he had an outlet for his clothing chain in a mob hotel/gambling casino, he would often invite Bioff along for the ride. Willie apparently saw another opportunity to cash in on a good thing and tried to insinuate himself into the Las Vegas scene. There he was spotted by a visiting Chicago mobster named Marshall Caifano. One day in Phoenix, when Bioff came out of his car, he noticed a device wired to the inside of the vehicle. He called his attorney and told him that the police had planted a bug on him. The attorney told him to bring it right down to his office, implying that they would hold a press conference to discredit law enforcement. Willie went back to the car and when he started the engine it exploded, killing him. By then, Goldwater was a United States Senator and he was in no doubt about who Bioff was. Still he wept at Willie's funeral.

Amidst major increases in crime, Senator McClellan's committee put through an omnibus crime control and safe streets act. Among other things it provided for the use of electronic surveillance under court authorization. Johnson did not want to sign such a bill; however, in the climate of the times he had no other choice.

In 1968, Johnson's final year in office, America was swept by a wave of political protests following the assassination of Dr. Martin

Luther King in Memphis where he had gone to aid a garbagemen's strike. In June, Robert Kennedy, who was running for president and winning a number of primaries, was shot to death in Los Angeles after topping the California Democratic presidential primary. The killer, an Arab-American who was anti-Israel, did not appear to have any mob ties.

The mantle of family leadership fell to Senator Ted Kennedy and it was assumed that he would run for president in 1972 against Richard Nixon. However, the drowning of a young woman because Kennedy drove off of a bridge on Martha's Vineyard produced such a furor that he could not make the run. He did eventually challenge President Carter in the 1980 Democratic primary, but was unsuccessful. Despite hopes for the younger generation to enter presidential politics, since 1980 the family has not offered any of its members as a candidate for the highest office. While the public still spends a great deal of time digesting the troubles of the Kennedy family, it is not because of their political primacy but because the soap opera quality of their lives keeps them in the spotlight.

Lyndon Johnson, who served twice as long in the White House as Jack Kennedy, and had some solid legislative accomplishments to boast of, was ruined by the Vietnam War. As the bitterness from Vietnam fades from American life, he is currently benefiting from the rewriting of history, which awards him great credit for passing civil rights legislation; however, his conversion came after he no longer had to face the Texas voters. Though he was stubborn enough to pursue an unpopular war that eventually brought down his party, he did not opt to wage what might have been a popular war against organized crime. For the second time in a generation, an accidental president had served the interests of the American Mafia. The assassination of Kennedy in 1963 literally killed the opportunity for an American president to lead a real fight on the mob. It now fell to others below White House level to carry out JFK's task

Chapter 9

Fatal Attraction I:
President Nixon and the Hoffa Wars

G. Robert Blakey was a North Carolina Protestant who enrolled in the most famous Catholic college in America, Notre Dame. The school maintained high academic standards, but its fame came from its legendary football teams which regularly contended for and frequently won a national championship. Blakey would spend seven years on the South Bend campus earning a bachelor's and a law degree. He then went off to the Department of Justice where he was assigned to the organized crime and racketeering section. When Attorney General Kennedy took over the DOJ, Blakey became one of his key aides in the war on the Mafia.

After the assassination of President John Kennedy and the departure of Attorney General Bobby, Blakey witnessed the return of the Department of Justice to "its old lackadaisical ways" in dealing with the mobs. Eventually he became a staff member of the organized crime task force that President Johnson did not want as part of his national commission.

Blakey recognized the basic defect of the federal government's efforts against the Mafia. Cops and prosecutors were employing the same tactics used against regular criminals: charge individuals with the specific crimes they were alleged to have committed. Even when successful it did nothing to combat criminal enterprises. The challenge was to find a way to take down the leadership of an entire Mafia family until the organization itself was destroyed or reduced to the status of a local street gang. Under the old system, if the lawmen got convictions against individuals, their organizations would go on. In the past, when Capone was sent to prison, Frank Nitti built a more powerful crime syndicate. In New York, after Dewey sent Lucky Luciano and some of his lieutenants to the penitentiary, Frank Costello took over and the family became even stronger. In 1970, while working as counsel to Senator McClellan's investigating committee, Blakey drafted a Racketeer Influenced Corrupt Organizations (RICO) law which made it illegal to participate in an organization or enterprise involved in a pattern of racketeering. Under RICO a pattern could comprise as few as two of thirty-four common state and federal crimes committed within a ten-year period. An individual defendant could be convicted of both the RICO violation and conspiracy with a twenty-year maximum for each offense, and a life sentence if a murder was involved.

In 1972, Blakey attempted to sell RICO to the staff of the United States Attorney for the Southern District of New York. Not only was it the most important federal prosecutorial office in America—under Bobby Kennedy's favorite prosecutor, Robert Morgenthau—it had secured half of the DOJ's organized crime convictions. If the Southern District were able to win a RICO case, the rest of the country would follow suit. However, Morgenthau was no longer in office. The Nixon administration had replaced him with Whitney North Seymour, Jr., formerly a New York State senator from the "silk stocking" district. In a race for a congressional seat, Seymour had come over as pompous, while his opponent, Ed Koch, later mayor of New York City, appeared a feisty and funny regular guy. As Koch would write "I creamed him." Blakey would later relate to journalist Selwyn Raab that when he tried to explain RICO, Seymour terminated the meeting, calling it a waste of time and ordered him to leave the room. Despite his humiliation and rebuff, Blakey continued to push for the use of RICO from his position as a professor at Cornell Law School where he established an organized crime institute. There he began to train federal agents and prosecutors in how to employ the statute, though after the setback in the Southern District, it would take nearly a decade for the law to bear fruit.

*

In January 1969, when Richard Nixon became president, there were few Republican administrations in cities where the Mafia flourished. So a Department of Justice attack on organized crime would not have upset local apple carts the way Kefauver and Bobby Kennedy had done to members of their own party in places like New York and Chicago. When he was in California, Nixon did not have ties to Mickey Cohen, Jack Dragna, or other Los Angeles mobsters. His attorney general John Mitchell was a New York bond lawyer with the firm Nixon had worked in before becoming president.

California lawyer Murray Chotiner, who had represented many gambling defendants, directed some of Nixon's early campaigns and supervised fundraising. But he had performed the same function for California governor Earl Warren. When Nixon was vice president, Chotiner was one of his special assistants. Such arrangements were not uncommon in politics. Hubert Humphrey, as mayor of Minneapolis and senator from Minnesota, maintained ties with the local organized crime leader Isidore Blumenfeld, known as "Kid Cann"—the nickname denoting his propensity to frequently wind up in the can (prison). He also appointed a petty racketeer named Fred Gates as his campaign finance manager. When Humphrey was sworn in as vice president it was Gates who held the Bible.

If there been a Mafia man of the year award, President Lyndon Johnson certainly would have won it for his cut back on the Kennedys' anti-mobster drive and his refusal to allow his own national crime commission to have an organized crime task force. But Nixon, Humphrey, and Johnson were not "mobbed up" in the traditional sense.

The temptation which drove President Nixon into an unwise involvement with the mobs was to gain the support of the International Brotherhood of Teamsters when he ran for reelection in 1972. With

2.5 million members, the IBT was the largest union in the country, constituting ten percent of the entire organized labor movement. Like many other blue-collar workers, Teamsters tended to vote Democratic and in FDR's time, under the leadership of Dan Tobin, the IBT was a bastion of New Deal strength. After Tobin stepped down in 1952, he was succeeded by West Coast Teamster boss Dave Beck. As often happened with men who rise above their modest origins, Beck sought the company of civic and business leaders and, although a school drop-out, wangled an appointment as a member of the Board of Trustees of the University of Washington. In 1952 he switched IBT support to the Republicans and moved the national headquarters from Indianapolis to Washington, D.C., where he could be close to the new Eisenhower administration. In 1957 Beck was compelled to step down and later sent to prison.

In 1960, under Hoffa, the union supported Richard Nixon for president, not because of the new-found Republicanism of some of its leaders but because Jimmy hated the Kennedys. In 1968, with Hoffa in prison and the union run by his designated seat warmer, Frank Fitzsimmons, the IBT backed Hubert Humphrey over Nixon. Ironically, Fitzsimmons was more open to Mafia influence than Hoffa ever had been. Under Jimmy all decisions had been centralized, when the mob wanted favors they had to come to him, and he was a tough negotiator. Fitzsimmons decentralized the union leadership and the thirteen regional vice presidents ran their own fiefdoms. Fitzsimmons allowed Bill Presser, the Teamster boss in Ohio, and Allen Dorfman, the head of the $628 million IBT pension fund, to have the final say on loans, many of which went to organized crime enterprises such as casinos in Las Vegas. This type of monopoly distressed some other mobs and one night some bullets flew past Dorfman's head. They weren't meant to kill him but rather to send a message, after which he apportioned the loan money more broadly than he had before.

After Hoffa went to prison a number of efforts were made to overturn his conviction. For a while great pressure was put on a key witness from the Louisiana Teamsters to recant his testimony. Even Hollywood was recruited in the cause with movie star/war hero Audie Murphy attempting to persuade the witness to repudiate his sworn remarks. But it was to no avail. A Senate subcommittee investigating government wiretapping sought to exploit its findings to buttress Hoffa's claim that he had been illegally wiretapped. An exposé in *Life* magazine revealed that the committee chairman, Senator Ed Long of Missouri, who had not practiced law since the 1950s, had received a fee of $60,000 from a St. Louis Teamsters leader to purportedly work on IBT legal business. The notion of a Missouri Senator working on behalf of an imprisoned criminal was a very old one. Harry Truman had constantly lobbied for Tom Pendergast's parole and blasted the Bureau of Prisons for their treatment of the fallen boss. In this instance, Hoffa remained in jail and Senator Long's career was terminated by the Missouri voters.

In the 1970s the Department of Justice conducted an investigation of racketeering in the International Longshoremen's Association (ILA) on the East Coast. This led to the conviction of 130 union leaders. One of those snagged was Anthony Scotto, boss of the Brooklyn waterfront. Scotto had a sterling pedigree. He was the son-in-law of the previous union boss Anthony Anastasio, the brother of the late Lord High Executioner of Brooklyn, Albert Anastasia. Yet at his trial, Scotto managed to secure character testimony from New York governor Hugh Carey and New York City mayors Robert Wagner, John Lindsay, and Abe Beame. The jury was not impressed and Scotto was sent to prison for three years. When he was released a huge welcome home party held for him was attended by many prominent political figures. Louis Freeh, later FBI director, was then a young agent assigned to the investigation. In 2005 he wrote, "All that was a lesson for me... In how politics can sometimes destroy judgment and corrupt moral sense."[1]

During Hoffa's imprisonment, Fitzsimmons was under heavy pressure from Jimmy's family and supporters to use political influence to get him out of Lewisburg Federal Prison. However, that meant that Fitzsimmons would no longer run the union. The prospect of Hoffa returning distressed a number of union leaders and mob bosses who

---

1. As FBI director, Freeh became an uncompromising opponent of President Bill Clinton, who had appointed him to head the Bureau. So strongly did Freeh feel about Clinton's conduct in the Monica Lewinsky affair that he delayed his departure from the FBI until after Clinton's presidential term ended so that the president could not appoint a successor.

were doing very well and did not look forward to having Jimmy back. As part of a plan to reelect President Nixon in 1972, a White House lawyer named Charles "Chuck" Colson conceived the idea of winning over conservative, blue-collar Democrats. These were people who were angered by antiwar marches, civil rights demonstrations, and campus protests, as well as the rising crime rate in the cities. In 1968 a number of them had voted Republican for the first time in their lives. After the election, the liberals, who took over the Democratic Party from the Southerners and big-city bosses, alienated more blue-collar Democrats. Colson reasoned that the Nixon administration could receive even more votes from such people if it played up to the huge Teamsters membership. In December 1970 Fitzsimmons was invited to the White House and given VIP treatment. At the end of 1971 President Nixon commuted Hoffa's sentence but John Mitchell's Justice Department inserted a provision that Jimmy could not run again for union office until 1980, thus ensuring that he would not return to power in the Teamsters. Hoffa was infuriated and blamed Fitzsimmons for the government's actions. In the 1972 presidential election, the IBT endorsed Nixon over Democratic candidate George McGovern. Even more Democrats voted Republican that year, allowing Nixon to win by a huge margin.

When Chuck Colson left the White House for the private practice of law, Fitzsimmons transferred the IBT's business from the firm of Edward Bennett Williams to Colson's new firm, even though Williams was a star while Colson was just another lawyer.

Jimmy Hoffa always believed he could have anything he wanted despite the obstacles. While this attitude has led some individuals to great success, the prisons and graveyards of America are full of people who have learned the hard way that there are limits to ambition. Jimmy's first step back to power was to get the restrictions on his activities overturned. If successful, after his parole ended in 1973 he could hold union office. So he sued the Department of Justice on the grounds that the executive branch did not have the authority to add to a judicial sentence by forbidding him to return to office before 1980. Many Teamsters were still pro-Hoffa and if he ran for his old job, most observers believed he would win handily.

The Fitzsimmons forces moved to counter Hoffa. In 1971 Teamster heavyweights Allen Dorfman and Bill Presser met with U.S. Internal Revenue agents in California. As bosses of the union pension fund, Dorfman and Presser had as much to lose from Hoffa's return as Fitzsimmons did. Their pitch was that they were revealing secrets in order to clean up the union. The agents took this with a grain of salt, knowing that Dorfman was sponsored by the Chicago mob and that Presser's Teamster board in Ohio was commonly referred to as a who's who of the local Mafia. Now, like two hoods in the back room of a police station, they were "spilling their guts" to the law. The agents kept a straight face and listened.

With the White House behind them, Fitzsimmons, Dorfman, and Presser might have been able to continue business as usual. Nixon's re-election victory in 1972 made it look that way. However, the Watergate scandal began to engulf the president and his inner circle. Fitzsimmon stood behind the president until the bitter end. At the time there were rumors that Dorfman had raised a half million dollars and a New Jersey Teamster leader, Tony Provenzano, had raised the same amount with the sum being delivered to the White House to help with Nixon's legal expenses.[2]

Out of prison Provenzano had teamed up with Russ Bufalino, head of the Mafia family in northeastern Pennsylvania, to put together a slick racket with Fitzsimmons' blessing. They received permission to allow employers to use Teamsters members to haul freight without paying them union wages. The businesses would terminate all their regular drivers and then rehire them at lower wages through a mob-backed leasing firm. When some of their drivers protested they were intimidated into silence. It was behavior that Jimmy Hoffa would not have approved of, or at the very least he would have wanted his own cut.

In August 1974 Nixon resigned the presidency. His successor Gerald Ford had been a Michigan congressman and minority leader of the House of Representatives. As such, he was fully acquainted with

---

2. While in Lewisburg prison, Jimmy had made an enemy of Provenzano, who had formerly been one of his biggest supporters. Tony was serving time on an extortion conviction and had been denied a pension by his own IBT local. So he asked his buddy Jimmy to arrange for the IBT to reverse the decision. Hoffa refused and allegedly the two men had a fistfight. When he was released Provenzano became a bitter foe of Hoffa.

the nature of the IBT, so he was wise enough not to become involved with them. He appointed as attorney general Edward Levi, president of the University of Chicago and former dean of its law school. Levi was a man of high standing in both academic and legal affairs and any attempt to approach him would have met with a severe rebuff. Rumors began to abound that the Justice Department might find that the restrictions on Hoffa were unconstitutional. To run for union president, Jimmy had to be an IBT official and the most likely place for him to achieve such a post was from his old Local 299 in Detroit. The president of the local was his friend and could be relied upon to name Jimmy a business agent, thereby making him eligible to run for office. Fitzsimmons put up his own son as a candidate for head of the local. During the campaign, shots were fired and bombs exploded. One of the latter destroyed young Fitzsimmons' car outside of a bar where he was drinking. Finally, a compromise was reached whereby the incumbent union president would remain while young Fitzsimmons would be designated vice president.

Some of Jimmy's gangster friends approached him as peacemakers. Tony Giacalone, a Detroit mafioso who was a longtime intimate of Jimmy's, and Russ Bufalino tried to persuade him to back off. They made the usual arguments that one does to an older CEO who wants to continue in power. They pointed out that he was financially well fixed and should go off and enjoy himself by playing with the grandchildren. Anybody who knew Jimmy Hoffa would have realized that he would never roll over and play dead while somebody stole "his union." In contrast, Tony Provenzano threatened not only to tear Jimmy's guts out but to kidnap his little granddaughter. Some of Jimmy's friends warned him that he better start carrying a gun and hire bodyguards. He always played the tough guy and would not do either. Worse, he was threatening that when he got back in power he would open the IBT books and reveal the corruption that had gone on, thereby presenting the government with evidence for criminal charges against many Mafia figures and union leaders. He also agreed to co-author a book with Oscar Fraley, who had written the best-selling *The Untouchables* with Eliot Ness.

It is questionable whether Hoffa would have followed through with his threats. To open the files would reveal his own criminality and he might have ended up back in prison. It was the same thing with writing a tell-all book. But the Mafia always followed the rule, "Resolve all doubts in favor of the organization." In some instances men who were mob capos, much liked by their colleagues, ended up being murdered because someone thought they just might cooperate with the government or cause some other trouble. For his part, Hoffa reasoned that the gangsters would never dare kill someone as famous as himself, because it would create a national sensation and only lead to greater difficulties for all of organized crime. In the aftermath of the Kennedy assassination, half the country believed that the Mafia had killed him. Yet the organization was not destroyed because of that belief. It was not likely that the murder of someone like Hoffa would create even more outrage than the murder of a popular president.

On July 30, 1975, Jimmy Hoffa left his vacation home in Lake Orion, Michigan, and told his wife he was meeting someone at 2 p.m. at Machus Red Fox Restaurant in Bloomfield, a suburb of Detroit. At 2:15 he called to tell her that the person he was supposed to meet had not arrived yet. It was the last time she heard from him. When he did not return home, Mrs. Hoffa began phoning family and friends seeking information. She notified the Bloomfield Township Police Department the next morning, and, within a short time, they located Hoffa's green Pontiac in the Red Fox parking lot. Though the FBI would not have jurisdiction until at least twenty-four hours had elapsed, the Detroit office immediately contacted Washington headquarters and received permission to open an investigation. Early on several things seemed apparent: Jimmy had not been kidnapped for ransom and was not the type to voluntarily disappear. He was the sort that if he had been taken prisoner and released, he would never have rested until he got revenge. So, it was likely he had been murdered. An examination of Jimmy's appointment calendar showed a 2:30 luncheon meeting on July 30 with Tony G (who was assumed to be Tony Giacalone). Thus, investigators followed a working hypothesis that Hoffa has been murdered and the Detroit Mafia was involved. Other than those who wish to blame government agents, as they do in almost every major case ranging from the

Kennedy assassination to the fall of the World Trade Center, most investigators subscribe to that hypothesis. Following through on that supposition, investigators believe the people who arranged for the carrying out of the hit were Jimmy's friend Giacalone and his enemy Provenzano and the hit could not have been carried out in Detroit without an okay from the local Mafia family.

Several people have been singled out as the actual assassins, including the Briguglio brothers, who worked for Provenzano in New Jersey and had accompanied Russ Bufalino and a Teamster from the Pennsylvania/Delaware area, Frank Sheeran, to attend a wedding in Detroit. Years later, as he was dying, Sheeran told an author that he had shot Hoffa, but no traces of blood were found in the house where it was supposed to have occurred. While there have been claims that Hoffa's body is buried in the Caribbean, a construction site in New Jersey, or various farms around Michigan, most likely it was compacted to avoid it ever being found. To date no one has been formally charged in the case; however, a number of people suspected of being involved have been given stiff prison sentences for other crimes. Privately government officials will tell journalists and others that although the case was never officially solved, those who committed the crime have been punished. Despite the government's contention, one can confidently assert that books claiming "I killed Hoffa" or "I know who killed Hoffa" will continue to appear. The subject is ideal: the man was a fascinating character. He was probably the most famous private citizen ever murdered in the United States, linked to the Kennedys, and the details of his death are still not clear.[3]

As it turned out Richard Nixon did not need the Teamsters to get reelected president in 1972, nor did he need to send operatives into the Watergate to look for any Democratic secrets. Following the disasters of 1968, the Democratic Party was still tearing itself apart and alienating many voters. All he had to do to serve two terms was to conduct a law-abiding administration. If he had done that, because of his historic openings to Russia and China, he would have been hailed as a great statesman. Even his enemies recognized that he was the only

---

3. The passage of time has foreclosed the possibility of a book claiming Hoffa is still alive and has been seen having a drink with Elvis Presley. If Hoffa were around today he would be over 100.

person who could have pulled off rapprochement with the two Communist giants because he was previously so identified as such a fierce enemy of both that no one could accuse him of being soft.

As with the Kennedys, there was no one in Washington who could steer Nixon away from the trouble the mobs (or the White House plumbers) would bring him. Because of the mistakes J. Edgar Hoover made in the 1960s in combating civil rights protesters and antiwar activists, he had lost considerable prestige. Seventy-four years old at the time Nixon took office, with but three years to live, Hoover had neither the standing nor the vigor to stop the president from courting the Teamsters or employing the Watergate burglars.

When Hoover died one of his top assistants, Mark Felt, expected to be named director. Instead the job went to a Nixon loyalist, Pat Grey (who had been a career naval officer and a Justice Department lawyer but never a cop). During the investigation, Felt fed inside information to *Washington Post* reporters Bob Woodward and Carl Bernstein. At the time many people suspected he was their "Deep Throat," though his motive was most likely revenge for being passed over for director rather than serving the interests of justice. Later, when he was indicted for authorizing agents to break into the offices of alleged subversive groups, even though Nixon must have suspected that Felt was "Deep Throat," the former president testified on his behalf.[4]

*

In the confusion and collapse of the Nixon administration, very little was accomplished against the Mafia but there were some bright spots. Since Frank Hague's assumption of power in New Jersey in 1917, corrupt politics and organized crime were rampant in the state. In 1969, after G. Robert Blakey, while testifying before the New Jersey legislature, said, "I think New Jersey has as large a corruption problem as any state in the union, organized crime is so powerful in New Jersey that they can have almost anything they want," the state attorney

---

4. Half of the Washington law enforcement community thought it was obvious that Felt had to be the source of the stories because they were based upon the ongoing FBI investigation.

general became so furious that he impaneled a special grand jury to look into the situation. The prosecutor who ran the probe, William Brennan, Jr., son of a sitting justice of the United States Supreme Court, confirmed the mob's power. In a speech he declared that "organized crime has infiltrated virtually every facet of life in the Garden State with the exception of the church." According to him, "Too many local governments are responsive more to the mob than to the electorate that puts them in office," and he declared that some legislators were "Entirely too comfortable with members of organized crime."

The following year President Nixon appointed Frederick Lacey United States attorney for New Jersey. His first target was the state's largest city, Newark. There the mob boss was Ruggiero "Richie the Boot" Boiardo, Genovese family overseer of organized crime in the area. In December 1969, a federal grand jury indicted Mayor Hugh Addonizio and seven former or current members of the Newark City Council on extortion charges. Included in the indictment was Boiardo's son, Tony, who was co-boss with his father. The mayor received ten years in prison. Young Boiardo suffered a heart attack that led to his death a few years later.

New Jersey's only homegrown mob family made their headquarters in a plumbing shop in Kenilworth. The boss was Sam "The Plumber" DeCavalcante, who preferred to be called "Princeton Sam" for the university town in which he resided. The dapper DeCavalcante claimed descent from nobility and his mob associates often referred to him as "The Count." Though his family was small—only fifty members—and did not have a seat on the national commission, he was highly respected within the Mafia.[5] Federal agents listening to a microphone planted in his plumbing store picked up a great deal of information about New Jersey congressmen, mayors, politicians, and police chiefs and their relationships with mobsters.

Following Lacey in office was his chief assistant Herb "The Hawk" Stern who went after Frank Hague's old machine, the Hudson County Democratic organization, then led by Boss John Kenney. It was

---

5. In later years there would be arguments over whether the Boiardos or the DeCavalcantes were the inspiration for the hit television show *The Sopranos*. Most likely it was a combination of both.

Kenney who sponsored the political career of U.S. senator Harrison "Pete" Williams, a New Jersey aristocrat who described the Boss as a "great humanitarian." Prosecutor Stern managed to win sentences of seventeen and fifteen years respectively against Boss Kenney and Jersey City mayor Thomas Whalen, though Kenney died before he could begin serving his sentence.

In one instance there was a report that New Jersey congressman Cornelius Gallagher had been entertaining a loan shark in his home when the man suddenly expired of natural causes. The congressman, not knowing what to do, allegedly called a well-known mob enforcer, the much-feared Harold "Kayo" Konigsberg, to his home and asked him to dispose of the body. Kayo, whom *Life* magazine described as an "uncaged killer who ranged up and down the eastern seaboard," said he would not do it unless he received permission from the capo who controlled Hudson County organized crime. Later, while serving a prison term, Kayo revealed the story but the congressman denied it. By the time federal and state prosecutors completed their investigation, ten New Jersey mayors had been found guilty of various crimes, along with two secretaries of state, two state treasurers, the assembly speaker, and the senate president. Among those convicted were Sam DeCavalcante, who received a five-year sentence on interstate gambling charges, and Congressman Gallagher, who pleaded guilty to income tax evasion.

On the other side of the country the Justice Department made some progress against the Mafia's glamour playground, Las Vegas. It was Benjamin "Bugsy" Siegel who had first brought the mobsters to the desert when he built the Flamingo Hotel and Casino. However, his arithmetic was bad. He short-changed such backers as Frank Costello and Meyer Lansky, and what he did not steal his mistress, Virginia Hill, did. So after Bugsy was murdered in Los Angeles on orders from the eastern bosses, Virginia wisely gave back her money to Lansky.

Vegas was designated an "open city" where any mob family could operate. So several of them secured Teamster loans to build casinos, thanks to Allen Dorfman. In addition to the regular profits, specialists were sent in to "skim" money off the top and distribute an estimated $160,000 a month to the four Mafia families who controlled Vegas:

Chicago, Milwaukee, Cleveland, and Kansas City. Morris "Moe" Dalitz, who had flourished as the top Jewish mobster in Cleveland, where he had maintained friendly relations with the Italian faction, was the leading mob star in Vegas, though he posed as a great philanthropist and civic figure. Dalitz left the rough stuff to the boys from the Windy City, who by common consent, were the most skilled at enforcing discipline. Al Capone's claim to fame had been based on the way his gunmen played "the Chicago piano" in the North Clark Street garage on Valentine's Day. The memory still sent a shiver down many tough guys' spines. So Chicago supplied the resident overseer for the area. The first was Johnny Roselli, who had long experience doing the same work for the Mafia in Hollywood. His gentlemanly manner, combined with his ability to call on hit men, kept things pretty much in order. When the usual hustlers and burglars showed up to get their share of the free-flowing cash in Vegas, Johnny's boys would advise them that it was better for their health that they leave immediately. If some recalcitrant had to be hit, the mob shooters waited to kill him until he was out of town, in a place like Los Angeles or Phoenix, so as not to produce lurid local headlines and scare casino patrons. In an emergency they could bury a body in the desert around Vegas.

When Johnny was replaced by Marshall Caifano, things began to go wrong. Back in Chicago, Marshall and his brother, "Fat Lenny," threw their weight around with abandon. In 1951, during the syndicate takeover of a policy (numbers) operation from its African American owner, Lenny, accompanied by some of his boys, curbed a car carrying the policy chief, waved a gun, and yelled that he was a detective from the state attorney's office. The gambler in the car was accompanied by some real Chicago detectives, acting as bodyguards. They realized that Lenny was not a cop, so they killed him. Because of the somewhat embarrassing circumstances of the incident, the gambler had to drive to the local police station and claim he killed Caifano. No charges were ever brought. The affair taught the Chicago mob not to try to kidnap a man riding in a car with police officers. So, a few months later two gentlemen parked outside the policy boss's house one night and shot him to death when he came home.

When Tony Accardo sent Caifano to Vegas he warned him to keep a low profile but Marshall ignored him. It was Caifano who earlier had spotted Senator Goldwater's friend Willie Bioff in Vegas at the senator's store in Moe Dalitz's casino hotel. The word was flashed to Chicago and back in Phoenix the mob put a bomb in Bioff's car that blew him to bits. At least Caifano had enough sense not to shoot Willie while he was standing next to Senator Goldwater. Otherwise Caifano acted as if he were still on the West Side of Chicago. He openly defied the Nevada Casino Control Commission by appearing in gambling joints where individuals on a blacklist of gangsters were forbidden to enter. Thanks to Caifano parading around the casinos and openly advertising his presence, and later his big boss Sam Giancana doing the same, in 1963 Frank Sinatra lost his license for a resort he owned on the California-Nevada border.

In 1971 a small-time Chicago gunmen and gambler, Tony Spilotro, was appointed overseer in Las Vegas. A worse choice could not have been made. Not only did Spilotro openly throw his weight around the casinos, he brought in a crew of his burglar friends to break into expensive homes and jewelry stores in the area. When the Midwestern mobs made a smooth Chicago gambler named Lefty Rosenthal the hidden boss of the Stardust Casino, he and Spilotro spent half their time feuding with one another. Another problem with Spilotro was that he kept being hauled back to Chicago every couple of years to face old murder charges. In one case the leading defendant was a vicious Chicago character named Sam DeStefano, who was known to turn trials into circuses, causing a lot of bad publicity for the outfit. To prevent that happening, he was murdered. The trial then proceeded quietly and Spilotro was found not guilty. Two years after that he was charged in a Teamsters extortion scheme along with Allen Dorfman. This time the government's chief witness had his head blown off in front of his wife. After that the prosecution's case collapsed. The fundamental problem in Vegas was that the real bosses back in the Midwest were too far away to supervise what was going on or even learn about it.

*

When the Carter administration took office at the beginning of 1977, its inner circle was relatively unknown in Washington and the president himself was unknowing of the capital's ways. His choice for attorney general was Griffin Bell, a former federal circuit court judge from Atlanta and principal partner in a leading law firm. It appeared to signal that the administration would have no interest in fighting organized crime. In 1978 Carter appointed another federal circuit court judge, William Webster of St. Louis, to head the FBI. Both were old-fashioned men of integrity and they did not back down from gangsters and crooked politicians.

At the time a New York con man named Marvin Weinberg, who had been arrested by the FBI for securities fraud, was offered the chance to keep out of jail by becoming an informant. He was initially assigned to work on an organized crime case where four potential witnesses had already been murdered. However, within three months sufficient evidence was assembled to charge the suspects. So Weinberg was put to work hunting art thieves. To assist him, a team of federal agents was assembled to impersonate the retinue of a rich Arab sheik and lure the sellers of stolen art into a trap. Weinberg spread the word that his client, the Emir Kambir Abdul Rahman, was anxious to purchase some paintings—no questions asked.

Because the first criminal that Weinberg had hooked was arrested in the Eastern District of New York, where there was an active organized crime strike force, in order for Weinberg to keep working, his FBI handlers had to appeal to the strike force chief, Thomas Puccio, to hold off prosecution until Weinberg's other investigations were completed. The strike forces were actually a remnant of the Kennedy Justice Department meant to operate in districts where the local U.S. attorney was not particularly enthusiastic about prosecuting organized crime. Puccio agreed to let the sting play out.

Emir Abdul's first meeting with sellers of stolen art in a hotel room at New York's posh Plaza Hotel turned into a farce. The FBI agent who impersonated him spoke no Arabic and the agents who had rented Arab dress from a local theatrical customer found that when the robes arrived they were so wrinkled that the Emir had to settle for wearing a headdress and an ordinary business suit. Eyebrows were also raised because the FBI had ordered hors d'oeuvres from a Jewish deli as snacks for the supposedly Muslim emir. Some agents, unable to suppress their laughter, had to make sudden exits from the room. After that fiasco another FBI agent was brought in who spoke Arabic and some more suitable agents were added to the team. The FBI named the case Abdul scam, or ABSCAM for short.

The investigations eventually led to Atlantic City, New Jersey, where a con man friend of Weinberg suggested that he get the sheikh to invest in the casino boom going on there.[6] This led to a meeting with the politician who supposedly could deliver anything in Atlantic City for the right price, the mayor of Camden, New Jersey, Angelo Erichetti, who (as was permitted under New Jersey law), also served as a state senator. The meeting was held on Long Island so that it would be within the jurisdiction of the Eastern District strike force. Erichetti was a money hungry politician of the type that New Jersey had in abundant supply. As Tom Puccio would later write, "His idea of economic development was to use the port of Camden to smuggle guns and drugs into the country." He was also very tight with Paul Castellano, leader of the Gambino family, who had been instrumental in persuading the Philadelphia family of Angelo Bruno to make Erichetti the mob's main fixer in Atlantic City.

As the investigation progressed there were many moments in which the targets should have recognized that it was a federal scam. One FBI agent got her picture in the paper at an airplane hijacking. Yet the other agents were able to assure the targets that it was not her. In another instance the FBI used a yacht seized from drug smugglers to host a party in Florida to which they invited a number of crooks whom they were operating stings against. The New Jersey contingent managed to persuade United States senator Harrison "Pete" Williams to come to the party and welcome the emir. Eventually word got to the underworld that the yacht party was a sting, but the ABSCAM team convinced their targets that information was wrong. Another tipoff that the meetings were phony was that they were held in an unim-

---

6. Despite the conviction of so many of officials in his state, Governor Brendan Byrne had ignored the advice of law enforcement and pushed through a bill authorizing casino gambling in Atlantic City.

pressive ordinary Long Island office building. A real Arab sheik would have occupied a fancy suite of offices in Manhattan.

Erichetti began to introduce the ABSCAM crew to New Jersey politicians, particularly members of Congress. All discussions between the federal scammers and the targets were scripted. Conversations were taped and filmed by hidden cameras and monitored from a nearby room by a strike force attorney to ensure that any statements made by agents were within the law. In some cases the attorney would phone the agent's room to suggest particular questions that should be asked of the target so as to produce legally admissible evidence. A favorite topic was the possibility of the congressmen introducing private bills to allow the emir to reside in the United States.

The various members of Congress who were roped in were a cross-section of political types. Erichetti was bold. In one instance he personally accepted $25,000 from the ABSCAM team. Investigators were also able to pass over a $100,000 bribe meant for Erichetti in the presence of an official of the New Jersey Casino Control Commission. A Philadelphia congressman, Ozzie Myers, was a blunt, profane individual. At his swearing in as a congressman in Washington, he celebrated by getting arrested for punching out a waitress in a local cocktail lounge. When he was filmed taking $50,000 in cash, he complained afterward that he expected $100,000. Another congressman was so greedy that he stuffed his pockets with bills as the cameras rolled. Senator Williams, chairman of the powerful Labor Committee, was ill at ease and somewhat reticent. Still he made it clear that he would work to obtain government funds for a titanium mine in which he secretly held shares. One congressman, a West Point graduate, was more cautious. He sent private detectives to investigate Abdul Enterprises. They quickly concluded that the scammers were government agents. However, it was too late to save him.

As the investigation began to target members of Congress concern was expressed from the White House on down. Lawyers argued that Congress was a separate branch of the government and the executive branch had no right to test their integrity. If the politically astute J. Edgar Hoover had still been director of the FBI, it is doubtful that he would have authorized arresting congressmen. FBI director William

Webster was not a politician or professional bureaucrat, but a public servant in the true sense and his personal status was such that he was not dependent upon a government paycheck. He gave his full support to the ABSCAM team. At the highest level, President Carter had to consider that he was the head of a Democratic administration and Senator Williams and all the congressmen involved were Democrats. In his time President Roosevelt had stopped investigations of Democrats like Mayors Hague and Kelly. In addition to the problems in Washington, federal and state prosecutors in New Jersey were not happy with the Eastern District of New York strike force coming into their territory. Finally, the decision was made by Attorney General Griffin Bell, who ruled that the investigation should go on.

In February 1980, with newspapers about to break the story, the FBI arrested Senator Williams and six congressmen. All were later convicted of bribery and given sentences in the two-to-three-years range. Various lawyers and lesser officials were also convicted. In one hilarious case, Erichetti brought a man to Abdul who was supposedly the deputy commissioner of the United States Department of Immigration. FBI agents were suspicious when the man did not resemble pictures of the commissioner and was unable to spell his own name correctly. It turned out he was just a Philadelphia lawyer looking to make a quick score.

At the time of the ABSCAM investigation there were also a number of Koreans involved in schemes to bribe congressmen. Some journalists believed that the story about the Koreans and ABSCAM were leaked to the press in order to halt both investigations, before they could bring down some of the top figures in Congress.

In the final analysis, the New Jersey cases were successful because the political climate in the state had been so corrupt for so long that no one really feared arrest. From an investigative standpoint, bribing some of the state's politicians was like shooting fish in a barrel.

The roundup of crooked congressmen was not the greatest scandal in post-Kennedy Washington. The biggest was Watergate, which caused some of the president's aides to be imprisoned and Nixon himself to resign. Nevertheless the permanent government of Washington insiders continued, always in and never out. Their uncrowned king was

Clark Clifford, who had learned his trade in Truman's White House and perfected it afterward. Had Clifford and the others been operating in a state capital they would have been called "fixers," but in the national capital they were known as "statesmen." So loose was the ethical climate in the Nixon White House that the president's hand-picked vice president, Spiro Agnew, behaved like a Chicago alderman—taking bribes in his White House office that were handed over by individuals from his home state of Maryland who owed him money for his services to them at the time he was governor.

Post-Watergate, with the doors to the White House barred by Presidents Ford and Carter, the boys with the suitcases full of dollars turned to Congress. The Korean lobby and other individuals found that they were able to do business on Capitol Hill. The ABSCAM investigation revealed that some congressmen were just as hungry as any mob figure and their ethical level was no higher. Outside Washington, states like New Jersey and Nevada were virtually owned by mobsters, and they were not the only places. Louisiana was traditionally corrupt and Massachusetts, Illinois, New York, Florida, and several other jurisdictions could not have stood too close a scrutiny. Given the state of corruption and organized crime in the late 1970s, it was as though there had not been a Kefauver investigation or an Apalachin raid and the Kennedy brothers had never lived. If further proof was needed, the next Republican president, Ronald Reagan, picked up with the IBT where Nixon had left off. It might have been expected that after forty years of embarrassment, the White House doors would have been locked and bolted against the mob-influenced Teamsters. The problem was that some politicians still needed the Mafia (or thought they did) and that the Mafia needed the politicians.

Chapter 10

Fatal Attraction II:
The Gipper Embraces the Teamsters

In 1983, President Ronald Reagan appointed a commission to study the problem of organized crime in America. Commissions and committees had been examining the subject for thirty years. Usually they did not accomplish a great deal. Bobby Kennedy had once told his aides who complained that it was hard to define what was the Mafia or organized crime, "Don't define it, do something about it." The country did not need another commission to tell them that there was such a thing as the Mafia. They had seen it on the screen in the *Godfather* movies, where a bunch of well-dressed, mostly Italian, gentlemen sat around like a corporate board deciding which enterprises to muscle in on and whom to kill.

Reagan chose as chairman of the commission a U.S. Circuit Court judge from New York named Irving Kaufman, a man widely regarded as pompous, and self-seeking. Other than the fact that he had been the district court judge who sentenced the defendants in the Apalachin case to prison and then was reversed by a higher court, he knew very little about the subject. He was also the judge who had sentenced Soviet agents Julius and Ethel Rosenberg to death with the absurd claim that by stealing atomic secrets they were responsible for starting the Korean War. Still, he considered himself an expert on everything and he frequently took to the op-ed pages of the *New York Times* to expound on a wide range of topics. His commission turned out to be one of the least effective such bodies ever constituted.

As with the Warren Commission, the question could again be asked what was a federal judge doing investigating criminal activity which might come before his court. Despite the fact that there were some real organized crime experts on his commission, Kaufman ignored them and proceeded to run his hearings like a circus. Jimmy "The Weasel" Fratianno, a mob turncoat from California where he had been acting boss of the Los Angeles family, was called to testify in New York. To protect Fratianno's identity, he spoke from a closed booth. Since the Weasel had appeared without any disguises on a number of TV shows, it was obviously a ploy to make the hearings appear more sensational.

To add to the drama, just before the hearings were called to order, a commission functionary stood up and, in a loud voice, said "Marshals, draw your guns, there are mafiosos in the room," or words to that effect. If there were any, they had been checked in by those very same marshals. As a practical matter, if there were really dangerous people around, it would have been better to quietly eject them rather than invite lawmen to start pegging shots all over the place. When I had entered it there were no seats available except on the far side of the room, so I plunked myself down there. Only one other person occupied the same bench. When I looked him over, I understood why the bench was vacant. He was a burly character who was obviously a mob enforcer and he looked at me as if to ask why are you sitting here? As it turned out he was not there to initiate a bloodbath but in response to a subpoena from the commission. When the call was made for the marshals to draw their revolvers, I worried that an excited fed might start shooting at my seatmate and accidentally hit me. My first thought was to stand up and yell to a marshal, "Toss me a shooting iron, pardner, so I can get the drop on this varmint next to me." This might have won me some praise from Judge Kaufman but it could have also have landed me in Bellevue Hospital where I would have ended up talking to a nice man in a white coat. So I simply shifted as far away from José (I later learned that was his name and that he allegedly headed a Latin organized crime crew in New Jersey) and gave the marshals a look that said "Shoot him not me." The next day José and I were pictured together in a newspaper with the inference that I was his lawyer. At least the commission hearing was good for laughs. Throughout its investigations some of the members openly criticized their chairman and in the final report, the majority characterized the whole effort as "a saga of missed opportunities."

*

In January 1981, a man had ridden out of the West to save America. His name was not Lochinvar but "The Gipper," a Marlboro man tall in the saddle, who was expected to run the baddies out-of-town or plant them in Boot Hill and return America to its Norman Rockwell past. People were confident that he could accomplish all that because they had seen him do it many times before—on the screen.

Ronald Reagan, who acquired the nickname of "The Gipper" from his movie role as Notre Dame football hero George Gipp, had been born and raised in mid-America along the Illinois-Iowa border. As a young man out of college, he had broadcast baseball games, often in a somewhat imaginative form, because when the game was out of town the action was telegraphed to him in terse phrases like "base hit," "walk," "stole 2B." His good looks and pleasant personality earned him a Hollywood contract. There he followed the usual path of the time playing lead roles in B movies and supporting ones in As. He married rising star Jane Wyman. After military service and in his 30s, his career began to decline. As he himself said, "I could have phoned in my parts." His best known role was playing opposite a chimp named Bonzo. Eventually his principal public exposure was as host for a TV show, *Death Valley Days*. He divorced Jane Wyman, whose career had taken off after she received the academy award for best actress, and married a Chicago socialite who played minor roles on the screen. Strangely, considering his later career, he was a liberal Democrat and president of the Screen Actors Guild (SAG), a leading Hollywood union.

The difference between Reagan and 100 other fading Hollywood actors was that his warm, friendly manner and strong persona attracted people. So he parlayed this into a career as a corporate spokesperson, then into politics where he became governor of California and eventually president of the United States. On Inauguration Day, January 20, 1981, the country waited to see what he would do about the American hostages held in our embassy in Tehran. They had been prisoners for 444 days and President Carter's attempts to obtain their release or rescue them had failed, leaving eight American servicemen dead and the U.S. embarrassed before the world. Ironically, Jimmy Carter was an Annapolis graduate and a submarine commander, while Reagan had spent the war in Hollywood making military training films. Yet to the American public, it was "The Gipper" who appeared strong and Carter weak. Reagan also looked tough to the Iranians. As soon as he was sworn in as president they released the American prisoners, who were put on a plane and flown out of the country. During his two terms in office he would constantly castigate the Soviet Union, which he referred to as the "Evil Empire," and demand that the Berlin Wall be torn down. Once he scared the Russians so badly that they went to virtual full alert in anticipation of an American nuclear attack. Only when one of their spies high up in NATO assured them that there was no attack contemplated did they stand down. At the end of his administration and in the years shortly afterward, the Soviet Union collapsed. Ronald Reagan had won the Cold War.

Reagan also managed to instill conservative values into American politics where they would remain strong for the next quarter of a century. Despite Kaufman's missteps, during the Reagan administration the Mafia, which the president characterized as "the evil Empire within,"[1] would be dealt such heavy blows that it would be reduced to a shadow of its former self. However, most of the credit for accomplishing that rested with people like Professor Blakey, who gave law

---

1. The last part came from Robert Kennedy's book on the Mafia entitled *The Enemy Within*

enforcement the key to breaking the Mafia with his RICO law, and prosecutors and investigators across the country who successfully applied it.

*

If a national anticrime drive were to be successful it had to, in a phrase borrowed from Hollywood, "play well in Peoria." In this instance one of the Mafia's Peorias was Cleveland, Ohio. In the 1980s both the president and the local FBI would stumble badly in Cleveland. It was not the first time the city on the lake witnessed law-enforcement embarrassments. In 1921 the chief justice of the local municipal court was accused of being involved in a gang shooting. In 1928, when Cleveland cops raided a Mafia summit meeting being held in the Statler Hilton, they had shoved the hotel manager through the door first to shield themselves from bullets if the attendees began shooting. From 1935 to 1942 Eliot Ness was director of public safety. He did a good job of cleaning up the police department but could not catch a serial killer who murdered a dozen people in the city. The police lieutenant who was Ness' right-hand man in his drive against organized crime was later found to be on a mob payroll. Unlike many cities, the Italian faction, and the Jewish faction that been run out of Detroit when the Italians took over that city's Purple Gang, got along well. While the principal Jewish mobster Morris "Moe" Dalitz went off to Vegas and became a respected businessman, or at least posed as one, the long-time Mafia boss of Cleveland, John Scalish, stood still. Under his leadership the Mafia failed to recruit new blood because Scalish did not want to have to share the profits with any more people. At one time his underboss was ninety years old.

In 1976 Scalish died and a war broke out between the faction headed by James Licavoli (*aka* Jack White) and his lieutenant Angelo "Big Ange" Lonardo and on the other side the insurgents John Nardi and a flamboyant Irishman named Danny Greene. In the year 1977, thirty-seven bombs exploded in Cleveland. One sent Danny Greene and his girlfriend, who were sleeping in a bed on the third floor of his house, hurtling to the basement. They emerged unharmed and Greene immediately went on television to challenge his enemies to renew the battle. During the fighting, Greene managed to avoid bombs and bullets that had his name on them. Eventually, though, Nardi and Greene were blown up by car bombs in separate incidents.

A key Jewish figure in Cleveland organized crime was Bill Presser, whose Board of Directors was composed of many local Mafia figures. At testimonials for him, the guest lists would not only include the mayor of Cleveland and the governor of Ohio, but a number of other high-ranking political, business, and civic officials. While Bill was always a strong figure, his son Jackie was just a lucky sperm. He dropped out of school in the eighth grade and the only real work he had done was as a member of an interstate auto theft gang. Through his father's influence, at twenty-one he was made business agent for the Hotel and Restaurant Workers local. Mostly the job involved union organizing in which the chief persuasive device was a baseball bat, and the principal task was listening sympathetically to individuals who claimed that the union was pushing them too hard. If they came up with a pay off, Jackie would resolve the problem. Within a few years he was made president of the local.

Young Presser presented a somewhat odd appearance. He weighed over 300 pounds and was fond of orange suits with green shirts and ties. It was an ensemble that gave him the appearance of a Halloween pumpkin. Despite his looks, Jackie collected a string of wives and mistresses. In 1957 he was removed from leadership of the restaurant workers local for using union funds to pay personal expenses.

Again, Daddy Bill was available to help his son. Presser Sr. arranged for Jackie to receive a Teamster loan to build an entertainment complex. After a few years it went under. So Jackie, at forty, was made secretary-treasurer of a newly chartered Teamsters local. In middle age, he changed his appearance, although not his weight, and began to dress like a banker and involve himself in civic affairs. Somehow he got the notion that he was a great public relations expert, so he edited the monthly *Ohio Teamsters,* a magazine that had been largely used by his father to sell advertisements to people seeking favors from the union. The funds collected went into the pockets of the Pressers.

In 1976 Bill retired in favor of his son. Jackie followed the same policies as his father but he had to walk a narrow line. He was not a made man in the Mafia and there was always the possibility that someday the mob would decide to eliminate him. He backed Licavoli and Lonardo in the Italian civil war, but he could not become too involved with them. As James Ragen of Chicago, head of the National Racing Wire Service, said when he declined a partnership with that city's syndicate, "If I accept, someday I'll wake up dead in an alley." So Ragen held out and even complained to the FBI that he was being menaced by Chicago mobsters. J. Edgar Hoover ordered a squad of agents to investigate and gave the case the name "reassembly of the Capone gang" (abbreviated in Bureau communications as CAPGA). As some agents observed, it was as if Hoover believed the mobsters had been on sabbatical since Capone was sent to prison in 1932. In June 1946, as Ragen was driving along at the height of the evening rush hour, a truck pulled alongside him and opened fire. He was badly wounded but doctors believed he would survive. So the mob sent a second team into the hospital and it managed to slip some poison to Ragen. The deceased man's partner, Arthur "Mickey" McBride, who operated out of Cleveland, was a former Chicagoan but he took a different approach. He always went to along with the Cleveland mob and the national syndicate and managed to live a long time and die in his bed.

Jackie was close to a prizefighter named Tony Hughes, who worked as a business agent for his union and served as a sort of bodyguard for him. In 1968 a loan shark who was a friend of Hughes was playing golf at a suburban course. As the man lined up his shot on the 16th hole, a sniper lined up a shot on the shark and killed him.. The incident terrified Hughes, so he decided to get a little insurance of the kind issued by a bewhiskered individual named Uncle Sam. He went to the local FBI office and consented to become an informer for the organized crime squad. The agents noticed after a few years that his information was exceptionally good and obviously had to have come from higher up in the union than Hughes. When questioned, Tony admitted to his handler that he was getting it from Jackie Presser. So the FBI was able to persuade Jackie to become an informer too. Presser was considered so special by the Bureau that he was not assigned the usual informant number. Where Hughes was CV (Cleveland office) 882TE (top echelon), Presser was given the codename "Tailor" and his file was kept at Washington headquarters. It was a wise decision because a civilian clerk in the Cleveland FBI office would later begin stealing informer lists, smuggling them out in her girdle and selling them to mobsters, one of them a man who had done twenty years for killing two Cleveland cops. After a while, FBI officials realized that "Tailor"—a related operation to a presser—was a bit obvious for a codename and Presser's was changed to "Alpro." In a town where a car might have a bomb wired to it or a sniper might be lurking in the bushes, a mobster really needed Uncle Sam with all his informers to at least be able to provide a warning if rivals were planning to kill him.

*

Until 1977 the Interstate Commerce Commission (ICC) had set freight rates and restricted entry to the trucking industry. This was to the benefit of the Teamsters because they were able to obtain hefty wage increases that the employers could pass on to the shippers by gaining rate increases from a compliant ICC. However, as an anti-inflation measure, the Carter administration proposed deregulation of the industry. Defeating the deregulation bill became a major IBT priority so Allen Dorfman and Kansas City Teamster boss, Roy Williams, who was soon to be named general president of the IBT took the lead in opposing it. Williams had started his labor career as a truck driver. Then, as a union official in Kansas City, he became friendly with mob boss Nick Civella. Later, when Nick asked for a piece of the union, Williams consulted his friend Jimmy Hoffa. It was Williams who had taught the ex-freight handler, Hoffa, to drive a rig so he could be one of the boys, a real knight of the road. Hoffa had benefited from Mafia support in Detroit, so he advised Williams to cut a deal. Later, Williams would claim he didn't know Nick was a Mafia leader. Even Harry Truman never claimed he thought Johnny Lazia sold apples and that the 1933 affair at the Union Station had been a pillow fight. With the mob behind him, Williams rose rapidly in the

Teamsters international and was the mob's chosen successor to Frank Fitzsimmons when he died in 1981.

In 1979 the Chicago FBI had commenced Operation Pendorf (penetrate Allen Dorfman) by planting a bug in the target's office. On it they heard Dorfman, Roy Williams, and the Chicago outfit's[2] Joe Lombardi discussing a deal whereby they would let the chairman of the U.S. Senate Commerce Committee, Howard Cannon of Nevada, purchase some Teamster property in Las Vegas at a discounted price. In return for which he would help to block the deregulation bill. So casual was the political situation in Vegas that it had been Senator Cannon who approached Dorfman rather than the reverse. Cannon even held meetings with Dorfman and Williams in his private office. The Justice Department hesitated to include the senator in the indictment against Williams, Dorfman, and Lombardi so soon after it had brought charges against Senator Williams of New Jersey and a group of Democratic Congressmen. Instead he was allowed to testify as a government witness. Although when he stood for reelection in 1982 he was defeated by the voters.

During the 1980 presidential campaign, Ronald Reagan had come out against the Carter administration's proposals for deregulating the trucking industry. Because of Reagan's stand, Jackie Presser's IBT council endorsed him. It was an important boost because no Republican had ever been elected without winning Ohio. When Reagan won he named Jackie to his transition team as a senior advisor. Only a few years earlier President Nixon had gotten himself involved with the troubles of the Teamsters union by backing Frank Fitzsimmons against Jimmy Hoffa. There was nothing wrong with the Teamsters supporting Reagan because the union had an honest difference with Carter, who was Reagan's opponent. However, there was no need for the Reagan White House to honor Jackie Presser by giving him a top position on the transition team. Jackie immediately drew unfavorable publicity by announcing that he would be picking the secretary of labor and having a significant say on who was appointed to run the ICC and

---

2. A name used for the Chicago Mafia. In the 1920s and for a while afterwards it was the Capone gang, then it became the syndicate. Now reporters refer to it as "the outfit." Cops called it the mob.

the Department of Transportation. This should have demonstrated to the new administration that they should not get too close to him.

*

The mistakes of the White House carried over all the way down to the federal agents in Cleveland. In the first instance, the FBI wanted complete control over any investigation it conducted. In fairness to their view, over many years the G-men had been burned by local cops leaking information to their favorite reporter or gangster. The agents also did not trust some local U.S. attorneys who received their appointments through politics. The alternative U.S. attorneys, known as strike forces, had only been created in the '60s. In some places the local U.S. attorney, like Robert Morgenthau of New York's Southern District, would not allow a strike force to operate in his territory.

In the midst of the internecine fighting in Cleveland a new player appeared on the law enforcement scene. For years the Department of Labor had been criticized by Congress for failure to combat corrupt unions. On the labor beat, the DOL was the good cop and the FBI was the bad cop. In 1978, when the Carter administration decided to put an inspector general in every federal department, the one appointed to the Labor Department was given the authority to investigate organized crime. While the FBI was glad to have people from the DOL helping them—Labor Department investigators could audit union books at any time, whereas the FBI was required to obtain a subpoena—they did not want them playing Sherlock Holmes. When the Cleveland DOL agents started looking into Presser and his IBT, the FBI kept secret from them (the U.S. attorney and the local strike force) the fact that Jackie was a government informer. One impediment to the DOL gaining acceptance was problem was that they did not have guns or the power of arrest. Thus to the law enforcement world they were not really cops. The FBI also had an obligation to protect their informers and if Presser had been identified as such, he might have been blown to pieces or picked off by a sniper.

Despite FBI secrecy, word leaked out that Presser was working for the government and it was not in the form of whispered rumors. In

August 1981 the story appeared on the front page of the city's leading newspaper, *The Plain Dealer*. Jackie would either have to convince mob leaders that the story was false or go into the witness protection program which the feds had set up to provide refuge for their informers. It was a question of going into exile, which meant being buried in some place like Wyoming—or literally being buried in Cleveland. Except in the latter town, sometimes there was not enough left of the deceased to inter him. Danny Greene, who had also been an FBI informant as well as a gangster, had been scattered all over the parking lot by the bomb that killed him.

The Presser family had always been close to Maishe Rockman, one of the Jewish gangsters, who was also John Scalish's brother-in-law. Maishe was popular with Italian mobsters from Chicago to New York and because of his marital connections he was considered an honorary mafioso. Bill Presser, who had died a month before the story appeared, had always been known as a standup guy, so Rockman felt that the son must be one too. Since Scalish died Cleveland did not have a seat on the national Mafia commission. Instead it was represented there by Tony Salerno of New York's Genovese family. Rockman was able to convince Salerno that the charges against Presser were false. Salerno in turn was acquainted with Roy Cohn, a man who had made his reputation as counsel to Senator Joseph McCarthy's Red-hunting committee. It so happened that one of Cohn's clients was the Newhouse Publishing Company, which owned *The Plain Dealer*. Based on Cohn's arguments, the newspaper withdrew the charges against Presser, prompting an informational picket line to be set up in protest by the papers reporters.

After Roy Williams was convicted with Dorfman in the Senator Cannon case, Jackie Presser appeared to be one of the logical successors as head of the international union. Again, Maishe Rockman persuaded the Chicago bosses that Jackie was the right choice and he was given the job. This meant that the president of the International Brotherhood of Teamsters, the largest union in the United States, and a frequent target of investigation, was headed by a man who was a corrupt union leader, closely affiliated with organized crime and a top-level informer for the FBI all at once. Many years earlier there had been a television show about a man who served as an FBI informer within the Communist Party, entitled *I Led Three Lives*. If you threw in the fact that Jackie Presser had gone through four wives and numerous mistresses, he might have been a good subject for a series entitled *I Led Four Lives*, though there was always the possibility that a bomb or a bullet could take away all of them.

The FBI now had a tiger by the tail. It could be accused of setting union policy through Presser in which case it would be open to lawsuits from aggrieved parties. The White House might not like the fact that an FBI informer was allowed into its circle of influence. If the United States attorney in Cleveland learned of the arrangement, he might complain to the attorney general that the Bureau was playing the old Hoover game of ignoring the DOJ. FBI director William Webster ruled that the Bureau could no longer assign tasks to Presser, but it could receive information he volunteered to give it.

For a time things went well for America's newest labor statesman, which was how young Presser fancied himself. After Jackie's election as Teamster president, Reagan himself called and pledged to work with him. The union threw a big party for its new leader and among the attendees were President Reagan, his chief of staff, James Baker, Vice President George Bush, Senate leader Robert Dole, and other members of the Washington elite.

As president of the International and a White House favorite, Jackie was riding high. In the run-up to the 1984 presidential election, he manipulated a poll of IBT members to show that they favored the reelection of President Reagan over Senator Walter Mondale. Two weeks after Reagan's victory, he visited Teamster headquarters near the capital. There, he greeted the president and vice president on the front steps, then ushered them through a throng of clapping and cheering employees.

Amidst the celebrating over Jackie's new status the Department of Labor began looking into no-show jobs in his union. It was common in unions—as well as many state and local governments—that people were given paid positions but not required to show up or do any work. Even Senator Harry Truman had provided a no-show job for a relative in Missouri, and he was far from alone in the practice. When the DOL began asking questions, Jackie worried, but his FBI handlers made light of the charges. They assured him that he could not be brought down by a few Keystone Cops.

The Cleveland mafia itself was experiencing difficulties. After the assassinations of Greene and Nardi, there had been some people convicted of the crime but none were the top individuals involved. Now the government had witnesses like Jimmy Fratianno. Because he was on the California FBI informer list, Jimmy had suspected it would not be long before he was exposed—the head of the San Diego family, who was also on the California list, had already been murdered. So Fratianno agreed to be a government witness against the Cleveland bosses like Licavoli and Lonardo. The conviction of the leadership practically wiped out the Cleveland mob.

In August 1985, with all the various investigations pending and the ramifications reverberating to Washington, White House political director Ed Rollins appeared at a Teamsters rally in Dearborn, Michigan. There he told the assemblage, "Jackie Presser shares Ronald Reagan's faith in the men and women who made America great... With leaders like Jackie Presser, we can make America stronger, better." Two months later when Rollins left the White House to become a partner in a lobbying firm, he brought in the Teamsters as a client. It looked to be a rerun of the Chuck Colson/Frank Fitzsimmons love affair.

In January 1986, at a White House ceremony, Judge Kaufman, chairman of the President's Commission on Organized Crime, handed the president the commission's report. In it, Reagan was criticized for the White House's contacts with Presser and the Teamsters union. That night a reporter questioned Reagan about what Kaufman had said to him while handing him the report. Reagan said he had not read the report, at which time an aide broke in reminding the president that he had to meet his guests at the dinner. A decade earlier, Nixon had stumbled over the IBT. Now even the Kaufman commission (thanks to some of its members) was criticizing Reagan for his handling of relations with the union.

Some FBI agents like Presser's handler, a clean-cut Annapolis graduate, who not only was head of the Cleveland office's organized crime squad but also its SWAT team, suggested that the Bureau simply tell prosecutors that they had authorized Presser to hire no-show employees. It did not work. Presser was indicted, as was the unfortunate FBI agent. A judge would eventually dismiss the charges against the G-man because he believed he had been granted immunity when he admitted that he had not been truthful in claiming that Presser had FBI permission to hire no-shows. Jackie would die in 1988 while still union president, and the charges pending. The Gipper suffered no ill effects from the IBT connection. Unlike Nixon, whom the country regarded as "Tricky Dick," presidents like Ronald Reagan and Jack Kennedy could smile their way out of any embarrassment and the country still loved them.

*

While the White House and Cleveland feds fumbled with the IBT problem, great progress was being made against the mobs elsewhere. For a decade Professor Blakey's RICO law had largely lain dormant. Under RICO previous crimes could be cited to prove that the defendants were members of a racketeering organization. Even if they had been acquitted it did not matter. To prove that a group was a criminal enterprise, or at least an association, that engaged in a pattern of racketeering, the jury might be given the criminal history of the organization—including offenses committed before some of the individual defendants had joined the group. The notion that evidence of previous crimes—including ones the defendant did not commit or ones that he had been acquitted of could be part of the charges—sounded unconstitutional to many attorneys. Even the name RICO itself was seen as an ethnic slur. However, Blakey denied that he had taken the title of the law from Edward G Robinson's character Little Caesar in the movie of the same name. In it, as Enrico Bandello lays dying from police bullets, he says "Mother of Mercy, can this be the end of Rico?"

The law also did not mesh with the traditional culture of criminal justice. Lawyers and cops were used to working on individual cases. A RICO prosecution would require extensive investigation to catalog all of an organization's activities. Then a jury might be so overwhelmed by the complexity of a case which involved so many individuals and activities, that it would simply acquit the defendants.[3] RICO cases also seemed too much akin to civil suits which dragged on forever and contained little drama. Often at the end there was no clear-cut resolution. Some money changed hands but no one went to jail. The typical prosecutor was a tough, cigar smoking, former college boxer or football player who had led a company of marines across a desert or through a jungle. They preferred to go mano-a-mano with the bad guys and their hired gun lawyers, winner take all, and not settle for a fine. In the criminal justice world fining a criminal was like forbidding him to eat strawberry ice cream for three months.

G-men and cops did not want to pour over reams of documents and write long reports. They wanted to slap the cuffs on the crooks and take them on a perp walk before the cameras, the modern equivalent of a Roman victory parade. In the FBI analytical types who like to compile reports gravitated to national security work where they kept their eyes on foreign spies who only rarely would they be able to arrest, because they had diplomatic immunity. It was easy to tell who was in what section of the Bureau. The agent with the ankle holster was on the bank robbery squad and the one carrying the attaché case was in a security squad.

Despite some setbacks in the late 1970s, the national Mafia syndicate was still flourishing. In 1977 a *Time* magazine cover story (written by a reporter known to have a direct pipeline to FBI intelligence) estimated that nationally the Mafia was grossing an annual 48 billion—of which half was net profit. Only Exxon oil with 51 billion in sales made more, but it netted just 5%. In New York City the Five Families continued to control produce (whether it was meat, fish, or chicken), the garment manufacturing center, the construction industry, and JFK airport's cargo operations. With their hold on food, housing, clothing, and transportation, the mobs possessed enormous economic power and their decisions affected millions of people.

In the '70s however, some of the toughest FBI agents and most aggressive assistant U.S. attorneys developed RICO into an operational

---

3. As happened in a major RICO trial in New Jersey.

concept. Some of them had been officers in the Vietnam War and they were determined that the United States of America would not be defeated by the Mafia as it was by the Vietcong, so they were open to new ideas. The U.S. attorneys were different from some of the ones in the past. Many were like Rudy Giuliani of New York, who had not been born into a comfortable WASP background and attended Ivy League colleges. Instead he came from a modest urban Italian family, attended Catholic schools and New York University Law School in the heart of Greenwich Village. His grades got him a job in the U.S. attorney's office. While there he prosecuted a crew of corrupt NYPD narcotics cops.[4] After his government service he became a partner in a prestigious law firm. In 1981, when he was only thirty-six, the incoming Reagan administration appointed him to the number three job in the Department of Justice.

From his position in Washington, Giuliani watched the FBI building RICO cases in New York. He had already decided he wanted to return to the city and enter politics. If he could convict the mob en mass it would likely propel him into a top elective office. So he sought and received appointment as United States attorney for the Southern District of New York, even though, on paper, it was a lesser position than the one he already held in the DOJ. His Washington service gave him a big advantage in New York. If any federal employees refused to cooperate with him, Giuliani could call main Justice and get the problem straightened out to his satisfaction.

On the other side the Mafia could no longer call a friend in Washington or even local politicians who had connections there. At a time when the drug wars were filling the streets of American cities with bodies, no politician could risk being identified as a protector of organized crime. Unlike Presidents Johnson or Truman, Reagan had no objection to a war on the Mafia. He still had the mindset of a western law man he had often portrayed. Giuliani was familiar with the concept of RICO and when he read a book by Joe Bonanno, boss of the New York family of the same name, in which he described how the Mafia functioned and mentioned the fact that there were both local

---

4. In the movie *Prince of the City*, he is the handsome young AUSA who champions the cop who turns government witness.

and national commissions, Giuliani observed "If he can write about it, I can prosecute it."

In February 1985 Giuliani brought an indictment against the leadership of all five New York City families. One of those he targeted was the boss of the Gambino family, Paul Castellano. Many people regarded the Gambinos as the city's leading Mafia family. However, it was a house divided. Castellano, known as "The Pope," was the brother-in-law of his predecessor Carlo Gambino, and lived in a multi-million dollar mansion on Staten Island which his mob soldiers called "The White House." To the troops he was a remote figure. The head of the other faction was Aniello "Neil" Dellacroce, who was also named in the indictment. When Gambino had died of natural causes in 1976, most of the crew members thought Neil should be made boss. However, his candidacy was hampered by the fact that he was in jail for failing to pay taxes on money he had obtained in an extortion scheme. Instead, Castellano and Dellacroce agreed to split control of the family's twenty crews. Unlike the remote Castellano, Dellacroce was popular and accessible, and was a familiar figure in Manhattan's Little Italy district. At the time of the indictment, he was suffering from a serious case of cancer which would kill him. Before the trial ended, Paul Castellano was assassinated by a crew under the leadership of a Dellacroce protégé named John Gotti.

Probably the best-known individual arrested was Anthony "Ducks" Corallo, boss of the Lucchese family. The Luccheses were a small family but they were united and they controlled many of the most lucrative operations in the garment center as well as operating a major drug trafficking ring. The only problem with Corallo was that he was always being arrested. In 1963 he had gone to jail with state judge James Keogh over a scheme to bribe a federal judge. When Tommy Lucchese died, Corallo, like Dellacroce, was the man the crews wanted to become boss but Ducks was in prison at the time after his conviction in the extortion scheme he had worked with Carmine DeSapio. So an older capo kept the seat warm. Along with Corallo, his underboss and consigliere were also indicted.

Some people felt that the most powerful mafiosos in New York were the Genovese family. It had been created by Lucky Luciano and then was headed by Frank Costello. After Costello's fall, Vito Genovese took over, giving the family its name. According to the indictment the leader was Anthony "Fat Tony" Salerno. With a cigar in his mouth and a cloth cap perched on his head, Tony had the look of an old-time mafioso. It was Fat Tony who had acted as liaison with out-of-town mobs and as such guaranteed that Jackie Presser of Cleveland was not an informer. Unknown to the federal government, Salerno was not the boss of the family. He was second to Vincenzo "Chin" Gigante, the man who shot Frank Costello twenty-eight years earlier. Chin[5] did not seem to enjoy any of the glory of being a mob boss. He posed as a poor, mentally ill nobody who lived with his mother in a cheap Greenwich Village walk-up. On one occasion he had accepted a subpoena standing in the shower dressed in a raincoat and holding an umbrella. Sometimes he would wander the streets in his pajamas and relieve himself in broad daylight. Once when examined by psychiatrists, Gigante pretended that he thought he was at a wedding, asking "Where's the bride?" His family explained that poor Vincenzo had taken one too many punches to the chin during his career as a light heavyweight boxer. Even some psychiatrists believed that story. When Chin was not playacting he lived with his wife in an expensive home in New Jersey and simultaneously with his girlfriend in an equally expensive townhouse in upper Manhattan. Luckily for Chin's domestic peace, both women had the same first name. He somehow got the idea that FBI agents did not work at night: when his chauffeur would race him through the streets of New York and New Jersey so he could fulfill his familial obligations, an FBI tail car followed at a discreet distance.

The Colombo family was represented by Carmine Persico, whom most people referred to as "The Snake," although usually not to his face. Since the Gallo-Profaci war more than twenty years earlier, the Colombos had been a divided family. After the shooting of Joe Colombo, which left him comatose, and the murder of Joey Gallo at Umberto's Clam House, the family was thrown into chaos. Eventually, Persico emerged as boss. Indicted with him was his underboss Ralph

---

5. The nickname supposedly came because his mother called him by the diminutive of Cincenzo. Others thought it was because of his lantern jaw.

Scopo, who was a key figure in the "concrete cartel" racket upon which the commission case was based.

The Bonanno family, whose longtime head, Joe Bonanno, was in a way responsible for the indictments, was represented by its current boss, Philip "Rusty" Rastelli. The Bonannos were another family that was in turmoil since Joe had been kicked off the local New York commission and exiled to Arizona. For a time Carmine Galante had been family head but he had been murdered in 1979. Indicted with Rusty were some of his gang who had been involved in the Galante murder.

To overcome concerns by his superiors in the Justice Department that the mass prosecution would fail, Giuliani agreed to personally try the case. However, at the time a huge political corruption scandal broke out in the administration of Mayor Ed Koch and the big shot defendants had their cases moved to New Haven, Connecticut.[6] So Giuliani took over that prosecution and assigned the so-called "commission case" to Michael Chertoff.

The corruption case involved the political leaders of the Bronx, Queens, and Brooklyn. The leader in Brooklyn, Meade Esposito, was a long-time ally of organized crime, which included a group that in 1986 shot and killed a New York detective and seriously wounded his partner. Though Mayor Koch was not mobbed up, he had allowed Esposito and the other bosses to receive a share of city patronage and remained friendly with them because he wanted their support. Koch always declared that he wanted to be mayor for life, so he made a number of compromises. As it turned out he was defeated in the 1989 election. In assessing Koch's support of the bosses, all of whom, including Esposito, were convicted, one can only recall Louis Freeh's statement about how politics corrupts moral judgment.

Michael Chertoff, who would later become a judge of the United States Court of Appeals and then secretary of Homeland Security, presented a masterful case in the complex RICO prosecution. Defense lawyers took the line that there was no such thing as a Mafia. However, the Southern District prosecution would trace the story of the organi-

---

6. They thought a Connecticut jury would be less shocked by corruption than a New York City jury. They learned to their sorrow that just the opposite was true.

zation from 1900, evoking long-forgotten episodes. The government also brought in turncoats such as Angelo Lonardo, former underboss of the Cleveland family, and Jimmy "The Weasel" Fratianno, one-time acting boss of the Los Angeles family, to testify that in fact there was a New York Mafia commission. Chertoff even called to the stand New York State troopers who had participated in the raid at Apalachin in 1957.

Carmine "The Snake" Persico acted as his own lawyer, which permitted him to address the jury without being sworn as a witness or subjected to cross examination. However, his contribution was more helpful to the prosecution than the defense. He became confused in his remarks and during his questioning of a man who had received a beating for an unpaid loan shark debt, he declared "You was angry because you was beat up, and you was beat up because you didn't pay back the money." He attempted to prove that another government witness was untrustworthy by claiming he had failed to make a promised payoff to the Colombos.

At the heart of the government's case was the concrete cartel. This was a setup whereby the mob steered contracts to supply concrete to construction companies by rigging the bids to ensure their applicant won. On concrete jobs under 2 million the Colombos took a 1% cut. Jobs between 2 and 15 million were divided among seven contractors who submitted rigged bids and paid off 2% to the New York commission. On jobs over 15 million, the payoff belonged exclusively to the Genovese family. The system had been in effect for many years and the rules were so well known that no outsiders dared to make a bid if they valued their health. Historically, the greatest fortunes in New York came from land ownership and development. Any mayor or mayoral candidate knew it would be hard to get elected without the support of the landlords, who were veritable princes of the city. Yet, despite the immense political power the builders wielded, they were willing to pay the highest price for concrete in the United States simply because the Mafia wanted it that way and they were afraid to challenge them.[7]

---

7. When the writer chaired the New York governor's advisory committee on racketeering in the construction industry, it was very difficult to recruit business leaders to serve on the committee. At the time I was informed that government wiretaps picked up racketeers asking who I was. I wondered if they were

In November 1986 the defendants were found guilty and all but one were sentenced to 100 years in prison. The verdict was upheld on appeal. Later, each New York family would be charged and convicted in its own separate RICO case. Once other DAs saw how successful the New York prosecutions had been they began employing similar tactics in their own jurisdictions. By then, Blakey was a highly respected figure in American criminal justice, while Rudy Giuliani's successful use of RICO contributed greatly to his election as mayor.

Following up on the indictment of Presser, the government decided to file a civil suit against the IBT board in the Southern District of New York where Giuliani's office would prosecute it. The Teamsters fought back in their usual free swinging fashion. However, when the board learned that they faced the prospect of individual civil liability, for the sins of the union, they agreed to accept supervision by monitors appointed by the government. The judge in the case, David Edelstein, appointed former New Jersey U.S. attorney, Frederick Lacey, the man who had cleaned up Newark in the 1970s, as an independent administrator of the union with the same powers as the IBT president and executive board. Other monitors were appointed to conduct investigations of, or to oversee, individual locals. The IBT lawyers sought to undercut the monitors' authority by filing suits in federal courts around the country so that the government would be bogged down in a multiplicity of cases. Edelstein simply consolidated all of them in his court. The IBT board believed that charges would not be brought for actions predating the consent decree, but this was not the monitors' view. Union officials were dismissed or punished for practices that had previously been widespread, such as using union funds to pay personal expenses or to purchase a new car as a gift for a retiring officer. Union officials who associated with organized crime figures were removed from their posts. When they appealed the monitors' decisions to Judge Edelstein he generally upheld them and in some cases increased the penalties. When one official filed suit against a monitor, the judge held him in contempt of court.

considering whether a lead pipe might discourage my interest in the subject. However, the answer that they received, i.e., that I was "just a glorified cop," either pacified them or scared them off.

*

The Chinese have a saying that an individual who always succeeds has "the mandate of heaven." The American version is that, "it's better to be lucky than good." In his career, Ronald Reagan was a very lucky man. Under his administration, both the old Soviet Union and the Mafia collapsed. In its later stages the Reagan administration ran into difficulty because of attempts to overthrow the Sandinista regime in Nicaragua. The blame largely fell on Lieutenant Colonel Oliver North. Reagan was just too popular with the American people to ever really lose their confidence.[8] The IBT was brought to heel and Reagan never suffered any consequences for his administration's close relationship with Presser.

President Reagan's political views not only prevailed but even many scholars—who initially dismissed him as just a Hollywood actor, manipulated by other people—now rank him as one of America's best presidents. Jimmy Carter, who allowed ABSCAM to proceed and appointed William Webster as director of the FBI, kept mobsters out of the White House, and the Department of Justice away from their influence, is rated as a not very good president. As the Iranian hostage crisis illustrated, Carter did not have the mandate of heaven.

---

8. Once in a TV address, President Reagan told a story about a bomber in World War II whose crew was bailing out over Germany. Suddenly the pilot heard his tail gunner scream and went back and found him pinned under debris. To comfort the young airman, the pilot told him, "That's okay son, we will ride it down together."

Many of those listening had tears in their eyes when the president spoke. So the media began to research the incident with a view to writing it up. However, no record of such an event could be found and some bomber pilots of that time said it would have been impossible, because of the noise in the plane, for the pilot to hear the gunner calling out. Finally, the story was traced to a wartime movie entitled *Coming in on a Wing and a Prayer*. Instead of criticizing the president, most Americans believed (no doubt rightly) that such incidents of self-sacrifice had occurred in the war and that the president was simply bringing them to life. Ironically, in World War II the 1972 Democratic presidential candidate, George McGovern, had been a bomber pilot and actually experienced a similar incident. After his plane sustained serious damage, the crew prepared to bail out. However, McGovern told them to resume their stations, and with great skill landed the plane safely.

Ironically, McGovern and Jimmy Carter, who as a submarine commander, would have had to order nuclear missiles fired at Russia, both came across to the American public as virtual pacifists. Whereas the Gipper was seen as such a swashbuckler that he even terrified the Russians.

Chapter 11

The Great Divide:
Politicians Divorce the Mafia

On an afternoon in 1980 a thief snatched the brief case of a man walking down a Chicago street. The victim began pursuing him and finally brought him down with a football tackle. When police arrived on the scene, they encountered an unusual situation. Witnesses came up to them and volunteered to tell what they had seen. Cops also noticed that the witnesses and the victim gave comprehensive and coherent accounts of what had happened. Even the thief was cooperative. Later the police would learn that the victim, witnesses, and thief were all FBI agents and the purpose of their little charade was to develop a case that could be prosecuted through the Chicago court system. The incident was part of a larger plan called "Operation Greylord." This time the target was not the Chicago outfit but the political organization that had given it protection.

Worse was to come for the mob and its long-time ally, the Cook County Democratic party. The feds would follow up Greylord with a new assault that would bring down the fount of Chicago political corruption since the 19th century, the First Ward Democratic organization. Not only would its leaders be jailed or drop dead as a result of a sting operation, the Ward would be redistricted away from its rich pickings.

In the past the mobs could rely on politicians to neutralize law enforcement even at the federal level. During Prohibition the bootleggers had so much influence with politicians that they were able to emasculate the Prohibition Bureau. With the rise of the Mafia gangs at the end of the '20s, the only weapon the government could use effectively against them was to bring an income tax evasion case, as happened to Al Capone. Even then it required the White House to prod the Treasury Department after President Hoover had been appealed to by Chicago business leaders. In the 1930s, the politicians and mob bosses were able to avoid criminal tax evasion charges by settling for a fraction of their liability. This arose from a decision by President Roosevelt that he needed men like Frank Hague of New Jersey and Ed Kelly of Chicago to ensure his victories in the presidential elections.

In each mob-dominated city there were individuals who acted as liaisons to Congress and the White House. In New York, it was Bronx boss Ed Flynn, who was Roosevelt's man. Although Flynn had no direct ties with gangsters like Luciano, Costello, or Anastasia, he had to go along with the Manhattan and Brooklyn organizations that the Mafia controlled. In the 1941 mayoral election Flynn spurned Roosevelt's request to back LaGuardia and chose to throw his support to Bill O'Dwyer in order to maintain his political standing in the city. In 1945, after receiving the backing of Frank Costello, O'Dwyer ran successfully for mayor. This meant that the mobs of New York could reach into the White House through City Hall. When Eisenhower was president, despite the fact that racket buster Dewey's assistants ran the Department of Justice, no serious action would be taken against organized crime until the Apalachin Conference and even then it was minimal.

In Chicago Mayor Kelly himself was the one who could influence the White House and after his ouster in 1947 that role fell to County Chairman Jake Arvey. When Richard Daley took over party leadership and the mayor's office, he did not serve as a link between the syndicate and the presidents. However, some congressmen like "Blind Tom" O'Brien, leader of the Illinois delegation, were influenced by their fellow West Side politicians. During the Kennedy administration the Chicago mob was reduced to relying on a congressman with so little influence it was doubtful he could have obtained a new letter bag for a postman.

In the east, after President Truman appointed O'Dwyer ambassador to Mexico, where he would be safe from criminal charges, the president told Massachusetts' powerful congressman John McCormick, "I did it for you John." New England's boss Raymond Patriarca had his headquarters in Providence, Rhode Island, adjacent to the state capital where he maintained close ties to officials. In the Truman administration Rhode Island Senator J. Howard McGrath was chairman of the Democratic Party, then attorney general of the United States (where he tried to block the appointment of the Kefauver committee to investigate organized crime).

With the Missouri gang in the White House, the Kansas City mob had a direct link to the pinnacle of American government. Truman personally disliked some of the gangsters who ran Kansas City's First Ward and other facets of local politics. Still, he was a loyal party man, so nothing was done by the federal government to attack the local Mafia.

Florida politicians were always sympathetic to organized crime. Santo Trafficante ran part of the state and Miami was a city open to all of the mobs. However, Florida was virtually honest compared to Louisiana, where corruption, for practical purposes, was written into the state constitution. In that environment Carlos Marcello of New Orleans was able to operate without interference.

Ohio was a strong IBT state and the politicians were compelled to kiss the ring of Cleveland Teamster leader Bill Presser. The Cleveland mayor, later governor and senator, Frank Lausche, was an honest official, but he too did nothing against John Scalish's mob. The temper of public opinion in Cleveland was shown in 1947, when Eliot Ness sought the mayoralty and was badly defeated.

During LBJ's five-year tenure local politicians were once again able to exert influence but not to the extent they once had. In that time mayors of increasingly poor and riot-torn big cities were primarily interested in obtaining federal funds. In the '70s and '80s the greatest amount of organized crime influence in Washington was exercised by the Teamsters union, largely through the unwise decisions of Presidents Nixon and Reagan to placate the IBT. Even after the takedown of Jackie Presser, when the federal government proposed to take over the union, presidential candidates as diverse as Al Haig, Jack Kemp, and Jesse Jackson backed the union in opposing the measure.

Beginning in the '80s, politicians around the country would learn that it was not only dangerous to be a Mafia boss but it was equally perilous to be an organized crime protector. As Assistant Director Neil Welch of the FBI, whose agents carried out the ABSCAM investigation, would write, "I defy anyone to investigate organized crime apart from political corruption—the actors play on the same stage." A prominent Michigan crimefighter told historian Arthur Sloan, "The mobsters have always been wedded to the political system. That's how they survive. Without that wedding they would be terrorists and we would get rid of them." Cases like ABSCAM, which sent seven members of Congress to prison, Greylord and other Chicago stings aimed at corrupt officials began to convince political leaders it was time to end their long marriage to the Mafia.

Thanks to Professor Blakey, law enforcement officials had learned how to use the RICO law not only against organized crime but against political organizations. One place the government won a great victory over the Mafia was in the mobs' Shangri-La, Las Vegas. The desert resort town was always a tough place for law enforcement to operate because gambling was a pillar of the state's economy. In the postwar years Nevada's powerful U.S. senator Pat McCarran had chaired the judiciary committee. As such, he had huge influence in the White House. The willingness of Senator Howard Cannon to discuss his personal finances with Lombardo, Dorfman, and Williams was an example of how lightly ethical concerns were taken in Nevada

In January 1980 Joe Yablonsky took over as SAC of the Las Vegas FBI office. He had previously served in New York and Miami, becoming so adept at undercover work against organized crime that he became known as "The King of Sting." In the post-Hoover era, he was called to Washington to establish the Bureau's undercover operations program. When he was sent to Nevada, Yablonsky, like any new SAC, tried to develop community support for his agency. He became active in his local synagogue and frequently gave talks to civic groups where he openly charged local politicians with responsibility for the Mafia's free reign in Vegas. His remarks were not well received. Powerful officials such as Senator Paul Laxalt, an intimate of President Reagan, began protesting to Washington. The ABSCAM sting in Atlantic City had terrified politicians all over the country because it raised the possibility that the federal government would routinely institute sting operations against public officials. Now the King of Sting was in Las Vegas. The state's politicians demanded that Washington remove Yablonsky as SAC. However, when their complaints reached FBI director William Webster, they fell on deaf ears.

A simple way for politicians to prevent becoming involved with organized criminals was to keep their hands in their pockets, and when favor seekers' words began to stray into illegal areas, smile and say "But that's against the law." If that didn't work, and with some of the greediest and most overbearing it wouldn't, the right thing to do was to throw them out the door. Of course politicians wanted to get reelected or move on to higher office and they also wanted to make sure their families could keep up with the Joneses. Vegas was a town built around money and its politicians sought their share of it. As it turned out, the key to breaking Vegas would come from places like Kansas City and Chicago.

At the end of the 1970s the FBI obtained a court order to plant a bug in the back of a Kansas City pizzeria where the local boss, Nick Civella, and his top lieutenants held discussions. The purpose of the bug was to gather information about a murder that had occurred in a dispute among Civella and some other local gangsters. However, the listening FBI agents began to pick up some strange conversations. The gangsters talked about Las Vegas, where it appeared that the Chicagoan Lefty Rosenthal was part of a group trying to purchase control of the Stardust Hotel while another group was competing against him. The FBI wondered how a few hoods half a continent away could knows so much about the corporate secrets of the Vegas casinos. Yet, a few days later the owner of the Stardust announced he was selling off his property. On Valentine's Day, 1979, FBI agents intercepted

$80,000 in skim money from Vegas being brought in through the Kansas City airport. As a result, they obtained a search warrant for the home of the local underboss, Carl "Tuffy" Deluna. In it they found meticulous records that he had kept over the years detailing all of the Kansas City mob's business operations, including some involving other cities. The investigation named "Straw Man 1"[1] would lead to the indictment of Nick Civella and his brother, Tuffy Deluna, and Kansas City's man in Vegas, Joe Agosto. Nick died before the trial was completed and Agosto flipped over and became a government witness (although shortly after the trial he died of a heart attack).

Straw Man 1, Pendorf, and another skimming investigation involving Chicago and the Stardust Casino (which would become known as Straw Man 2) began to take its toll. In Vegas too many people were becoming government witnesses. To head them off the Mafia bosses instituted a preventive program. In October 1982 Lefty Rosenthal came out of a local restaurant, got into his Cadillac, and started the engine. The car burst into flames and he barely managed to get out before it exploded. The leading suspect in the case was Frank Balistrieri, boss of the Milwaukee family, because of his propensity for using explosives. Still it was hardly likely that the men who owned Vegas would set off bombs and scare the tourists away. Other investigators believed it was Tony Spilotro who arranged for it. When Rosenthal was questioned about who did it, he replied, "It was not the Boy Scouts of America." The bomb may have been meant to eliminate the possibility of Lefty turning government witness or it may just have been Spilotro in one of his crazy moods. Tony was recalled to Chicago and in June 1986 he and his brother Mikey were found beaten to death in an Indiana cornfield. Spilotro may have been killed to ensure his silence; however, the fact that he was so badly beaten suggests that he was being punished for screwing up the mob's operation in Vegas.

Rosenthal and Spilotro were small fry in the Chicago syndicate. Even if they had talked their knowledge was limited. In contrast, Allen Dorfman, though not a made man, was a major figure in the American Mafia. He had provided loans from the Teamsters pension fund to

---

1. Straw man was a term for individuals the Mafia used as the official owners of some of their Vegas casinos because the real owners could never receive a license from the Nevada Gambling Control Commission.

mobs all over the country. He knew the secrets of Teamster leaders like Hoffa, Fitzsimmons, and the Pressers. He could provide reams of information on the Vegas casinos. In Nevada, Senator Cannon would not have approached Dorfman if he did not believe that he could be trusted by the Nevada political leadership that had rented Vegas to the Mafia. Between Dorfman and his stepfather they could have written an inside history of the Chicago syndicate/outfit since the 1920s.

Released on bail after his conviction in Pendorf, Allen Dorfman had to decide whether or not to cooperate with the government. According to sources, he was considering the possibility. For the mob's point of view it was logical that they would believe a man like Dorfman, long accustomed to the affluent life, might not be able to face spending the rest of his days in prison. So mob bosses Joey Aiuppa and Jackie Cerone, who were also caught up in the Vegas skim case, invoked the rule that anyone who could hurt them must be eliminated. In January 1983, as Dorfman and a companion were walking through the parking lot of a suburban Chicago restaurant, two men ran up behind them and allegedly yelled "This is a robbery!" One of the men fired a .22 automatic at least half a dozen times but only Dorfman was hit. As the head of the Chicago Crime Commission told the *New York Times*, "There is no doubt in my mind that Mr. Dorfman was killed to keep him quiet... if he ever coughed up to investigators...this country would be shaking for a month." The fact that Dorfman's companion had not been shot suggested that he had set up the victim. Someone with access to the crime scene, probably a law enforcement officer, decided to ensure that at least some of Dorfman's secrets did not die with him. He made a photocopy of the dead man's memo book and sent it to the Chicago Crime Commission.

Worse blows were to fall on the Chicago Mafia over its own foibles. Its chief assassin was Harry Aleman, known as "the mob's killing machine." Aleman and his crew were the ones who collected the street tax from independent bookies, burglars, and other hoods. A few who were foolish enough to say no, or even to insult Aleman to his face, ended up six feet under the ground. On one occasion, though, Aleman stepped out of his professional role and committed a murder on behalf of a relative. The victim, one Billy Logan, had been involved in a dispute with his ex-wife over visiting rights to their two children. The lady was Aleman's cousin and she threatened to "call Harry." Not long afterward, as Logan was leaving his house to go to work, he was hit by a shotgun blast, then given the coup de grace with a pistol. Because of some official foot dragging it took several years to bring a charge against Aleman but it was a strong one, including an eyewitness identification. It was tried before a judge known for being a tough law enforcer. However, he declared he did not believe the state's leading witness and Aleman was acquitted. Fixing cases was common in Chicago and usually no one was really shocked by it. This time the public was outraged and the judge was defeated in a retention election.

The decision sparked so much outrage that the FBI decided to strike directly at the courts. It began by initiating "Operation Greylord."[2] During the course of the investigation, agents installed the first legal bug ever to be placed in the judge's chambers of an American courtroom, in the Criminal Court building on Chicago's west side. The Cook County Circuit Court would be cited in a federal RICO indictment as a "criminal enterprise." The agents started in traffic court where ticket fixing was the order of the day and moved to more prestigious judicial divisions which dealt with felonies and major civil matters.

To gain appointment to the bench required strong political support. Some judges had spent a lifetime of service to the local machine. Others were individuals with wealthy relatives in a position to make generous contributions to the party's coffers. Judges were men of respect in the city, with license plates that listed their judicial status. Other than a major elective office a judgeship was the most prestigious post the machine could bestow upon one of its favorites.

One key figure in the investigation was a downstate judge who had been transferred into the Cook County court system to deal with its heavy caseload. His Chicago judicial colleagues referred to him as the "hillbilly judge" because he wore cowboy boots. However, in one of his boots he had a concealed microphone—courtesy of the FBI. To gain the trust of corrupt officials he posed as a playboy and womanizer. The FBI also recruited a young assistant state's attorney

---

2. A pun on English judges who wore wigs and were addressed as "my Lord."

who was labeled by them "The White Knight" and described by associate as someone "with the face of an altar boy and the demeanor of an Eagle Scout." The prosecutor, Terry Hake, eventually moved on to private practice and began fixing cases on a regular basis. Whenever he handed over money he would immediately phone into the FBI office and dictate a report. A typical one would be:

> This is project development specialist Leo Murphy [a cover name]. The time is now 3:08 p.m., approximately 8 minutes after I paid [the name of the court official] in the back of the jury room. The day is July 7, 1981. Thank you.

During the course of the investigation, while still a prosecutor, Hake succeeded in taping one judge as he explained to him how to present a case so that the defendant was sure to be acquitted. The undercover operation became so extensive that in one matter heard before Judge Lockwood, all of the parties except the prosecuting assistant state's attorney were wearing wires. As a reward for his services, Hake would realize his lifetime's ambition: an appointment as an FBI agent.[3]

Greylord began eyeing well-connected jurists like a Chancery judge named Reginald Holzer, who had been a top assistant to Republican "reform" sheriff Richard Ogilvie. Supposedly the scourge of Chicago mobsters, Ogilvie had appointed as his chief investigator Richard Cain, who moonlighted as a hit man for the mob. Cain and Holzer became partners in a record company the cop set up to promote his girlfriend's singing career. While Cain went to prison, Holzer ascended to the bench. In 1985, Holzer was indicted under the RICO statute for mail fraud and extortion and the case was prosecuted by assistant U.S. attorney (and later best-selling novelist) Scott Turow. By the time the government was finished, Greylord had led to the conviction of twenty judges, fifty-seven lawyers, and sixteen police officers or deputy sheriffs.

Next, a mob-connected defense lawyer, with heavy gambling debts, volunteered to be an informer for the local federal strike force. During

---

3. An appointment resented by other FBI agents who had obtained their posts through the normal recruitment process.

the investigation code-named "Gambat" (for gambling attorney), the feds taped politicians, judges, and mob figures. Their principal target was the First Ward Democratic organization, the entity which had provided political protection for Jim Colosimo, Johnny Torrio, and Al Capone. By the end of the 1920s the shoe was on the other foot and the mob was telling politicians all over the Chicago area what to do. The FBI managed to plant a bug in a restaurant booth where the Ward leaders met. They also set up a camera that filmed the people who stopped by to engage in conversations. The targets thought that having the booth was an advantage in doing business. Though their offices were only a short distance from the restaurant, many so-called "respectables" did not want to be seen walking into them. Whereas a short conversation at the booth could pass as a simple friendly greeting. In addition the mob believed that the noise in the restaurant would drown out any conversation. Eventually an alderman and a state senator were sent to prison, another man died of a heart attack. Following the convictions, Mayor Richard M. Daley (son of Mayor Richard J.) took advantage of the case to redraw the Ward boundaries removing the lucrative Loop business district from its jurisdiction. It was the death knell of the old First.

A byproduct of Gambat was the indictment of Harry Aleman on the murder that he had originally been acquitted of. The gambling lawyer had been the one who passed over the $10,000 bribe to the judge to fix the case. When Gambat squealed, the crooked judge, then living in Arizona after being ousted from the bench, killed himself. Most legal experts thought it would be difficult to convict Aleman because it is supposedly a principle of American law that an individual cannot be tried twice for the same crime.[4] However, because the 1977 case had been fixed, the state's attorney argued that Aleman had never been in jeopardy in the first place. Appeals all the way up to the United States Supreme Court were unsuccessful. Harry, who was already

---

4. That is one of the enduring myths which have sent some crooks to jail. For example, despite the widely held belief that a murder conviction cannot be obtained unless a body is recovered, a number of criminals have been found guilty though their victim's corpse was never discovered. By the same token, individuals can be tried for crimes they were previously acquitted of. The theory is that the federal government and a state government are separate sovereignties, so on occasion an individual acquitted in state court is retried on the same set of facts by the federal government. Other times it works in reverse. In New York, the legislature, always concerned with the rights of defendants—particularly their own members—has voluntarily waived the state's sovereign right to try a defendant acquitted by the feds.

serving time in federal prison, was sentenced to a minimum of 100 years in a state one.

By the end of the 20th century the federal pressure was so intense that being identified as the leader of the Chicago mob was equivalent to someone having a target pasted on his back. In 1992, when Joe Lombardo finished doing time on his Pendorf conviction, he ran a series of classified ads in the newspapers declaring that he was not a "made man" and urging, "if anyone hears my name used in connection with criminal activity, please notify the FBI, the local police, and my parole officer." It didn't do any good. Joe got into trouble again in 2005 and was sent to prison on new charges. The U.S. attorney in Chicago observed that if all it took to avoid prosecution was a notice in a newspaper, there would be a lot more ads.

Another shocker for the mob came when Lenny Patrick, a long-time top figure, agreed to wear a wire for the government. As a result he brought down Gus Alex, who ranked even higher than Patrick in the outfit. The news broke in April 1992 and the following month Tony Accardo died. The old mob was not dead but it was not what it once was. Before his death Accardo had warned his troops to stop committing murders, because it was bad for the gangsters' public image. But Tony was a bit late in issuing his warning. He had always been a bad man to cross and had ordered some spectacularly gruesome hits.[5] Even defense lawyers had to change their tactics. At RICO trials they used to argue that there was no such thing as the Mafia. After former bosses in other cities testified that in fact there was one, the lawyers claimed that it was mostly a social organization. Chicago jurors who had seen TV clips of bodies being removed from car trunks knew that the "social activities" often involved homicide. So common was it to stuff a body in a trunk that a local term, "trunk music," was used to describe it.

---

5. In 1978, some thieves had broken into his suburban home while he was on vacation in California, seeking stolen jewelry that Accardo had recovered for a friend. Over the next few months, seven top Chicago burglars were found dead. Not only had they been shot, but in some instances their throats were slit, their faces burned with acetylene torches, or they had been castrated. A federal grand jury was convened to look into the killings. Accardo appeared before it and took the Fifth Amendment. Later, the two hit men suspected of carrying out the murders of the burglars were themselves killed. Accardo could probably have applied for the title of Chicago crime fighter of the year since he had rid the community of nine career criminals.

Despite the success of Greylord and Gambat, the political climate in Illinois did not change. Though politicians might not do business with the Mafia, some governors continued to swap their expensive suits for convict's duds after being caught taking or soliciting a bribe.

Back in New York the mob attempted to stage a revival after John Gotti, who had arranged the hit on Castellano, took over as Gambino family boss in 1986. Gotti, unlike most gang leaders, maintained a high profile swaggering around, giving interviews on TV and having his picture taken. Although by an astute use of bribery and intimidation he managed to beat several cases against him, in April 1992 Gotti was convicted on a number of RICO charges. It had taken five years, three unsuccessful prosecutions, and an estimated $75 million for law enforcement to nail the man people were beginning to call the "Teflon Don." Gotti was sentenced to prison for life. Once, the mob could count mayors and governors as allies, or at least get them to take the stand and urge leniency for the defendant or attest to his good character. Now no member of Congress, mayor, or governor ever appeared as a character witness at Gotti's trials. The only place where he was still respected was in the media and when he died in 1997 it gave him virtually a state funeral with four news helicopters hovering overhead. Wisely, most mob figures stayed away.

Even the man that no one thought would ever stand trial, Chin Gigante, boss of the Genovese family, was convicted. In 1978 the Department of Housing and Urban Development had instituted a program to install glazed thermal windows in New York City housing projects. Mafia-controlled construction businesses quickly snapped up $150 million in contracts. Non-mob contractors were warned not to bid on the jobs or forced to pay a kickback of two dollars on each window they installed. Chin's crazy act was beginning to wear thin. One day when he was walking through lower Manhattan with a handler, appearing infirm or befuddled, a traffic light changed unexpectedly and he sprinted to the sidewalk ahead of his protector. In 1990 when Gigante was indicted in the "windows case," he was still able to obtain testimony from psychiatrists that his ailments made it impossible for him to take the stand. While the case was being argued, the government indicted Gigante again, this time charging him with conspiracy to kill John and his brother Gene Gotti. Finally, after six years of hearings, a judge ruled that Chin was competent to be tried and in 1997 he was convicted on RICO charges. However, the judge showed leniency by only giving him twelve years in prison. He would continue to run his family from his cell until his death in 2005.

The same thing happened in the Lucchese family. They had always been a united group and controlled some of the choice areas in the city. Now under the leadership of Anthony "Gas Pipe" Casso,[6] they began to experience revolts from disgruntled members and a powerful New Jersey faction of the gang. After forty-one murders, Casso's succession was confirmed. Gas Pipe had no respect for mob protocol. He broke a long-standing Mafia rule by ordering a hit on a woman whose only link with the mob was that she was the sister of a person on Casso's hit list. He followed up by having the non-mob brother of another gangster murdered. Eventually, Casso too was indicted by the feds in the windows case and imprisoned.

In 2004, when Big Joe Massino, boss of the New York Bonanno family, was indicted, his underboss, who was his own brother-in-law, testified against him. After Joe was convicted, he too became a government informer and entered the witness protection program. In doing so he was emulating bosses all over the country. By the end of the century some mobs had virtually disappeared and in others there was such a rapid turnover of leaders that there was no time for them to deal with organizational business.

New York politicians such as members of both houses of the legislature and the New York City Council, were imprisoned for bribery. Even individuals who were seen as paragons of virtue fell off their pedestals. The state comptroller, who had previously had a good reputation, was imprisoned for accepting bribes. Governor Eliot Spitzer had to resign after it was revealed he was a patron of an expensive prostitution ring and had arranged to have one of its ladies transported across state lines to service him. His case was a real shocker. As an assistant district attorney in Manhattan he had prosecuted mob leader Tommy Gambino, son of Carlo Gambino, nephew by marriage

---

6. Casso's nickname came from his father who was also known as Gas Pipe for wielding lead pipes on union dissidents. The son hated it but it stuck.

of Paul Castellano and son-in-law of Tommy Lucchese. Tommy Gambino was more of a businessman than a gangster because he actually ran his garment center enterprises. This caused some mobsters to give him the sneering nickname "The Dressmaker." Under Spitzer a sting was set up and bugs planted in Gambino's office. In 1990 he, his brother, two of his employees, and four other trucking companies were charged with racketeering under New York's "little RICO" law and with restraint of trade in violation of the state antitrust law. In 1992 Gambino and the other defendants agreed to plead guilty to a single felony antitrust count, sell their trucking company and pay a $12 million fine. Later Spitzer moved up to attorney general and there he earned the title "The Sheriff of Wall Street" for his vigorous prosecutions of financial leaders. When elected governor in 2006, he was widely touted as the man who would clean up Albany. His fall was a heavy blow to good government groups.

The murder of long-time Philadelphia boss Angelo Bruno in 1980 ended twenty years of stability in that city. It was followed by twenty years of internecine warfare that did as much to destroy the family as law enforcement attacks. Bruno's successor was blown up in 1981 and Nicky Scarfo became boss. Despite the fact that ABSCAM had taken down two Pennsylvania congressman, two Philadelphia city council members and the mayor of nearby Camden, the lesson did not seem to sink in. In 1986 Willard Rouse III, a nationally known developer sought to build a half-billion dollar shopping and entertainment complex, known as "Penn's Landing," on the Delaware River at the foot of Market Street. Scarfo saw an opportunity to get a share. He had one of his lieutenants, Nick Caramandi, tell Rouse's representative, Jim Vance, that a $1 million bribe was necessary to ensure that City Councilman Leland Beloff give the necessary approval for the development to commence. Scarfo anticipated it was only the start of the payoffs. As in ABSCAM, greed blinded the conspirators to danger. Rouse was known to be so honest that he did not even make political contributions, yet he was expected to give a $1 million bribe to the Mafia. When Jim Vance turned out to be FBI agent Jim Vaules, Caramandi and Beloff were arrested. After Caramandi turned government witness, Scarfo himself was brought down in 1988.

While Scarfo was imprisoned, he tried to run the family through his son Nicky, Jr., but was unable to do so. In the early 1990s, John Stanfa, the man who had been driving Angelo Bruno on the night he was assassinated and had always been suspected of having a role in it, tried to take over the leadership. In 1995 he was convicted on RICO charges. The next boss was Ralph Natalli, who contended for power with Joseph Merlino. In 2000 Merlino and some of his associates were indicted. Natalli had the distinction of becoming the first top boss of an American mob family to testify for the prosecution.

In the end the Mafia families were never able to get control of the Atlantic City casinos, though they operated in ancillary areas, such as bribing public officials to award contracts to mob-controlled companies. One of those convicted in a federal sting operation was the mayor of Atlantic City, Mike Matthews. He too had ignored the lessons of ABSCAM. As he told the federal judge who sentenced him to prison, "Greed got the better of me." It could serve as an epitaph for many politicians who were caught on the take.

Perhaps the strangest story in the FBI's war against the Mafia was what happened in Boston. The leader of the Italian faction in New England was Raymond Patriarca of Providence, who died in 1984. Under Patriarca, his lieutenant in Boston was Jerry Angiulo. However, after the FBI won plaudits for sending Angiulo and the Italian mob to prison, it was revealed that some of the agents were working hand in glove with Whitey Bulger, the top Irish gangster in the Boston area and brother of the powerful leader of the state senate, William Bulger. So bad was the situation that two FBI agents were indicted for murder. One of them died before he could be brought to trial and the other was convicted and is serving time in Florida. A number of other FBI agents were embarrassed, as were federal prosecutors. In retrospect J. Edgar Hoover had been right: assigning FBI agents to attack politically connected mobsters was dangerous. It was inevitable that some of them would make mistakes or even go over to the other side. When Whitey Bulger's brother, Senator Billy Bulger, stepped down as leader of the Massachusetts state senate, the Republican Brahmin governor, William Weld, named Bulger president of the University of Massachusetts. Billy, a self-declared "rednecked mick," had gained fame when he led resistance to school integration in South Boston. No one ever thought of him as a great educator. When reporters started to write stories about Billy, brother Whitey threatened to kill them. Bill refused to answer questions about his brother and Governor Weld would not order him to do so. The governor's only contribution to the affair was to sing a comic song about Whitey at a political breakfast. Apparently he thought a man responsible for a score of murders and the corruption of the FBI was a suitable subject for humor.

After Mitt Romney became governor of Massachusetts, he ordered Bulger to answer questions. By that time Whitey was a fugitive. In his testimony, Bill took the line that he had no knowledge of his brother's activities or where he might be. When Romney removed Bill Bulger from the University of Massachusetts's presidency, American higher education survived the blow.

The FBI posted a million-dollar reward for Whitey, but for some reason they could not capture him and he remained a fugitive for eighteen years. Only when a woman recognized him from his wanted photos and turned him in to get the reward, was Whitey caught. There had long been rumors that he was hiding in some secret place in Europe, but he was actually in an apartment building in California. When he was brought back to Boston for trial he tried to make the FBI a virtual co-defendant in his case but the judge would not allow that line of defense.

In New Jersey after the retirement of Sam DeCavalcante, John Riggi ran the family for the next twenty years. After the 1993 attack on the World Trade Center, the owners of the building, the Port Authority of New York and New Jersey, installed a tight new security system. However, the DeCavalcantes were not kept out. One of them obtained a pass that enabled him to move about the complex freely. He used it to arrange for a $2 million holdup of a Brink's crew delivering money to a bank in the Trade Center. The men carried out the robbery in ski masks but they exited the bank without them and were caught by security cameras. One of the robbers became an informer and Riggi and other members of the family were indicted on RICO charges resulting in a ten-year sentence for him.

By the end of the century stories about the Mafia generally described it as a dying or in disarray. In 1999 an analyst for the Department of Justice wrote that in some of its previous strongholds such as Cleveland, Detroit, Kansas City, Las Vegas, Los Angeles, and New Orleans, the Mafia was "weak or nonexistent." In Cleveland there were reported to be no more than five made members still around. Former underboss Angelo Lonardo, who had been a witness for the government in the Commission case, moved back home after he finished his own prison sentence and walked around without bodyguards. Detroit never recovered from the law enforcement blanketing of the area after Hoffa's disappearance. According to the Kansas City Crime Commission, the local mob had nearly died out.

Once upon a time politicians got rich from mob money but they made the fatal mistake of allowing gangsters to be co-equals with them and even to have access to some presidential administrations. In the past few years politicians have run away from any involvement with gangsters. If organized crime, especially of the Mafia variety, and politicians were once wedded, they are now divorced.

Chapter 12

The 21st Century:
The Emergence of the Modern Mafia

In January 1934, when French detectives entered the Alpine chalet of a fugitive swindler named Serge Alexandre Stavisky, *aka* Sacha, they reportedly found him dying of a gunshot wound to the head. However, the public did not buy the story. They believed that Stavisky had been murdered by the police to keep him from revealing what he knew about bribes to politicians, judges, and officials—including police officers. In 1926, Stavisky had been accused of selling worthless bonds of the Bayonne municipal pawnshop to investors. He had also deposited, what he claimed were the emeralds of the late German empress. In fact they were cheap glass imitations he used to inflate the pawnshop's books. Since 1927 he had been free on judicial bail. In 1934 it was revealed that the bonds had been sold to insurance companies on the recommendation of a cabinet minister.

To many people, what became known as "the Stavisky affair" seemed to illustrate the sickness of French society and the corruption of its government. As questions arose about the case the French premier, Camille Chautemps, refused to resign. Coincidentally, the prosecutor who had authorized Stavisky's release on bail so many times was Chautemps' brother-in-law. Finally, public outrage compelled the premier to vacate his office. In his place the Radical-Socialist Party (despite the title, a moderately left group) replaced him with another party stalwart, Edouard Daladier, the so-called "Bull of the Vaucluse." Daladier was a forceful individual. Though a few years later, while serving as premier at the time of Munich and in the first year of World War II, he would prove to be more like a frightened cow, bossed around by his titled mistress.

Daladier's first act was to demand the resignation of Jean Chiappe, the prefect of police of Paris who was a hero to the right wing elements in France. However, Daladier undercut his own position by offering Chiappe an appointment as governor general of Morocco. The public wondered how a man deemed unsuitable to be chief of police of Paris was good enough to hold a post once occupied by France's great colonial pro-counsel, Marshal Hubert Lyautey. Because Chaippe was a right-wing prefect of the Paris police, Daladier's government sought to balance the ledger by transferring the director general of France's other police force, the left-leaning Sûreté, to head the Comedy Français. Parisians jeered that a cop heading the "House of Molière" was a fitting subject for one of the great writer's comedies. Apparently the reason for the appointment was because the company had presented a play which offended left-wing sentiments.

In response to Chiappe's dismissal the right-wing elements of the nation, war veterans, royalists, and anti-Semites, took to the streets. Sensing revolution in the air, the Communists ordered out their own followers. The Paris police, under a newly appointed and inexperienced prefect, moved to deal with the disturbances. Not so coincidentally, two of his top commanders who had been loyal to Chiappe called in sick. At about 6 p.m. on February 6th, hundreds of thousands of people gathered to march to the bridges spanning the River Seine that led to the French parliament building. There were some encounters between supporters of the left and the right but mostly the two groups worked together against the police. To defend the Parliament, a force of Paris police and national gendarmerie, the latter including members of the Republican guard that performed a similar function in Paris to

Britain's Royal guards, were mobilized. Political riots were common in France since the storming of the Bastille in 1789, and on more than one occasion a Paris mob had overthrown the government. Everyone recognized that the fate of the Third Republic, which had existed since 1871, was at stake.

When the demonstrators surged down the streets toward the Seine they were stopped by police. In the melee that followed, many officers were struck by missiles, including park railings that had been uprooted by the mob and used as weapons. Some police officers, feeling threatened by the rioters, opened fire without receiving orders to do so. Fire hoses were brought in to douse the demonstrators but they had little effect.

Within the Parliament building members of the chamber of deputies urged Daladier to send for the army before they were all lynched. The premier hesitated because the military leaders were sympathetic to the right and he feared that they would seize control of the country. As the evening wore on, the police in the streets were beginning to be overwhelmed. Horses were hit with paving stones and slashed with razors. Balls of coal thrown under their hoofs caused them to trip. More and more policeman were felled by missiles. When the mobs reached the bridge, a trumpeter was ordered to stand on a parapet and sound the call to bring the crowd to attention while a high-ranking police official read a proclamation warning that the authorities would open fire. Both men were badly injured by rocks. As the mobs began to push across the bridge, more police began firing on their own initiative. Finally, a leader emerged—Colonel Simon of the Republican guard arrived on the scene with 175 gendarmes, formed his troops, and personally led a charge against the mob, clearing them from the scene. Estimates of the dead in the riot ranged from thirty to seventy.

After a few less tumultuous disturbances, Daladier was forced to resign and a coalition government was formed. Across the Rhine, the new German chancellor, Adolf Hitler, noted the affair and drew conclusions unfavorable to the French government

The Stavisky affair and France between the two world wars provides a model for study because in many ways it closely resembles problems of present-day America. In the '20s and '30s France was a great power with the strongest army in the world. It was allied diplomatically with Britain and on friendly terms with the United States. It was not likely that the former World War I allies would engage in conflict with each other. In a crisis France could always rely on British support. However, a menace worse than Imperial Germany had arisen from Soviet Russia because not only did it threaten Europe, internally Communists were a major force in the Third Republic.

In the 1920s, Paris had been the arts and entertainment capital of the world; still there was great unrest among French citizens. In its colonial possessions France put down revolutions in Indochina and Islamic countries like Syria and Morocco. During the Depression era of the 1930s, within France the struggle between left and right was intense. The average Frenchman had low regard for most of the country's political leaders of whatever faction. The dominant parliamentary body, the Chamber of Deputies, was commonly believed to be a den of thieves and high officials of the government were regarded as incompetent or worse. Governments changed every six months or so, but the same individuals who were in a previous cabinet would be given portfolios in the new one. In the interwar years, making money became the prime goal of many people and a common saying was "All the world is for sale; it's just necessary to name the price." Many Frenchman saw their country slipping away from the grandeur of its past.

In the big cities violent criminals such as the Paris apache gangs robbed people in the streets or committed assaults. Marseille was run by big-time crime bosses. French police were well known for using forceful methods. Exceptionally troublesome criminals were sent to a prison colony at Cayenne in French Guiana known as "Devil's Island." Murder was punishable by the guillotine.

Police corruption was common and the rivalry between the Paris police and the Sûreté hampered law enforcement. The Sûreté was scattered about France and politicians had a great deal of influence with local police. A municipal police chief who ran afoul of an important politician was likely to be transferred to a distant and less desirable post.

The fact that an insignificant man like Stavisky could rise in France showed how easy it was for a fraudster to operate. Serge Alexander Stavisky was born in 1886 in the Jewish pale of czarist Russia and at four was taken by his parents to France. There, beginning in 1906, he worked as a café singer, nightclub manager, and the operator of a gambling den. His good looks brought him the name of "Le Beau (handsome) Sasha." Eventually he came to manage the municipal pawnshop in Bayonne. When questioned closely by inquiring newsmen, Sasha would bribe the reporter's paper by buying a great deal of advertising space. If that didn't work he would buy the paper itself. In 1927, when he was put on trial for fraud, the repeated postponements permitted him to remain at liberty.

The Stavisky affair was the culmination of a series of scandals that caused public outrage in France. In 1928, a man named Julian Klotz, formerly minister of finance, was arrested on charges of issuing bad checks. That same year a woman named Martha Hanau was accused of swindling hundreds of investors in a series of fraudulent schemes. However, it took seven years to get her convicted, during which time she was frequently set free to continue her operations. When she was finally given a long prison sentence she committed suicide, although many people believed that her death was faked and she had simply left the country. In 1930 Albert Oustric, a Parisian banker, was authorized by the minister of finance, Raoul Praet, to float some overvalued Italian stocks on the Paris Bourse. Later the minister went to work as one of Oustric's lawyers. When Oustric's bank collapsed, ruining many of its investors, an investigation was conducted by Praet, who had returned to government as minister of justice. Not surprisingly nothing came of the probe. Another who was involved was René Besnard, former French ambassador to Rome who had assisted Oustric in his schemes and then also went to work for him. Praet and Besnard were reprimanded by the French Senate but no criminal charges were filed.

Finally, in January 1934, Sûreté inspectors (detectives) were ordered to locate Stavisky and arrest him. It took a long while for them to find him and when they arrived at a ski lodge in Chaminoix they hesitated before moving in. Finally, when one of the officers knocked on the door and identified himself as a policeman, he reported that he heard a shot inside. When they entered the room Stavisky was supposedly still alive, but instead of taking him to a hospital immediately, they called their superior in Paris. Eventually, Stavisky was transported to a hospital but he had lost so much blood that he could not be saved. One rumor was that the police did not want to bring him in for fear that he would make politically embarrassing revelations. Some French writers called it "suicide by persuasion." The affair was too much for the French people and the riot of February 6th resulted. In the aftermath, many attempts were made to get to the bottom of the Stavisky case. Georges Simenon, who was the country's leading mystery writer, was hired by a newspaper to investigate the case, as was Sir Basil Thomson, a former police official at Scotland Yard. No resolution of the affair resulted from their efforts, though their stories were good for circulation.

In 1936 an alliance of left wing, socialists, and Communists formed "the Popular Front" and won the elections. Their government only lasted for two years and was kept busy coping with, not only opposition from the right, but with strikes by their own followers. In 1938 Daladier returned as premier and the country began to face up to the Nazi threat. In 1940, when France fell after a mere seven weeks of resistance, many of the rightist elements joined the Vichy government while both left and right worked in resistance movements and the more traditional patriots joined Charles de Gaulle. Despite being on the winning side in World War II, France would never regain its status as a great world power.

*

There are obvious similarities between present-day America and interwar France. Despite the country's military strength, Americans do not feel safe. The United States has fought wars in Vietnam and the Middle East without achieving lasting victory in any of them. Russia under the leadership of Vladimir Putin is being restored to the power once held by the Soviet Union. The proliferation of nuclear weapons leaves America open to attack not only by great powers like Russia or China, but by smaller states or terrorist groups. The 9/11 destruction of the World Trade Center could easily be repeated anywhere in the country.

The brightest of young Americans flock to the financial services industry because of the fabulous rewards to be found there. Often it appears that the chief skill of such people is finding ways to get around legal and ethical rules. Politicians and bureaucrats are repeatedly arrested for bribery at all levels of government. Regulators often do not perform their duties because they are either fixed or receive the promise of lucrative jobs after they leave federal service from the very people they are supposed to be regulating. Under the revolving door system, after a bureaucrat has resigned he can use his government knowledge and contacts to help his private employer or clients. He can also return to the government where his work may require him to regulate his previous employers.[1]

Few people believe that Bernie Madoff's operations were so well concealed that they defied discovery. Many question how he could have delivered consistently high returns. Most suspect that a number of people who knew what was going on were either prevented from exposing him or did not choose to do so. Madoff might be tagged as the American Stavisky, except his frauds dwarf those of the French swindler. Since the crash of 2008 many of the individuals responsible for it have remained in their jobs or skipped off with their golden parachutes. No one has been punished by a criminal court for the reckless, often legally questionable, activities that led to the financial meltdown.

The well-known financial writer Charles Gasparino, in his book, *Circle of Friends*, has recently explained why the government has been able to convict so many people for insider trading and no one for offenses committed that brought on the great crash. Inside traders are easy to ferret out and successfully prosecute. The individuals who brought down the financial system in 2008 are much more difficult to bring charges against and one suspects the government is still applying the rule that some organizations are too big to fail and some top executives too big to jail. The notion that money and influence are

---

1. There are regulations requiring bureaucrats to recuse themselves for a year or two from working on matters that they previously dealt with while in the government. Incoming government officials are also not supposed to handle cases involving their former employers. However, unless the official leaves a paper trail, the regulations are very difficult to enforce.

everything, found in France between the wars, seems to have taken hold in America.

The political bitterness in Washington also resembles that of the French government between the wars. American opinion polls constantly find respect for Congress extremely low. Everywhere there is a feeling that the United States will soon pass from its status as the leading power of the world—if it has not already done so. The lesson of Stavisky is that businesses engaged in fraud and official corruption on their behalf demoralize a country so severely that people lose faith in their own government.

*

Until the mid-1980s, Mafia influence in the United States was not only strong in state and local government, but stretched as far as the White House. Then, as a result of certain social and political developments, the enactment of new laws and the adoption by federal law enforcement of successful strategies and tactics, the federal government was able to greatly reduce the power of organized crime. By the 1990s some experts felt that it would soon disappear. Others believed it could make a comeback. Certainly the current ethical climate in America makes this possible. However, if the Mafia does revive it will have to do so in a much revamped format.

In a 2006 book describing the war on the Mafia, I concluded that the old American Mafia could never restore its previous power unless it found a means to fend off federal law enforcement. In my research I examined various means by which the Mafia might accomplish this. For example, some observers have long argued that the phenomenon of "ethnic succession" would bring black and latin gangs to dominance in the cities and they would be able to use their power to demand that local politicians keep the federal authorities off their backs. In short, they would repeat the mid-20th century scenario where political machines, whose influence extended to White House level, protected their Mafia allies by holding the feds at bay. In those times only the imprisonment of Lucky Luciano by a Republican prosecutor, Tom Dewey, hurt the Mafia. However, Luciano's successor, Frank Costello, quickly repaired the damage. In 1944 the Chicago syndicate leadership was sent to prison for trying to take down America's fifth-largest industry, Hollywood. In that instance the case had been brought by federal prosecutors in New York City, one of them a very competent attorney and both trial and appellate cases were heard by distinguished judges who could not be fixed. Still, the defendants were paroled with record speed.

There were several problems with the ethnic succession theory. Blacks and Hispanics do not have the same kind of tight criminal structures that the traditional Italian gangs possessed. In addition, because of their drug dealing and the violence that accompanied it many politicians were fearful of helping them. Even though a gang like the Chicago Gangster Disciples, with 30,000 members, was a powerful force, they were unable to control City Hall, much less influence Washington. In 1990 Larry Hoover, *aka* King Larry, the head of the Disciples, where he ran a hundred-million-dollar-a-year drug business, branched out to engage in extensive political activity, registering voters and supporting candidates in city elections. When Hoover sought parole from prison, where he was serving two life sentences for murder, many politicians backed him, including a former Chicago mayor. It was argued that the gangsters had become a civic group. Then in 1997, the government convicted Hoover and many of his members on drug conspiracy charges. In recent times the Gangster Disciples have declined to only 18,000 members. In 2013, an Illinois senator urged the United States attorney in Chicago to lock up the entire lot. Since the country was not under martial law, the prosecutor could not comply with the request.

Another factor mitigating against a return of the traditional Mafia is that the political power of the cities that made organized crime so strong has eroded, along with the old-fashioned political machines. American elections are now won in the suburbs where people have different priorities than city dwellers.

For a while a popular notion was that the mob would "Marry Wall Street." While some gangsters did gain a foothold in the financial world, they lacked the skills or polish to do more than set up pump-and-dump bucket shop operations which quickly folded under law enforcement pressure. In many instances a gangster's idea of a good sales pitch was to point a gun at the customer. The kind of organized crime that flourishes in the financial world is fueled by money, not muscle, and the mafiosos have not able to develop multibillion dollar hedge funds that would make them big players on Wall Street.

A more likely possibility is that sophisticated foreign criminal organizations will use the American Mafia to carry out certain tasks for them in the United States. Overseas crooks have many advantages. They can conduct their operations in several countries, thereby concealing their finances and secrets from the regulatory authority of any one jurisdiction. Luxembourg and the Cayman Islands have more banks than New York City. Most of them exist to maintain depositors' secrets from regulators in their own countries. Individuals involved in unlawful activities can move money across national borders with the touch of a button. They have ties to various governments and their national intelligence services, through which an international organization can acquire information that is not even available for a White House briefing.

One possible example of how a foreign organization could penetrate the United States was furnished by the Bank of Commerce and Credit International (BCCI), which was set up in 1973 in the Middle East by a Pakistani named Agha Hasan Abedi. At the height of its operations it had $23 billion in assets, 14,000 employees, and 400 branches in 73 countries. Its clients included drug dealers, dictators, international arms traffickers, and those with flight capital such as politicians with bribe money to conceal. Its operations were no secret to law enforcement agents in many countries. However, BCCI distributed bribes and favors to top politicians to win the support of governments. Former British prime minister James Callaghan was a paid advisor to the bank. Abedi donated $500,000 to former President Jimmy Carter's presidential library. In other instances BCCI employed murder squads to silence individuals who posed threats to them.

In the United States the bank snagged as its front man Clark Clifford, dean of the Washington permanent government. Clifford had begun his career with his fellow Missourians in the Truman White House. From there he had gone on to be the man politicians and corporate CEOs in trouble sent for to straighten out their problems.[2] Lyndon Johnson made him secretary of defense, expecting him and the president's representative at the Paris peace talks, Ambassador Averill Harriman, to pull the United States out of the Vietnam quagmire. However, the leaders in Hanoi knew that Johnson and his advisors were on their way out. So they waited to deal with the Nixon administration and its chief foreign policy figure Henry Kissinger, who was able to arrange a truce in which the North Vietnamese waited for two years before they finally took over South Vietnam.

On the domestic side, Clifford had begun to lose some of his ability to work magic in the capital. When Georgia banker Bert Lance, Jimmy Carter's Director of OMB, got involved in a financial mess and the Senate started probing, Clifford was called in to save the day. However, his act no longer worked and Lance was forced out of the government.

Nearing the end of the end of his long career, Clifford looked to the BCCI as a financial windfall and prestigious post to add to his resume. For a time he was able to keep Washington regulators and congressional probers from looking too closely at the bank. It almost worked. Then a frustrated investigator told his story to New York County district attorney Robert Morgenthau. As Bobby Kennedy's U.S. attorney in New York, Morgenthau, and his father Henry, as President Roosevelt's treasury secretary, always opposed corrupt criminals and politicians. Just as Morgenthau was beginning to close in on Clifford, the latter was publishing memoirs in which he sought to cement his image as a great statesman who belonged in the pantheon with such figures as Daniel Webster, Henry Clay, Elihu Root, and Henry Kissinger. When Clifford's self-congratulatory tome came out, the BCCI scandal had broken open and reviews of his book spent less time on his supposed past triumphs than his present scandal-scarred banking activities. He was indicted, although he was excused from standing trial because of his age.[3] The investigation left his reputation

---

2. Men like Clifford were the successors to the New Dealers who portrayed themselves as noble figures. Today slick operators have their walls festooned with pictures of themselves when they were hippies and antiwar protesters.

3. It is interesting that in America men of advanced years who are active in business or politics suddenly become almost totally infirm when they are faced with scandal. The stories about them then change from puff pieces about their driving energy, to a recital of their many recently acquired diseases and disabilities.

in shreds and his public support was limited to people like Pamela Harriman (née Digby), daughter of an English Lord. Among her various husbands were Winston Churchill's son, Randolph, Broadway producer Leland Hayward, and Governor Averill Harriman. Most of her fame came from the gossip columns, particularly the cries of outrage from various of her husband's children whom she allegedly cheated out of their inheritance. At the time, her own position as chief hostess of the Democratic Washington establishment was rapidly deteriorating and when her obituaries appeared they were not flattering. The old guard in Washington, New York, and the international jet set had been replaced by the new guard of superrich, with retinues of lawyers and public relations persons. Such people looked on Clifford and Harriman as dinosaurs. While the BCCI structure was a clever one, and its choice of Clifford was a seemingly good investment, he could not maneuver past American law enforcement or open the doors of the White House. In the end he could not even save himself.

In the early years of the 20th century another foreign organization provided a model of how the American Mafia might function as a subsidiary of an international crime syndicate. This was the Bureau Zaharof that exercised influence from the turn of the century to the 1930s. Its leader, Basil Zaharof, was known as the mystery man of Europe. Born Basileios Zacharias, probably in Constantinople around 1850, he supplied the European states with arms. One element of his system was his ability to identify himself and his organization with diverse interests. As he said, "I was a Russian in Russia, a Greek in Greece, a Frenchman in France." The headquarters of his operation was in Paris where he maintained a lavish home, bought a newspaper, founded a bank, cultivated the French establishment and received the Legion of Honor. His various companies often had cabinet members, high-ranking military officers, and well-connected people from several nations on their board of directors.[4]

Though Zaharof did not possess any royal blood, one of his ambitions was to become king of Greece. On one occasion he employed

---

4. Older readers will recall Zaharof as the model for Undershaft in George Bernard Shaw's *Major Barbara*, Achille Weber in Robert Sherwood's *Idiot's Delight* and as a regular character in Upton Sinclair's Lanny Budd novels.

168 agents to stir up riots and set fire to the royal palace. Individuals who opposed him often met mysterious deaths. His spy networks were so well-connected that he had the best intelligence information in Europe.

His trump card was his standing in Britain. In 1895 he became the star salesman for the giant arms manufacturer Vickers. This permitted him to operate worldwide on behalf of the British imperial establishment. He sold machine guns and battleships to a number of countries, usually to both sides at once, and his annual commissions made him super rich.

Zaharof was very close to British prime minister David Lloyd George, who was frequently accused of accepting large sums from various individuals and survived more than one scandal, such as improper financial relations with the Marconi Radio Company and selling royal honors like knighthoods to the highest bidders. So close was their relationship that during World War I the prime minister put a destroyer at Zaharof's disposal so that he did not have to travel on passenger ships and risk being captured by the Germans. Eventually Zaharof was made a Knight of the Bath, which entitled him to be called Sir Basil. At that time, Sir Basil Thomson, Scotland Yard's director of intelligence, found evidence that British officials were acting as Zaharof's secret agents. Though Thomson was a son of the Archbishop of York and well connected in the British establishment, the Sir Basil who was dismissed by Lloyd George was the Scotland Yard chief. Zaharof died before World War II began and his organization did not last.

In the postwar era narcotics became the illicit commodity that was most lucrative. Among the leading drug rings were the so-called French connection in which the Italian Mafia secured Middle Eastern drugs and turned them over to French sources, who would refine them and smuggle them in the United States where they would be sold by the American Mafia. An even more powerful group came from Latin America, especially the Colombian cartels who used intermediaries to sell cocaine in American cities, thereby making billions. It was the Colombians who introduced the cheap, easily ingested cocaine derivative known as "crack," which in the 1980s sparked wars among dealers who turned U.S. cities into free-fire zones. However, neither the French connection nor the Colombian cartels sought to obtain major influence in American politics. After a while they were unable to deflect attacks by the United States government.

*

Criminal organizations do not arise because some ruthless gangsters decide to go corporate. Zaharof benefited from the continental arms races of his time. The American Mafia arose because Prohibition required groups that could carry on large-scale bootlegging. In the second half of the 20th century, when drugs became "cool," the U.S. market demanded its fix. In the post Prohibition era, the Mafia control over portions of the American labor movement provided a basis for their power in the business world. Many employers preferred dealing with the Mafia because it provided a rationalizing influence in certain industries. For example, in construction the mob was often a vital element. When the writer was involved in an investigation of the New York City construction rackets, it was disconcerting to find that, contrary to popular belief, housing and construction costs would be higher, not lower, if Mafia influence were removed from the industry.[5]

In imagining a crime syndicate of the future, some key components will be needed. It will have to be run from abroad and sheltered by foreign states. Its operation would also have to be high tech. Already in America many frauds originate offshore. Recently the NYPD and the Queens County district attorney broke a case labeled "House of Cards." This involved three dozen defendants who used fake credit cards to send shoppers on nationwide sprees buying high-end goods that were later fenced. The defendants were able to obtain account holders' checking and debit account numbers from an unknown supplier in China. The local boss of the operation was a 36-year-old Chinese resident of New York City, whose employees were also Chinese. The ring had a relationship with another unknown individual

---

5. When New York skyscrapers are going up, the Mafia will usually provide a general foreman to ensure that petty rivalries between craft unions or parking problems that prevent the delivery of building materials are quickly taken care of and the offending party does not make the same mistake again. As a result the building goes up on time, and the builder does not default on his bank loan. If the Mafia foreman (and his strong arm boys) were out of the picture, construction schedules would not be met, loans would be more costly to obtain and the builder would have to charge higher rents.

in China who was able to emboss cards with the color and artwork depicted on genuine credit cards. He would then inscribe false names and load information onto the magnetic strip where it would show on a store owner's machine that it was a legitimate account but would bear the name of the false shopper who used it. Utilizing court authorized electronic eavesdropping of thousands of conversations, most of which required translation from Chinese (both Mandarin and Cantonese), the participants in the ring were sent to prison. However, the principals in China were beyond American jurisdiction.

Another NYPD case known as "Plastic Pipe Line" involved nearly four dozen individuals using counterfeit credit cards to steal money and buy electronic goods. This scam was run from Nigeria. Again, after a long investigation, the police and the DA developed cases against the American criminals who received prison sentences but they were not able to apprehend any of the principals in Nigeria. Since the overseas leaders in both house of cards and plastic pipe line were safe from charges, their rings could easily be reconstituted.

Among the past examples of European crime syndicates, the Stavisky case offers little of value to a present-day international crime organization, rather it is a cautionary tale for governments that it cannot continue to excuse blatant wrongdoing by well-connected individuals, lest the government itself be brought down. The scandals that constantly occur in contemporary America will someday produce one that will shake the country to its foundations.

BCCI and Zaharof were both clever at the way they operated. They had bases in many countries which permitted them to hide transactions from various regulators. However, other than handing out money to select individuals, BCCI did nothing to help the United States. In contrast, Zaharof was not only well connected with such powerful people as Lloyd George, but he provided massive arms orders for British corporations like Vickers, and most importantly he supplied governments with useful information on the plans and weapons of other countries. In the years leading up to World War I he was better informed than the intelligence bureaus and general staffs of the great powers. In 1914, European statesmen and generals expected a short war and an easy victory. Zaharof knew better. When the British War Office failed to provide enough munitions for its troops, it was the Civilian Minister of Munitions, Lloyd George, and his close confidant, Basil Zaharof, who were able to make up the shortfall.

The new Mafia will furnish information to U.S. intelligence on terrorist plans, hacking, and cyber warfare groups. In some cases it will secure the capture of dangerous terrorists or other criminals who will be quietly shipped off to foreign countries where the criminal justice system is run in a no-nonsense manner. American law enforcement has reorganized its operations to combat current threats. One of the tasks will be to prevent a modern version of the Bureau Zaharof from penetrating the top levels of American government. However, if the international mob kingpins are providing useful information to U.S. security agencies, the latter will be reluctant to shut off the pipeline.

When the new international Mafia besieges the United States, it will likely confront a political system much like the present one, where the chief ingredient is money and those who control the levers of power are career politicians and lobbyists for the special interests. Such people operate by trading favors. In the final analysis, as FBI director Louis Freeh observed, "Politics can sometimes distort judgment and corrupt moral sense." Anyone who has seen the political world close-up knows that he expressed an eternal truth.

The new Mafia will not come forward as representing some particular ethnic group nor will it serve as a front for drug dealers and killers. That was a prime reason why the old Mafia failed. Instead, it will present itself as a modern, efficiently managed, technically expert, financial conglomerate that will enable government and private parties to undertake large projects for the benefit of mankind. In addition, while not broadcasting the fact, they will demonstrate to governments how they can be of help in maintaining national security in countries like the United States.

The new Mafia would have to share some of its wealth with American banks and corporations and serve as a diplomatic conduit between America and some foreign governments. It will also have to avoid Zaharof's mistake of putting his name and face to international intrigue. Although he was never brought down in his lifetime, his organization did not survive him. A modern international criminal organization will not have a clearly designated head but a number of less publicly known individuals directing it.

Of course, there will always be naysayers who will point out that the new Mafia front groups are making vast profits and that some politicians seem to have benefited personally from wise investments. Occasionally there will be stories about individuals who have met with fatal accidents after they ran afoul of some of these international groups. However, it will be difficult to link any of this to ostensibly respectable people and such stories will not have much impact. This is particularly true because such professions as investigative reporting are rapidly dying out.

As for the old American Mafia, if they have any place at all, it will be as foot soldiers in areas such as drugs and gun smuggling or providing domestic muscle for the international Mafia. In Dumas's novel, *The Count of Monte Cristo*, the hero, Edmond Dantès, seeks to revenge himself on the men who caused his false imprisonment. This involves maneuvering through the high levels of French society to bring down politicians and bankers. In one instance, though, he requires the services of a classic criminal gang led by Luigi Vampa, who controlled the bandits operating out of the catacombs of Rome. For the American Mafia, being reduced to this status would not be something new. Until Prohibition they were largely small-time gangsters and often worked as Election Day sluggers or performed other services for political machines. Their return to that sort of modest position, or to low-level smuggling operations, would be due to their failure to develop the managerial, technological, and intelligence skills required to operate large-scale 21st-century criminal organizations.

The U.S. criminal justice system will eventually find ways to cope with international conspiracies. It took the fifty years between 1930s and the 1980s to cripple the American Mafia. It may well be that victory was just World War I, and World War II is now starting. After we win that in thirty or forty years, it will be time for criminal world war three. By that time the U.S. may play such a reduced role on the world scene that even access to 1600 Pennsylvania Avenue will no longer be much of an achievement. If so, a 21st-century Zaharof will most likely seek to convince people he is actually Chinese.

Appendix I

The Strange Behavior of Governor Dewey

In 1940, Tom Dewey, though only thirty-eight and having held no higher office than a county district attorney, was considered a real possibility to win the Republican nomination for president of the United States. Every elected president for over sixty years had been a governor, Senator, or cabinet member. However, the 1940 Republican convention was so wide open that a Wall Street lawyer, Wendell Willkie, who had never held public office, received the nomination for president. The fact that Roosevelt was running for an unprecedented third term, and had accumulated the usual criticisms that a chief executive receives after eight years in office, meant the Republican nominee had a real chance to win. Only the fall of France persuaded voters to stay with FDR. In 1942, Dewey easily won election as New York governor. In 1944 he received the presidential nomination of the Republican Party. However, the country was at war and the voters again decided to go along with the president. In 1946, Dewey was reelected governor by a wide margin and with a strong GOP tide running and the weak, accidental President Harry Truman in the White House, it appeared as though Dewey would be moving to Pennsylvania

Avenue. To the surprise of many people, though, he lost the election. Dewey would remain governor until the end of 1954, and would exercise considerable influence in the Eisenhower administration which took office at the beginning of 1953. After the governorship, he would found a major law firm and continue to exert influence in Republican councils. Today he is largely forgotten, the only visible sign of his reign is a rural thruway named for him.

Between his election as governor in 1942 and his second presidential run in 1948, public opinion about Dewey changed. He went from being viewed as a crusading prosecutor to just another politician—and a stuffy one at that. The remark about him looking like "the little man on the wedding cake" resonated with voters. Part of the reason for the change in Dewey's image may have stemmed from his experiences with the American Mafia.

As a special prosecutor he had secured a fifty-year sentence for Lucky Luciano. He had even acquired a heroic aura because, for a time, the story was widely believed that Dutch Schultz had planned to assassinate him. As noted previously, Schultz's murder was more of a power-play by Luciano and Lepke to seize Dutch's holdings rather than protect Dewey from assassination.

After being elected governor, Dewey seemed to lose interest in organized crime fighting. He would not commute Lepke's death sentence in return for him providing information on Sidney Hillman, the American labor leader closest to the White House. Even though it might have been useful to Dewey in the '44 presidential election, where "clear it with Sidney" became an issue. Once he started talking, Lepke would have undoubtedly revealed secrets about powerful mob figures and the Mafia bosses would not have liked that. They in turn might have raised embarrassing questions about Dewey's tactics in Luciano's prosecution—or other matters.

At the end of World War II Dewey released Luciano from prison in return for him agreeing to accept deportation. Dewey cited the claim that Luciano had been helpful during World War II in preventing sabotage on the New York waterfront and providing information to American forces invading Sicily. However, he admitted "the actual value of the information [Luciano] procured is not clear." Later the Kefauver commission would demolish such claims.

It was much more likely that the decision to deport Luciano was based on the fact that Dewey did not want his prosecutorial conduct examined in a legal forum. Not only was the release and deportation unjustified, every insider knew that Luciano would not stay in Italy. He soon left for Cuba and was preparing to be smuggled back into the United States. When U.S. narcotics agents discovered his presence on the island, FBN commissioner Harry Anslinger exerted so much pressure on the Cuban government that they had to send Lucky back to Italy.

It is likely that Dewey's decline from crusader to ordinary politician arose from the fact that the Luciano case haunted him and he was fearful of it blowing up in his face. If so, the Mafia shadows over Dewey ended up preventing him from reaching the White House.

*

Another unanswered question is why Dewey's lieutenants did not carry on a war against the Mafia when they were elevated to attorney general of the United States. When General Eisenhower ran for president in 1952, Dewey had been governor New York for nearly ten years. The assistance of the Dewey machine to Eisenhower's candidacy was of great value. For example, a request from a New York banking firm to a Kansas business leader that he support Eisenhower over Senator Taft of Ohio, would be taken very seriously, particularly if the businessman was hoping for a renewal of an outstanding loan. In 1952, when Eisenhower was nominated at the Chicago Republican convention, Colonel McCormick was so furious at the maneuverings of the Dewey machine that, in his opinion, had stolen the nomination from McCormick's man, Senator Taft, he took it out on Ike's floor manager, Henry Cabot Lodge. McCormick's *Tribune* endorsed Lodge's Democratic opponent in the November's Massachusetts Senatorial election and that support was credited with persuading a number of conservatives in the Bay State to cast their ballots for the winning candidate, John F. Kennedy.

When he took office, Eisenhower named New York lawyer Herbert Brownell to serve as attorney general. Brownell had been Dewey's campaign manager in the '42 gubernatorial election and both presidential races. From 1944 to 1946 he served as chairman of the Republican national committee where he managed to keep the party lined up behind Dewey. If anyone was close to the New York governor it was Brownell. Eisenhower, having spent his life in the military, knew little about American domestic affairs such as criminal justice. Despite the Kefauver revelations being still fresh in the public's mind, Brownell did not choose to conduct a federal drive against organized crime. Instead, he spent much of his time placating FBI Director J. Edgar Hoover, who always resented the accolades given to Dewey as a crime fighter. In office, Brownell (as noted earlier) recognized the real hierarchy in the DOJ by mentioning how, one day when he forgot his entrance pass, and explained to the building guard that he was the attorney general of the United States, the guard replied, "I don't care if you're J. Edgar Hoover himself, you can't get into the building without a pass."

When Brownell stepped down his deputy attorney general, William Rogers, another New York lawyer, was named to succeed him. In 1938 Rogers had become an assistant district attorney under Dewey, where he served on a task force which attacked New York City's organized crime. So he was well-versed in Mafia affairs. In 1957, the year of his appointment, the Apalachin raid took place. Given the outcry across the country a major drive against the Mafia was in order. It even made great political sense. Rogers was always close to Vice President Richard Nixon. While serving as counsel to a U.S. Senate committee, at the request of Congressman Nixon, Rogers became involved in the investigation of Alger Hiss and advised him that the Hiss case should be vigorously pursued. In 1952, when Nixon's secret slush fund was discovered, Rogers counseled him and helped prepare the "Checkers Speech" that saved Nixon's place on the ticket. Everybody knew that he would be running for president in 1960 and his likely opponent was John F. Kennedy, who at the time was serving on a Senate committee, where his brother Bobby was chief counsel, and the two were attracting great attention by their attacks on the Mafia. Yet, Rogers did not launch a major drive against the Mafia to win good publicity for the Republicans.

While I cannot pretend to know what motivated Dewey's inner circle, particularly individuals like Brownell and Rogers, it is hard to explain why Dewey and his assistants, one of whose career had been made fighting the Mafia, wanted no part of mob busting.

Appendix II

Federal Law Enforcement:
From Hoover to Homeland Security

On May 1, 1936 FBI agents who had been tracking the notorious bank robber, Alvin "Creepy" Karpis, located him in New Orleans, Louisiana. Instead of immediately arresting him, they called Washington because the Bureau director, J. Edgar Hoover, had made it clear he wanted to be the one to personally collar the headline-making public enemy. So agents surrounded Karpis' apartment and waited for the big boss to fly down and make his first arrest in the twelve years he had been director. When Hoover arrived, he did not have long to wait. As Karpis emerged from the building, Hoover and some agents leveled their guns at him and yelled that he was under arrest. Creepy did not resist and Hoover barked, "Put the cuffs on him!" To everyone's chagrin none of the G-men was carrying handcuffs. So an agent put Karpis' hands behind his back, took off his own tie and secured the gangster's hands. Then Hoover briskly ordered "to headquarters." Nobody moved. The FBI agent at the wheel of the official car explained that he had just flown into town and did not know where the FBI office was located. It turned out only one of them knew—Karpis himself, who helpfully volunteered that it was in the main post office building. He explained that he knew this because he had been planning a hold up in the building. The whole affair was not exactly how the G-men were starting to be portrayed on the nation's movie screens. But it was enough for the Bureau's public relations department to turn it into a great personal triumph for their leader.

*

John Edgar Hoover was a native of Washington, DC, from a civil service family. As a boy he captained his high school Cadet Corps. However, in 1917, with a brand-new night school law degree and unmarried, he did not rush to a recruiting station. Instead he took a job in the Department of Justice working for the custodian of alien property, A. Mitchell Palmer. When Palmer became attorney general of the United States he brought Hoover with him and eventually named him director of intelligence for the DOJ. It was a surprising choice because Hoover was only twenty-four and had not served as a military or law enforcement officer. Nor did he ever travel far from Washington. In 1919 his credentials paled beside the many wartime intelligence officers available to fill the job that he got. During the era of Palmer's "red raids," it was young Hoover who compiled the list of those who were to be arrested or deported and provided overall supervision of the operations. On the night of January 2, 1920, when federal officers began a nationwide roundup of "Reds," they were told that if any problems arose they were to call Hoover at his desk in Washington. Later, he would deny any responsibility for the "red raid" excesses and put the blame on the attorney general and the Bureau of Investigation Director William Flynn. Both men were dismissed when the Republicans took over Washington in March 1921.[1]

After the Republican victory, Hoover was retained in the Department of Justice as the assistant director of the Bureau of Investigation (the prefix "federal" was not added until 1935). In 1924, Attorney General Daugherty and Bureau director William Burns were fired for spying on U.S. Senators who were probing the Teapot Dome

---

1. In later years Hoover would recall how he and Flynn went to New York harbor to wave goodbye to the famed anarchist Emma Goldman, who, thanks to them, was one of those being deported to Russia on an old scow nicknamed "The Soviet Ark." When Emma shook her fist at them, they both laughed in her face.

scandal, Hoover protested his innocence and moved up to head the Bureau. The young lawyer was proving himself a master at taking credit but never blame.

Hoover was probably the most successful federal bureaucrat in the history of the United States. He ran a force of several thousand agents with offices stretching from Hawaii to Puerto Rico, plus overseas posts in U.S. embassies. In any organization with such a geographical range, the normal tendency was for various field offices to assert their autonomy from headquarters. In some agencies the California office operated totally differently from the New York office. This did not happen in Hoover's Bureau. Every field office set up its records so that a headquarters inspector, on one of his frequent surprise visits, whether it be Detroit or Denver, knew which drawer to go into to find what he was looking for. Though Hoover's total force of agents was smaller than several police departments like New York or Chicago, and his G-men were not even true cops because they could only make arrests for violations of laws Congress specifically authorized them to enforce, in the three years following 1933, the FBI became the leading American law enforcement agency and Hoover, the nations "top cop." Though had it not been for certain decisions made by the White House and the Department of Justice, it is likely that the FBI story would never have happened.

Before 1933, the Bureau of Investigation was essentially a backwater until the Democrats took over the government that year. At the outset of the Roosevelt administration, Hoover was lucky not to be dismissed. The president named Wyoming senator Thomas Walsh to be attorney general. It was Walsh who, when he led the Senate investigation of Teapot Dome, had been harassed by Bureau of Investigation agents and he always blamed Hoover for it. Almost surely he would have fired the director. Fortunately for J. Edgar, on the way to being sworn in, the elderly Walsh died of a heart attack in the railroad sleeping compartment he shared with his new, vivacious young Cuban bride.

Hoover was still not out of danger. Jim Farley, the political boss of New York State, who managed FDR's campaign for the presidency, was a man well acquainted with the shady side of New York affairs.

When Roosevelt became president Farley was made postmaster general, the chief patronage dispensing post in the federal government. Jim's candidate for director of the Bureau of Investigation was a New York private detective, Valentine O'Farrell. One of O'Farrell's top clients had been New York racket boss Arnold Rothstein. If O'Farrell had gotten the job, the mob would have had nothing to fear from the Department of Justice. Again, Hoover was lucky. O'Farrell died before any action could be taken on his appointment.

Through the '30s, Roosevelt was pleased at the way Hoover won widespread praise for his war on public enemies. Though Homer Cummings remained attorney general until 1938, Hoover's propaganda machine essentially marginalized him in the story of the FBI's war against the gangsters. Despite the public acclaim, as late as 1940 Hoover's job would hang by a thread. That year FBI agents arrested American Communists who had served in Soviet-controlled loyalist forces in the Spanish Civil War. The impetus for this round up likely came from the White House. In 1939 Stalin had signed a pact with Hitler and American Communists were beginning to blast Roosevelt for trying to aid the allies.

Following the FBI round-up in Detroit, United States marshals chained the defendants when they brought them into court. Many liberals pounced on the case, denouncing FBI "chain gang methods" and demanding that Hoover be fired. So serious were the threats that Washington insiders predicted the president would replace the FBI director. One night at a correspondents dinner in Washington, DC, Roosevelt spotted Hoover in the audience and called out to him, "Edgar, what are they doing to you." Hoover responded, "I don't know, Mr. President." Then, in full view of many people, Roosevelt turned his thumb down and declared "That's for them." For the rest of the Roosevelt administration Hoover was fireproof.

Hoover ran his Bureau as a personal fiefdom. He dismissed Chicago SAC Melvin Purvis, who had led the squad that killed Dillinger, Floyd, and the notorious "Baby Face" Nelson (né Lester Gillis), because Purvis got too much publicity. Later he would erase all mention of Purvis from the history of the Bureau and dog him for twenty-five years until Purvis committed suicide. FBI agents did not enjoy civil service protection but served at the pleasure of the director. In the 1920s Hoover took over the government's identification files and in 1935 established a national academy for local police officers. He modestly named the thirteen-week course for experienced police officers "the West Point of law enforcement"—though a four-year school for cadets was hardly comparable to a short training session for middle-aged officials. The identification section and the creation of a top crime lab gave Hoover a considerable measure of influence over local police operations.

As World War II approached, Hoover sought control of all U.S. domestic intelligence and managed to push the Secret Service out of the picture while marginalizing local police departments like the NYPD. He even had the temerity to protest the activities of the United States Army director of military intelligence to the secretary of war, as though Hoover himself was a cabinet officer. Roosevelt appeased Hoover by giving him control of American intelligence operations in Latin America, though the FBI had little knowledge of the area. He was also allowed to station agents as legal attachés (LEGATS) at U.S. embassies as a move to control foreign intelligence.

When President Roosevelt created an intelligence group which became known as the Office of Strategic Services (OSS), Hoover battled the agency throughout the war. Even though the OSS, under General "Wild Bill" Donovan, was a Roosevelt creation, Hoover had little to fear. He always complied with the president's request to spy on his political enemies. When Roosevelt violated the U.S. Constitution by deploying armed forces to assist the British in the Battle of the Atlantic, Hoover knew all about it but kept his mouth shut. If he had told what he knew to Congress or the press, FDR might have been impeached.[2]

For all his protestations about carrying out law enforcement in a strictly constitutional manner—FBI agents were required to warn suspects of their right to silence, long before the courts handed down decisions mandating that for all police—he could fight viciously and

---

2. To readers who have grown up in the postwar world witnessing presidents fight covert or not so covert wars on their own authority, the notion of FDR being impeached may seem far-fetched. But in the pre-World War II era it was a very real possibility.

did not hesitate to utilize his secret files to intimidate a congressman and other critics or to leak the contents of the files to friendly reporters. Because Hoover regarded himself as the country's leading crimefighter, he looked with disfavor on Tom Dewey's rise or Commissioner Anslinger's aggressiveness. If he did not like a police chief like O. W. Wilson of Chicago, or Bill Parker of Los Angeles, he would refuse to allow any of their cops to attend the FBI Academy. No one in Congress or the executive branch challenged Hoover's view—it's my football, I'm captain, and I'll say who can play.

By being so accommodating to Roosevelt, Hoover was allowed to expand the size and scope of his agency and often to choose his targets as he saw fit. If the FBI wanted to intervene in a case they would always find some federal statute which permitted them to do so. On the other hand if they did not, they would cite some legal reason to avoid conducting an investigation. Hoover often claimed that there were no organized criminal groups like the Mafia but simply local gangs over which he had no authority. Yet, interstate vice activities were a federal crime which his Bureau was assigned to combat. In 1940 a new law made obstruction of interstate commerce a federal offense. Both statutes could have been used against Mafia activity. In the 1920s when, contrary to orders, Hoover was investigating suspected communists, he used his personnel to gather evidence and turned it over to state authorities for prosecution. He did not do the same in the organized crime area.

*

Post-Roosevelt, at least two American presidents, Truman and Kennedy, would have loved to have fired the FBI director but they realized that the political fallout would be enormous. While Truman managed to dismiss the national hero, General MacArthur, and Kennedy fired CIA director Allen Dulles, they never moved to oust Hoover. President Johnson saw Hoover as a man he could use.

From the 1930s to the 1970s federal law enforcement was set in stone. Nothing could be done without Hoover's okay and anybody who crossed him regretted it. Even the Kennedys had to back down.

Then, in 1970 with Hoover largely a spent force (he would die 1972), President Nixon attempted to reorganize the federal law enforcement system. At the time the new public enemies were the drug dealers. So he decided to create a powerful law enforcement agency outside of Hoover's jurisdiction, ostensibly to combat narcotics but in reality to serve as a general investigative bureau that he could personally rely on in the same way that Roosevelt had done with Hoover and the FBI. In effect he was going to create a presidential secret police. One element of his plan was to take Anslinger's old Federal Bureau of Narcotics (then known as the Bureau of Narcotics and Dangerous Drugs, BNDD), and make it responsible directly to the White House, along with elements of Treasury's Customs and the IRS, as well as certain state and local cops. The new force also included prosecutors and CIA agents. The keystone of the plan was the creation of an Office of Drug Abuse Law Enforcement (ODALE), which was to concentrate on low-level, easy to make drug arrests. In that way the total number of arrests would rise, thereby boosting the administration's statistical perfor-mance against the country's major crime problem. At the same time the narcotics bureau was renamed the Drug Enforcement Administra-tion (DEA). ODALE formed a number of strike forces with their own prosecutors and began making raids. In 1973 one task force made raids in southern Illinois, east of St. Louis, Missouri, where they broke into private homes and put guns to the heads of innocent residents. In their search for narcotics, they ransacked the house, smashing walls and breaking windows. None of the raiding parties had search warrants and apparently they had entered the various homes by mistake. Ten law enforcement officers from the DEA, the Internal Revenue Service, and the St. Louis Police Department were indicted (though later acquitted). The raids received widespread publicity and the criticism that resulted caused ODALE to be discontinued. Nixon himself soon had to resign as a result of the Watergate scandal. If ODALE had not made such clumsy mistakes, and Watergate had never happened, there would have been a federal law enforcement agency under White House control and the FBI would have had to take a backseat.

Following the 9/11 attack on the World Trade Center, the Bush administration merged twenty-one federal agencies into a Department of Homeland Security. Among those included in the mix were such established entities as the Secret Service and the Bureaus of Customs and Immigration. The FBI was allowed to remain independent. Depending on the perceived level of threat from terrorists, the DHS might very well become the key law enforcement organization in the federal government. At present, however, the FBI still retains the premier position. For a time it had to beat off proposals that its security duties be transferred to an American version of Britain's security service, MI5. If that were to happen, the next step would be to make the American MI5 part of DHS.

While some federal law enforcement agencies, including the FBI, have been headed by capable individuals, no new Hoover has arisen. If one does, it will most likely be in the DHS.

Appendix III

November 22, 1963:
The Shadow of Murder Over the
White House

Paul Dorfman was a journeyman featherweight boxer in 1920s
Chicago. Though small, he was tough and when his ring career
ended he began doing muscle jobs for Chicago gangsters. He proved
more successful at that than in the ring, and by the 1930s he had come
to the favorable attention of the local mobs' secretary of labor,
Llewelyn Murray "The Camel" Humphreys.[1] The Camel put Dorfman
to work in the area of labor relations. Many harsh things could be said
about the Capone gang, *aka* the syndicate, but they were semi-equal
opportunity employers. A Welshman like Humphreys and a Jew like
Dorfman might never become made men or head the syndicate, but
they could play important roles in the organization.

In 1940, the leader of the Chicago waste haulers union was
murdered, a not uncommon fate of mobbed-up union heads. The only
other official of the union was a fellow named Jake, a loudmouth,
oafish character from the West Side, whom no one thought should
take over. Though Dorfman had no experience in waste hauling,
Humphreys recommended him for the job. So Red walked into a

---

1. Camel was either a play on "hump" or referred to his preference for camel hair coats. He was also
known as "Curley." In tough Chicago, he never dared use the name Llewellyn.

union meeting one night, paid his membership dues, and was promptly elected secretary-treasurer. There were no dissenting votes cast. In his new job he was a persuasive negotiator. An employer who did not meet his demands could expect Dorfman to come into his office, drop two bullets on the desk, and announce, "The next one is going into your head."

In 1949 Dorfman would become acquainted with an upstart Teamsters union leader from Detroit named Jimmy Hoffa, who was signing up new IBT members throughout the Midwest. Dorfman arranged for Jimmy to obtain the support of the Chicago mob bosses for his organizing drives—in return for allowing gangsters to loot a local's funds and to go easy on employers who paid off mobsters. In 1950 Hoffa awarded the Central States Teamsters Health and Benefit Insurance account to Red Dorfman's 26-year-old stepson, Allen Dorfman, who had recently gone into the business, despite having neither a license nor an office. Young Dorfman was a wounded and decorated marine veteran of Iwo Jima and college-educated. At the time he joined the Teamsters he was working as a college physical instructor at a salary of $5,900 a year. As Teamster pension head, he would come to own fourteen insurance companies, ten other businesses, and maintain lavish homes in three different states. Dorfman would use the pension fund to build up Las Vegas as a mob cash cow. Step-daddy Paul would also do very well as he rose to a top position in the Chicago syndicate. Only in America.

Unlike the enterprising Dorfmans, Jake, the man passed over for head of the waste haulers union in 1940, was not very successful at anything. Around 1946 he found himself on the wrong side of a dispute among West Side Jewish gamblers. Realizing he had no future in Chicago, he set off for Dallas, Texas, where he had a sister and the Chicago mob was planning to expand. However, the expansion fell through, so Jake Rubenstein, now known as Jack Ruby, began running strip joints in Dallas. His place was, in Chicago terminology, "a bucket of blood." When a ruckus broke out, Ruby himself was usually in the middle of it, breaking customers' heads and pitching them out the door. Though not a particularly law-abiding man, he had a great liking for police officers and whenever one came into his place, everything would be on the house for John Law. Over the years Ruby also maintained his mob friendships. In 1963, his rough nature, liking for cops and mob associations, all came together when, on Sunday afternoon November 24, he shot and killed Lee Harvey Oswald in the Dallas police headquarters in front of national television cameras.

*

Prior to the assassination of President Kennedy in 1963, three other American presidents had been murdered. In 1865 Abraham Lincoln was shot to death by a disgruntled southerner, John Wilkes Booth. In 1881, President James Garfield was fatally wounded by a mentally ill, disappointed office seeker, Charles Guiteau. Both incidents took place in Washington, DC, at Ford's Theater and the Union Station respectively. In September 1901 President William McKinley was assassinated, at the Pan-American Exposition in Buffalo, New York, by Leon Czolgosz, a self-proclaimed anarchist. Czolgosz had joined a receiving line to shake hands with the president. As he stepped up to meet McKinley, he fired a gun in his bandaged hand. The wound proved fatal.[2]

All three assassins were caught. Booth was shot to death in Virginia while resisting capture by U.S. soldiers. Guiteau was arrested by a policeman who had been directing traffic outside the railroad station. Considered mentally ill, he was confined to an institution. Czolgosz, who was seized at the scene by the president's guards, was tried by the state of New York for murder and hanged.

In 1912 former president Theodore Roosevelt was shot by a mentally disturbed person in Milwaukee, Wisconsin. At the time Roosevelt was running for president on the Progressive ticket and was on his way to deliver a speech. Luckily his folded speech and his glass case took most of the impact from the bullet and, though wounded, he

---

2. At the time McKinley was being guarded by three Secret Service agents and two Buffalo detectives. A concealed weapon in the hand was a well-known tactic in Europe, and the year before, King Humbert of Italy was shot to death by a man with a gun hidden in a bouquet of flowers. The assassin, Gaetano Bresci, was an Italian who had journeyed from New Jersey back to Italy to carry out the deed. At the time the U.S. Secret Service had investigated his background and was aware of the concealed gun trick. However, none of the agents with McKinley checked Czolgosz's hand.

managed to go on to the meeting hall and deliver his remarks. The would-be assassin was sent to a mental institution.

In 1933 Giuseppe Zangara shot and fatally wounded Mayor Anton Cermak of Chicago while the mayor was sitting in an open car with president-elect Franklin Delano Roosevelt in a Miami park. Zangara was taken into custody at the scene and a month later was electrocuted by the state of Florida.

In the mid-1970s President Gerald Ford was shot at twice while on trips to California. One of his would-be assassins was a young woman who was part of the Charles Manson family. The other was a middle-aged woman with a history of mental illness. Both assassins were captured immediately and later incarcerated.

In 1981 President Ronald Reagan was shot and severely wounded, outside a Washington, DC, hotel by John Hinckley, a disturbed individual who was apparently seeking to impress actress Jodie Foster (at the time attending Yale), whom he had never met. Hinckley was captured at the scene and remains confined in a mental institution.

All of the shooters were at least borderline mentally ill, with the possible exception of Booth. In contrast, Lee Harvey Oswald, who is officially regarded as the assassin of President Kennedy, did not display overt signs of mental illness and his motive in the shooting is the subject of dispute. In the weeks before the assassination he had made a number of public statements in favor of Castro's Cuba. Two days after he was arrested Oswald was killed by Ruby who, three years later, would die in jail of cancer. In the decades following the assassination there have been many theories as to who was behind it. Some believe it was agents of the United States government or right-wing groups; others maintain it was Castroites. The most popular explanation in recent years has been that it was organized crime figures. The latter theory has received attention from both Congressional committees and serious scholars and is the one most favored by the public.

President Johnson appointed a committee of distinguished Americans, under the chairmanship of Chief Justice Earl Warren, to investigate the assassination. Besides the obvious mistake of appointing Warren, who as a member of the Supreme Court, might have to hear cases brought in connection with the murder, the commission also included CIA Director Allen Dulles; and a major influence behind the scenes was FBI director J. Edgar Hoover. Both should have been asked to explain why their agencies had not flagged Oswald as a potential assassin. Instead, they were allowed, in effect, to investigate themselves.

It was typical of President Johnson to want an investigation he could control, though he benefited more from the assassination than any other individual. It would have been more fitting if the investigation had been carried on by a joint congressional committee rather than appointees of the president. The fact that the commission was made up of Washington insiders was a major factor in causing many people to doubt its conclusions.

Fifty years afterwards, public opinion polls find that the majority of the American people either do not believe or at least question the Warren Commission's finding that the crime was carried out by Lee Harvey Oswald acting alone and unaided. Most Americans have made up their minds about the case long ago, based on movies like *JFK*, TV dramas, and books long on inference and short on facts. If, as many believe, the Mafia arranged the killing of the president, it would be the ultimate shadow over the White House. In effect gangsters would have staged a coup which changed history. While America in the '60s was inevitably going to be rocked by Vietnam and civil rights protests, the conflicts would likely have been less serious and easier to resolve under a popular figure like Jack Kennedy rather than an accidental president like LBJ.

There are several reasons to suspect organized crime involvement. Working backwards, the killing of Oswald by Jack Ruby, while in custody of the Dallas police, raised questions about his association with organized crime figures and the Dallas cops. Ruby had many mob friends. The night before the assassination he had dined with a local gangster, Joe Campisi, who was a member of the Dallas organized crime group that was a subsidiary of Carlos Marcello's operation in New Orleans. While I have no direct knowledge of Dallas police operations, in other cities simply buying a few drinks for the cops would not have been sufficient for Ruby to be allowed virtually free run of police headquarters for three days during which time an investigation of the murder of the president was being conducted.

Oswald, a U.S. marine sharpshooter and a defector to the Soviet Union, was a person who moved about frequently and had few close ties. Was he a government operative or a Communist agent on some kind of mission? His trips to the Cuban embassy in Mexico City and his defection to the Soviet Union brought him to the attention of both the FBI and the CIA. But J. Edgar Hoover and Allen Dulles never gave the Warren Commission a full account of their respective agency's relationships with Oswald.

Oswald had lived for a while in New Orleans with his cousin Dutz Murret, supposedly a gambler working for Carlos Marcello, who had a grudge against the Kennedys since his forcible expulsion from the United States in 1961. Thus it is easy to construct a scenario in which Oswald was recruited by Marcello to kill Kennedy. In some tellings, it was not Oswald who shot the president or at least not Oswald alone, but shooters stationed on the grassy knoll outside the book depository. That does not explain why Oswald was armed and killed Officer J. D. Tippit.[3]

Despite the many factors that point to organized crime involvement, there has never been any solid proof presented. The whole scenario of shooting the president while he was traveling in a motorcade in a strange city suggests the killers were not mafiosos or government agents. Stationing assassins at Dealy Plaza or in the book depository left too much to chance. The president might not have followed the scheduled route, or, because he was late roared past the assassination site at top speed. It is much harder to hit a moving target, so it would have been better to attack him when he was on foot, such as happened to Robert Kennedy in Los Angeles, Martin Luther King in Memphis, George Wallace in Maryland, twice to President Ford in California, and to President Reagan in Washington, DC.

In 1993 former mob attorney Frank Ragano co-authored a book in which he alleged that his client, Jimmy Hoffa, used him to relay a

---

3. Over the past half-century no investigation has found any connection between Officer Tippit and the plot against President Kennedy. Tippit appears to have been killed because he did not draw his gun on Oswald when he stopped him for questioning, probably because he did not know whom he was dealing with. However, many American police officers in those days would have leveled a gun at Oswald on the theory that it was better to be safe than sorry.

message to Santo Trafficante, Jr., to tell Marcello to kill the president. In the years after the assassination Ragano was convicted of crimes, disbarred, and served jail sentences, yet Trafficante never tried to help him. Then, according to Ragano, in 1987 he was summoned to the dying mafioso's home. There Trafficante, dressed only in pajamas, insisted that Ragano take him for an automobile ride—by then a standard practice to avoid hidden FBI microphones. During the ride Trafficante supposedly confessed that Marcello had carried out the assassination as a favor to Hoffa. However, the Trafficante family produced hospital records showing that on the day Ragano recollected as the one on which he took the automobile ride, Trafficante had been a dialysis patient in a Tampa hospital. Many organized crime experts found Ragano's assertions difficult to accept. In attributing the request to murder Kennedy to Hoffa, Ragano also diverges from accounts that claim it was Marcello's idea. If Hoffa relayed an assassination proposal to Marcello via Ragano, it was a very foolish move by Jimmy. He knew he was surrounded by informers and had been indicted and convicted in cases where people who were working for him had testified against him.

In probing organized crime involvement in the Kennedy assassination investigators may have looked at the wrong parties. One faction of the Mafia which should have been subject to more attention was the Chicago syndicate. Assassination was always an option in the Windy City's political conflicts. Colonel McCormick, Mayors Thompson and Kelly did not surround themselves with bodyguards to look impressive but because they felt they needed them to stay alive. In 1950, with Senator Kefauver headed to town, Chicago gangsters did not hesitate to murder an ex-police captain and a prominent attorney. It is also possible that the hit on Sam Giancana was connected to the Kennedy assassination. In 1975 Giancana was scheduled to testify at hearings of a Senate committee probing the CIA plot to kill Castro. However, before he could do so, he was shot in the back of the head while cooking a late-night snack in his suburban Chicago home.

If Marcello was mad at Bobby Kennedy for having him forcibly deported, Giancana was equally angry at what he regarded as a doublecross in the 1960 election and harassment of himself and his girlfriend, singer Phyllis McGuire, by Chicago FBI agents. So erratic was his behavior that Giancana's fellow Chicago gangsters eventually exiled him to Mexico.

Though the theory that organized crime killed Kennedy makes sense, the only thing it lacks is proof, and there it falls short. At the time of the assassination, leading mobsters all over the country were under heavy electronic surveillance. After a hiatus, during which Johnson ordered the bugs turned off, even more intense eaves-dropping was undertaken. While law enforcement officers listening to tapes have picked up gangsters discussing famous hits long before their own time (such as Jim Colosimo's murder in 1920), no one has been heard suggesting who might have killed Kennedy. At the time of the assassination and for several years after, the writer was a captain and then commander of detectives in the Chicago Police Department. Yet there were no rumors about the Chicago mob being involved in the case or that they knew who was behind the assassination.

Forensic examinations conducted for a congressional committee have determined that the shots that struck President Kennedy and Governor Connally came from the rifle found in a wrapping in the book depository, which witnesses claim Oswald was seen bringing into the building. Apparently he had used the same rifle to fire at retired army general Edwin Walker in Dallas a few weeks earlier. When a headcount was made of depository workers, only Oswald was missing. A congressional committee that posited the Mafia was behind the murder concluded that Oswald was the actual shooter.

The Cuban connection has yet to be fully explored. It may well be that post-Castro (and that time may not be far off) some Cubans will allege that he was behind the assassination. He did in fact give a warning shortly before it occurred, that because of the plots against him, the same thing might happen to Kennedy. Earl Warren, whose inept leadership of the ill-conceived commission investigating the assassination led to so many conspiracy theories emerging, said that all the facts were not being made public, allegedly because he feared it would prompt Americans to demand their country declare war on Cuba or possibly even Russia.

The truth is that Americans of the present era will never accept any explanation that does not confirm some sort of conspiracy theory. Partly this is because they don't trust the government—sometimes with good reason, other times unreasonably. Conspiracy theories in general are popular ranging from space aliens landing in flying saucers onto birthers and truthers who would have us believe the president of the United States is an alien or that the American government destroyed the World Trade Center on 9/11. Conspiracy theories confirm the belief of many people that the world is run by hidden forces. Even when facts are presented they are routinely dismissed. If a file from the Havana archives were to reveal that Castro was involved, some would accept it and others would label it a forgery. Indeed it is likely that some Cuban clerk will dummy up a document purporting to show that Castro's government was behind the killing and become a millionaire by selling it to a U.S. publisher, the same way that Hitler's fake diary was peddled.

One mystery of the assassination is why President Kennedy and his attorney general brother thought that they could bring down the Mafia at the same time their father was soliciting political support from mob chiefs like Giancana. Jack was carrying on a torrid affair with one of Sam's girlfriends, and Bobby, or at least his lieutenants, were recruiting Chicago hoodlums to kill Castro. The two young and relatively inexperienced men (at least compared to presidents like Eisenhower or FDR) never benefited from the advice of wise counsel that might have reined them in. Joe Kennedy had suffered a stroke in the first year of Jack's presidency that had left him paralyzed and unable to communicate coherently. J. Edgar Hoover was an enemy of the Kennedys, though if father Joe had been around, he might have been able to repair the breach. Bobby Kennedy never respected the wisdom of age. Jack had no standing among senior senators. When he served in the body his close associates were fellow playboy types like George Smathers of Florida.

Thus, two dynamic American leaders who might have rendered much service to the nation ended up in Arlington National Cemetery while still in their forties. Whatever one's opinion of them might be, their deaths were a great loss to America.

Sources

While the present work discusses nine American presidents, it is not meant to be a full or even partial portrait of any of them. Indeed, historians, political scientists, and journalists are constantly revising their views of various occupants of the White House. Instead, it seeks to trace the influence of the American Mafia at the highest levels of government. Since I have previously written on the Mafia, I have decided not to clutter the references with endless citations to my own work. Instead I just list where information on certain topics can be found.

*

The following are principal sources for the material presented in various chapters.

Preface

Hoover statements, *President's Commission on Law Enforcement and Administration of Justice: The Challenge of Crime in a Free Society* (1967), p. 192. On New York, Wallace Sayre and Herbert Kaufman, *Governing New York City* (1960).

Chapter 1 – The Fall of the Ohio Gang: The Rise of the Mafia Gangs

A full account of the Harding administration's Ohio gang is found in Francis Russell's *The Shadow of Blooming Grove* (1968).

The story of the rise of the American Mafia is contained in Stephen Fox, *Blood and Power: Organized Crime in 20th Century America* (1989); Humbert Nelli, *The Business of Crime: Italians and Syndicate Crime in the United* States (1976); and T. Reppetto, *American Mafia: A History of its Rise to Power* (2004).

Chapter 2 – New York City: Murder Incorporated

The usual reference on Murder Incorporated is Burton Turkus (who prosecuted some of the defendants) and Sid Feder, *Murder Incorporated: The Story of the Syndicate* (1959). However, it leaves important questions unanswered. Therefore, see also Virgil Peterson, *The Mob: 200 Years of*

Organized Crime in New York (1983); Selwyn Raab, *Five Families: The Rise, Decline and Resurgence of America's Most Powerful Mafia Empire* (2005); and Reppetto, *American Mafia.*

Chapter 3 – Chicago: The Legacy of Prohibition

The most informative work is long-time Chicago Crime Commission head Virgil Peterson's, *Barbarians in Our Midst: A History of Chicago Crime and Politics* (1952). A scholarly study of the Chicago machine is Roger Biles, *Big City Boss in Depression and War: Mayor Edward J Kelly of Chicago* (1984). Gus Russo, *The Outfit: The Role of the Chicago Underworld in the Shaping of Modern America* (2001) is an analysis of the Chicago mob in more recent times. Reppetto, *American Mafia* contains extensive information on Chicago during prohibition (1920-33) and the Kelly administration (1933-47).

Chapter 4 – Kansas City: Uncle Tom and his Henchmen

David McCullough, *Truman* (1992) provides a flattering portrait of the subject's life. For accounts of the criminality of the Pendergast machine see Elmer Irey and William Slocum's, *The Tax Dodgers: The Inside Story of the T-Men's War with the America's Political and Underworld Hoodlums* (1945); the former FBI SAC in Kansas City, Lear B. Reed's, *Human Wolves: 17 Years of War on Crime* (1941); and former U.S. Attorney Maurice Milligan's, *Missouri Waltz: The Inside Story of the Pendergast Machine by the Man who Brought it Down* (1948). An account of the gangster era of the mid-1930s is contained in Bryan Burrough's *Public Enemies*, 2004.

Chapter 5-Corruption Everywhere: The Real Governor of California; Crump of Tennessee; The Detroit Story; "I am the law" Hague

On Hague and Crump, Alfred Steinberg, *The Bosses* (1972). On Samish of California and the Detroit Story, see Fox, *Blood and Power.* On San Francisco see Jake Ehrlich, *A Life in My Hands* (1948).

Chapter 6 – 1944 Year of Decision: Clear It with Sidney

See Robert H Ferrell, *Choosing Truman: The Democratic Convention of 1944* (1994); Edward Flynn, *You're the Boss* (1947); Matthew Josephson, *Sidney Hillman* (1952). On Hillman, see also Fox, *Blood and Power*, pp. 215-20.

Chapter 7 – The Missouri Gang: Scandals and Exposure

Andrew J. Dunar, *The Truman Scandals and the Politics of Morality* (1984). See also U.S. Senate. Special Committee to Investigate Organized Crime in

Interstate Commerce (Kefauver Committee) *Hearings,* (1951), supplemented by Estes Kefauver, *Crime in America* (1951). Peterson's *Barbarians* describes the parole scandal. See also Fox, *Blood and Power* on Hubert Humphrey, especially page 159. Reppetto, *American Mafia* contains extensive information on the Kefauver investigation.

Chapter 8 – The Rise and the Fall of the Kennedys

There is a vast literature on the Kennedy administration, often by individuals who are acolytes. A useful study is Evan Thomas, *Robert Kennedy: His Life* (2000). A critical work is Victor S. Navasky, *Kennedy Justice* (1977). Since the Apalachin raid is so frequently misrepresented, it is useful to read the Circuit Court decision in the case *US v. Bufalino,* 285 Fed2d 408 (Cir, 1960). Reppetto, *Bringing Down the Mob: The War Against the American Mafia* contains an extended discussion of the Kennedy era and LBJ's dismantling of the government's anti-Mafia drive.

Chapter 9 – Fatal Attraction I: President Nixon and the Hoffa Wars

Steven Brill, *The Teamsters* (1978), Dan Moldea, *The Hoffa Wars* (1978), and Arthur D Sloane, *Hoffa* (1991) cover the topic. On ABSCAM see Thomas Puccio with Dan Collins, *In the Name of the Law: Confessions of a Trial Lawyer* (1995). FBI Director Louis J Freeh's rendering of the relationship between politics and organized crime is found in *My FBI: Bringing Down the Mafia, Investigating Bill Clinton and Fighting the War on Terror* (2005). On Humphrey, Fox, *Blood and Power*, pp. 163-70.

Chapter 10 – Fatal Attraction II: The Gipper Embraces the Teamsters

On Jackie Presser, a comprehensive account is James Neff, *Mobbed Up: Jackie Pressers High Wire Life in the Teamsters, the Mafia and the FBI* (1989). See also US Senate Committee on Governmental Affairs, Permanent Subcommittee on Investigations. *The Department of Justice's Handling of the Jackie Presser Ghost Workers Case* (1986).

Chapter 11 – The Great Divide: Politicians Divorce the Mafia

On the fall of the Mafia see Reppetto, *Bringing Down the Mob*. On the Whitey Bulger case in Massachusetts, Dick Lehr and Gerard O'Neill, *Black Mask: The True Story of the Unholy Alliance between the FBI and the Irish Mob* (2000). On the Vegas scene, Nicholas Pileggi, *Casino* (1995). On the Chicago corruption trials, James Touhy and Rob Warden, *Greylord: Justice Chicago Style* (1989); Robert Cooley and Hillel Levin's, *When Corruption Was King* (2004) relates the Gambat case. Comments by a Detroit law enforcement official on Mafia political influence is contained in Sloan, *Hoffa* and additional exposition on this topic can be found in Neil Welch and David Marston, *Inside Hoover's FBI: The Top Field Chief Reports* (1984).

Chapter 12 – The 21st Century: The Emergence of the Modern Mafia

On Stavisky, Paul F. Jankowski, *Stavisky: A Confidence Man in the Republic of Virtue* (2002). On BCCI, James Ring Adams and Douglas Frantz, *A Full Service Bank: How BCCI Stole Billions Around the World* (1992) and U.S. Senate Committee on Foreign Relations, Report of Senator John Kerry (1982). On Zaharof, Donald McCormick, *Peddler of Death: the Life and Times of Sir Basil Zaharoff* (1965). On a U.S. senator urging gang roundup, Mark Guarino, "Senator wants entire Chicago gang arrested. Would that work?" *The Christian Science Monitor* (CSMonitor.com), May 30, 2013.

Appendix I – The Strange Behavior of Governor Dewey

An anti-Dewey explanation of Luciano's release is Martin A. Gosch and Richard Hammer, *The Last Testament of Lucky Luciano* (1974). A pro-Dewey account is Rodney Campbell, *The Luciano Project* (1977). Neither is convincing.

Appendix II – Federal Law Enforcement: From Hoover to Homeland Security

There are almost as many books on J. Edgar Hoover as on George Washington. For a balanced account, I recommend Richard Gid Powers, *Secrecy and Power: The Life of J. Edgar Hoover* (1987). See also Ron Kessler, *The FBI* (1993).

On Nixon's plan to create a secret federal police force, see Edward J. Epstein, *Agency of Fear: Opiates and Political Power in America* (revised edition 1990).

Appendix III – November 22, 1963: Shadow of Murder over the White House

There is a vast literature on the Kennedy assassination. To accept some of it requires a great leap of faith. G. Robert Blakey and Richard N Billings,

Fatal Hour: The Assassination of President Kennedy by Organized Crime (1992), presents a well-reasoned case for a Mafia murder plot against the president. Gerald Posner, *Case Closed: Lee Harvey Oswald and the Assassination of JFK* (1993) and Vincent Bugliosi, *Four Days in November: The Assassination of President John F. Kennedy* (2008) are competent works which essentially accept the Warren Commission conclusion.

Acknowledgments

As I occasionally note in the chapters, my knowledge of organized crime and politics began in my preschool days. Later, it was supplemented by my observations as a police officer in the quiet little town of Chicago. There, I had a fairly wide acquaintanceship with various figures involved in both crime and politics. One of my former (military) superiors who was elected governor of Illinois ended up in a federal prison. It was a path taken by some of his successors, including at least one other I knew personally.

When I came east, I discovered that politics followed a somewhat different pattern from the Midwest, but the outcomes were essentially the same. Once again, I was shocked by the overnight fall of a state governor, whom I had admired.

Though I have met U.S. presidents, I have never known one personally. Once, I commanded a guard detail that spent half a day in a suite with a president. Before that I, like many Americans, had a high opinion of the man. I learned that, as with other celebrities, it is best never to meet your hero in person. I have had the opportunity to converse with some presidential aides and appointees. In one instance I was aware of facts about a certain cabinet appointee that the president apparently did not know about. The gentleman whom he had nominated for the cabinet had to quickly withdraw and eventually ended up donning convict garb.

Over many years I have asked a number of politicians and officials why they or their bosses allowed Mafia characters to have influence in their administration. The standard answer went something along the lines of, "We thought Mr. So-and-So had some rough edges, but we did not know he was controlled by the XYZ mob. In retrospect we made a mistake, but these things happen." In other words, their answer was "That's politics." As the present work relates, this is essentially the reason for organized crime's influence at all levels of government.

Most of the people I have questioned over the years are dead. Neither they nor the ones who are still alive expected that someday their answers would be used in a book. So I do not think it would be fair to identify them. Because the subject is so fraught with possible embarrassment, other people who have helped me in my research have preferred not to be acknowledged.

On a happier note, I must thank my principal editor Robert Miller and his assistant Jay Wynshaw of Enigma Books and my assistant Christa Carnegie for their help in compiling the present work. I should also acknowledge the cooperation of the Jersey City Free Public Library, the Library of the John Jay College of Criminal Justice of the City University of New York, The Library of Congress, The Harry S Truman Library and Museum, and the Westchester, New York, County Library System.

Index